BULLSHIT

and

the DEATH

of

COMMON SENSE

Reflections of a Cynical
Baby Boomer

After eating an entire bull, a mountain lion felt so good he started roaring. He kept it up until a hunter came along and shot him.

The Moral

When you're full of bull, keep your mouth shut.

—Will Rogers

Table of Contents

Foreword

Sometime during our childhood we have our first encounter with bullshit. For many of us in western societies it comes in the guise of Santa Claus, or possibly the Easter Bunny, the Tooth Fairy, or another such benevolent character, and what's not to like? That is a nice way to ease children into adult reality, for soon we come upon the stark realization that bullshit is endemic—in every phase of society. It's one of those harsh life lessons that leads many of us to grow into cynical, distrusting men and women.

My first lesson in adult-level bullshit came when I was only nine-and-a-half years old, in January 1959, when Fidel Castro's rebel army overthrew a corrupt, tyrannical government in Cuba, my native country. Immediately after assuming control of the island nation, the maximum leader promised to institute what amounted to a Nirvana of egalitarianism and economic progress for the people. Assuring the populace that his revolution was as green as the royal palms indigenous to the island, Castro enjoyed the support of a large segment of the population in the early going, but it wasn't long before people began to realize his revolution was as red as the communist flag of the now-defunct Soviet Union with which he aligned. Quickly introducing a Marxist system that brought equality only in the sense that everyone was now equally poor (except those in the government), "the liberator" ensured compliance by instituting a police state far more brutal than the one he helped depose. Scarcity, intense surveillance of citizens, relentless persecution of opponents, sham trials, executions, and propaganda ruled the day. In effect, the dream had become an Orwellian nightmare.

Fidel's speeches, which sometimes lasted from morning to evening and which were forcefully broadcasted via all television stations, kept the population on a steady diet of bullshit so effective that even with the country obviously headed toward ruin, many clamored for more (at least in those early days). Those seemingly endless discourses were loaded with what proved to be unfulfilled promises and rants against "enemies of the revolution," both real and fabricated. And the people believed, swallowing the crap as if manna from heaven, even if the stench lingered in the air for hours after every speech.

But that was only an introduction to bullshit for me. Since then, I have gradually come to understand how pervasive it really is—in every facet of life. We are drowning in it, an unshakable irritant in our society that has relegated concepts such as honesty, courtesy, trustworthiness, fairness, responsibility, empathy—in essence, core moral values—to the pages of nostalgic fiction and the fuzzy memories of grandparents, and it has become a formidable challenge to plain old common sense. I hope to make that clear in the pages that follow.

Roberto J. Herrera

December 13, 2016

Introduction

Inherently, we all know it. We live in a world that runs on bullshit. And by that I don't mean just the pedestrian lies and tall tales we so frequently encounter in our everyday lives. While a clear-cut lie is a form of bullshit—a very basic form—bullshit can be quite sophisticated, sneaking past our defenses and inflicting damage before we realize what has happened. That's the kind that should concern us.

For this book, I am using the widest possible definition of the word bullshit. I have expanded it to encompass not just plain old lies and exaggerations but also practices and policies that add unnecessary complexity and exasperation to our already busy and complex lives, distortions of cultural and aesthetic ideals in art and entertainment, and activities that work against society—actions that are harmful, or at least not conducive to anything good. I'm also taking the liberty to drop the word from the obscene/vulgar slang category, at least for the duration of this treatise, because there is no other utterance in the English language that even approximates its power to integrate so many concepts in so little space (the British "rubbish" is lame in comparison).

Bullshit, especially the really insidious kind, comes at us from innumerable sources. Whether it is the baby-kissing, flag-waving politician, the Bible-thumping Evangelist, the smooth-talking merchant, or the pamphlet-wielding Socialist, the general idea is to con people into parting either with their money, their values, or their beliefs (or all of them!). All too often our defenses—common sense, life experiences, and crap filters intrinsic to our rational minds—lack the sophistication to repel the attacks of carefully contrived political fabrications, ideological propaganda, unethical advertisement, corporate lip service, and the passionate diatribes of extremists of all kinds. In effect, it is difficult to defend against manipulative liars and misguided romantics with an agenda, and, sadly, as a society, we succumb to their tactics more frequently than we care to admit.

Not surprisingly, one of the consequences of bullshit's ubiquitousness is a widespread sense of distrust. Today, we are not just keenly aware and cautious; we are hyper-vigilant. We want to avoid being victimized by the con-artists forever looking for that easy prey. In fact, many of us have become fairly adept at protecting ourselves from the garden variety bullshitter, but, unfortunately, many are still easily duped by the more cunning players. Most damaging is when we fall prey to the crafty schemes of those in positions of power.

When intoxicated with power, bullshit artists can be extremely harmful, even lethal. They possess the ability to make us suspend critical thinking and act in ways otherwise inconceivable. Adolf Hitler's nearly hypnotic control of the German people is perhaps the quintessential image of the phenomenon, and it resulted in not only the most devastating war in history, but also in the unspeakable tragedy that led to the systematic extermination of *at least* six million people—likely even more—mostly Jews. Unfortunately, history is strewn with examples.

Consider the tragedy of Jonestown in 1978, where many of the 900-plus followers of cult leader Jim Jones willingly obeyed his orders to poison themselves and their children (from which the phrase "drinking the Kool-Aid" was coined). In the eighties, we saw untrained and poorly armed Iranian teens spearhead human-wave attacks against a professional Iraqi Army that slaughtered them by the thousands. It was said that in some battles the heavily indoctrinated young men charged across open fields, with "keys to heaven" hanging around their necks, complements of the Ayatollah Khomeini, Time Magazine's 1979 "Man of the Year," assuring them of entrance into God's kingdom should they be killed, as so many were. And who can forget the religious fanatics who, exhorted by bullshit from radical Islamic mullahs guaranteeing heavenly rewards (including 72 virgins each!), crashed passenger-laden jets into New York's Twin Towers and the Pentagon on September 11, 2001. I could go on.

As will be made clear later in the book, bullshit is also endemic in the entertainment industry, and that is particularly concerning because virtually all of us—and most importantly children—are exposed, in one form or another, to the bullshit streaming on television, the movies, and in some of the more popular music genres of the day. It is this industry, more than any other social force, that continually redefines the norms of behavior, especially among the young, dictating everything from fashion trends to moral codes.

As well, bullshit finds its way into education and science, where, ironically, scientifically unsubstantiated material is casually treated as fact and potentially new discoveries are delayed or possibly never bear fruit due to a stubborn resistance by scientists to any anomalous data that challenge existing paradigms. Bullshit also finds a comfortable niche in religion, as we shall see in one of the later chapters.

Thus, the purpose of this book is not just to talk about the preponderance of bullshit; you see it every day. Rather, it is to raise awareness of how widespread it really is and what it's doing to us—how it's negatively affecting our lives. I also want to have some fun writing this book and challenge myself to find the lighter side in what are, in many instances, concerning issues, meaning, I want my readers to enjoy a chuckle or two. And be warned: we are going to disagree on a few points, maybe more than a few, so please cut me a little slack because this tome is not short on personal opinion and contains more than a few tirades against aspects of bullshit in our society that really anger me but apparently do not have the same effect on a large segment of the population.

Because bullshit spreads (pun fully intended) across so many areas, I have sectioned the book by subject matter, dealing with each major topic separately, although they may sometimes overlap. This will not only allow for better organization and focus but also to emphatically underscore the extent to which bullshit has penetrated our lives. In fact, bullshit is so pervasive that any chapter or segment of this book could probably be expanded into a full book of its own. All that can be done here is lightly touch upon each area, a sort of sampling. We'll start with the easiest—politics—such a fertile terrain for bull.

Chapter 1

Politics

Politics is supposed to be the second-oldest profession. I have come to realize that it bears a very close resemblance to the first.

—Ronald Reagan

Without politicians, we'd have to spend all our time talking about the Kardashians.
—Joe Queenan, WSJ writer

One of my favorite political jokes is about a senator who visited an American Indian tribe in Arizona during a re-election campaign to deliver a speech in which he made many promises that would benefit the tribe. It went something like this: "And if I'm elected, there will be a new car parked outside every teepee...; Unga! Unga! the Indians would roar, seemingly in enthusiastic approval. "And every member of the tribe will receive high quality medical care—free, *and...*; Unga! Unga! would come the reply from the tribe's men and women increasingly excited. "And the children will benefit from the best schools the state can provide; Unga! Unga! Again and again the natives' response echoed across the canyon. Encouraged by the crowd's animated response, the senator continued dishing out more and more assurances: "And we will extend enhanced Social Security benefits exclusively for the tribe, with retirement beginning at age 45..." Unga! Unga! The yelling continued on cue, intensity growing with every pledge. At the conclusion of the speech, the candidate was being escorted back to his limousine by one of the tribesmen when, just before they reached the vehicle waiting on the dirt road, the escort suddenly pushed the congressman to one side, warning, "Watch it senator; don't step on the unga!"

This comic yarn is revelatory of the universal understanding that politicians deliver bullshit in abundance. No other profession—except, perhaps, law—can match them, and it is no coincidence that many politicians are lawyers. This would not be too concerning if it wasn't that these individuals make and interpret the laws that citizens are obligated to obey, laws that regulate our actions, from how much taxes we pay and what is legal or illegal to how involved we'll be in wars they've decided must be fought. They have the frightening power to criminalize actions most citizens do not view as crimes (e.g. use of cannabis) and then change their minds years or decades later so that a criminal today may be just a fine upstanding citizen tomorrow, but a tomorrow where those convicted of the "crime" in earlier years may still be forced to complete their sentences for something that is no longer a crime. It is no secret that most of these folks seek office to benefit themselves, and just as transparent is that the benefits of such appointments are so enormous that many candidates spend fortunes trying to become our "public servants."

In politics, hypocrisy and dishonesty reach unimaginable proportions. Who can forget Bill Clinton's "I did not have sexual relations with that woman," or, "I experimented with marijuana...but did not inhale." And, if you are old enough, Richard Nixon's "I am not a crook." There are (and have been) so many corrupt politicians in our country alone, it should be quite easy to assemble a pretty thick volume just to list them alphabetically. Be that as it may, I must limit the scope of this discussion because there is just so much room in this tome to cover the many facets of bullshit I want to address. So I'll choose just a handful of politicians as examples. Given the recent presidential elections, Donald Trump and Hillary Clinton are a must, of course, but I find it much easier to start with my favorite target—Florida's governor, Rick Scott.

Rick Scott — Florida's Criminal Governor

On the advice of counsel, I respectfully decline to answer the questions by asserting my rights and privileges under the Fifth Amendment of the U.S. Constitution.

I've absolutely lived the American dream.

—Rick Scott

A glaring example of political deviousness is Florida's governor, Rick Scott, who loves Floridians so much he spent over $75 million of his own money in the 2010 elections [1], all to be the people's servant. Scott won with less than half the vote, and only six months later he had pissed off so many people his approval rating was only 29 percent. For the 2014 elections he initially refused to use any of his money for campaigning, saying, "I won't have to" (he had enormous financial backing and much unfounded confidence), yet found himself having to throw in $12.8 million from his pocket and bring his own mother to vouch for him at the last minute as polls showed his re-election was in doubt.[2]

So, where did Scott's millions come from? It is well known that in March 1997 the FBI, IRS, and the Department of Health served search warrants on Columbia/HCA, a hospital-owning company headed by Scott (as Chairman and CEO). Among the accusations, which included kickbacks for doctors and signing illegal contracts with home care agencies, Columbia/HCA was suspected of gross Medicare fraud. A few months after the raid, Scott was forced to resign but left with a severance of nearly $10 million and over $350 million in stock shares. Then, after years of playing legal defense, in 2002, Columbia/HCA acknowledged guilt in fourteen felonies, which resulted in fines of over $600 million, *"the largest fraud settlement in U.S. history"* at that time.[3] A narrow escape for Scott.

While Columbia/HCA was under investigation for criminal activities, Scott was summoned for a deposition related to another case, one in which Columbia/HCA was accused of breach of contract by a communications company from Nevada.[4] It was at this July 27, 2000 meeting that Scott notoriously invoked the fifth amendment *seventy-five times* at least partly because his legal team feared that questions regarding the

Columbia/HCA on-going investigation would arise and Scott could end up saying something to incriminate himself. This blatant evasion further tarnished his character, as many saw it as his desperate effort to avoid conviction and jail time.

Of course, Scott and his political cronies deny such intent, but it would be somewhat naive to take him at his word. PolitiFact, the award-winning, fact-checking operation by the *Tampa Bay Times*, looked into this and had this to say:

> Does that mean Scott faced jail at all? In pleading the Fifth Amendment, it certainly seems like a possibility, former federal prosecutor Ryan O'Quinn told us. That's because the only legal reason to use your Fifth Amendment right in court is if you think your answer would incriminate you.
>
> Scott wasn't facing a jury, but we're trying to establish whether one could infer guilt for invoking the Fifth Amendment. In fact, there's no other reason to think otherwise, because by the letter of the law, Scott must have thought he would incriminate himself if he answered truthfully.
>
> "Given the adverse consequences of an assertion of the Fifth Amendment in a civil deposition, executives must have a significant concern that their response could contribute to their criminal prosecution," O'Quinn said. "A frivolous assertion of the Fifth Amendment would be an unethical act."
>
> So if Scott was avoiding incriminating himself and other executives were actually convicted and sentenced to prison (albeit later overturned), does that mean Scott faced jail? That's conjecture, but he certainly could have faced federal charges, which could have resulted in time in prison.[5]

I have long maintained (and I am not alone) that Rick Scott belongs in jail and not in the governor's mansion in Tallahassee. But as we know well, in our country money talks—and it talks very loudly. Besides, Americans—Floridians in particular—posses an enormous capacity to ignore, or at least forgive, corruption.

So we know that at least some of Scott's wealth, which he used to outspend his opponents in his governor races, came from a time when the company he led was convicted of flagrant, illegal business practices (He was not personally indicted; the corporation took the hit). He is also said to have made money as a "venture capitalist," putting his money (possibly much of it from what he took away from his sweet severance from Columbia/HCA) into various investments that produced many more millions for him. Among these investments was Solantic, an urgent care company founded in 2001. Solantic has also made the news. Why? Ding! Ding! Allegations of Medicare fraud! Does that sound familiar? The charges were brought forward by a physician, Dr. Randy Prokes, back during Scott's first gubernatorial race. [6] It has been suggested that this was only a ploy by Democrats to try to derail Scott's campaign, but we many never know, for to this date, quite curiously, no government agency has moved to investigate the claims, so this remains as just another red flag in the governor's résumé. Houdini would have been proud of Scott's escape tactics.

More recently, in 2015, Scott was found to have been using private email accounts to communicate with his staff for government business (remember Hillary Clinton?). He had *obstinately denied* the reality of those accounts but finally relented, astutely, when

Google was directed to submit all pertinent documents, something that could have exposed even more illegal emails and turned the issue into a really juicy, full-blown scandal—another narrow escape (Houdini, are you watching?). Actually, it is already scandalous, for Mr. Scott has had the gall to settle the lawsuits for violations of Florida's public-records law, totaling about $700,000, *with taxpayers' money*! As stated in a *Miami Herald* editorial:

> The governor violated the public's constitutional right of access, and the people of Florida now have the privilege of paying $700,000—for his denial of information to them. In other words, the public is both the injured party and the party liable for paying damages for the injury.[7]

As if that wasn't a big enough display of gubernatorial chutzpah, Scott has not fully revealed how much state money was spent to defend him from one of the lawsuits even though the *Herald* and several other parties have repeatedly requested the information for the public record. So it seems the governor not only used the people's money to pay for the penalties of his offenses but also for his legal fees, and the total tab (penalties plus legal expenses) is now estimated at upwards of one million dollars! Ouch! Scott violates; the people pay. It has a nice ring to it, doesn't it?

But that is not the only time Scott has plundered state funds to pay for his unethical conduct. Oh no! Another Tallahassee scandal saw him force the resignation of Florida Department of Law Enforcement commissioner Gerald Bailey in December 2014 for resisting repeated efforts by Scott and his top advisers to falsely name someone a target in a criminal case, hire political allies of Scott for state jobs, and intercede in an outside investigation of a prospective Scott appointee among other efforts to stage-manage the agency. In effect, the highly respected Bailey refused to cave in to Scott's attempted manipulations of the FDLE and got booted out.[8] When the issue escalated to a possible trial in which Scott would have to testify and explain why Bailey was fired, the governor shrewdly calculated the potential personal and political damage (read: the risk of his unscrupulous actions being publicly exposed) and thus wiggled out, Houdini-like, by settling a lawsuit for $55,000. Unfortunately for tax payers, that was only part of the cost. Oh, come on Scotty!

According to columnist Carl Hiassen, that was only "a fraction of its true cost to taxpayers," because Ricky's defense team consisted of more than a dozen private attorneys, and their fees came to about $365,000, all footed by those generous Floridians. Hiassen admits that it's still somewhat early to crown Scott as "Worst Governor Ever," but points out that no other governor in recent history "has worked harder to conceal his actions or spent more of the public's money covering them up." He adds cynically: "Scott wants to be remembered for creating jobs, and he will be. Lots of jobs for lawyers." [9]

I should be ending this segment, but there is so much controversy surrounding Florida's governor that I'm finding it difficult to keep my hands off the keyboard. So let me indulge my uncontrollable urge a little longer and tell you about a recent development in our state that is reflective not just of Rick Scott's unethical conduct, but of politicos in Florida in general. It deals with Dade Medical College, a for-profit "educational" institution that had to close its doors in November 2015 due to self-created financial problems. For the sake of brevity, let's itemize the bullshit surrounding the brouhaha, drawing on information extracted from several articles published in *The Miami Herald* during October and November 2015 [10 & 11]:

- The college's owner, Ernesto Perez, was a high school dropout who left school to join a rock band, was arrested in 2002 for aggravated battery, has still-pending 2013 charges for perjury, and in the 1990s was convicted and served time for exposing his genitals to a minor. His yearly salary was $431,999.

- Perez paid his father and mother $197,760 and $28,634 respectively to serve as "consultants." His wife also worked for the school. Her title? I kid you not: *Corporate Director of Ball Busting.*" Seriously.

- Perez hired the wife of the City of Homestead's Mayor, Steve Bateman, at $100,000 a year while the latter advocated for the sale of city-owned land to a Perez real estate associate at a steep markdown.

- Ninety percent of the school's money came from public funds, $100 million from taxpayers over the previous three years (for only two thousand students).

- One of the college's signature programs was a physical therapy assistant associate's degree costing $40,000, but it was *not accredited*, and students have complained that the school lied to them about accreditation.

- A state representative, Carlos Trujillo, who had worked for Perez, successfully pushed legislation to authorize the creation of *un*accredited physical therapy programs, *making Florida the only state in the union with such junk programs.*

- The college steered students into predatory loans that hooked them for years. Now many students are in debt for loans intended to cover the costs of a non-existent school and credits that cannot be transferred to traditional institutions.

- Eighty-seven percent of the nursing program graduates failed the state licensing exam in 2014 while the county's community college graduates passed the exam at five times the rate, paying only one-fifth the cost.

- The state's regulatory agency, CIE (Commission for Independent Education), never undertook *any* disciplinary action towards Dade Medical College nor could it document any instance of *ever* having disciplined *any* of the colleges it supervises due to student complaints.*

- Dismaying, but not surprising given Florida's scandal-ridden history, the CIE's board is controlled by representatives of the for-profit college industry, and, again, not surprisingly, Perez was a former CIE board member himself.

Now, *how* could Perez get away with this blatant bullshit? The short answer: he made political contributions—lots of them. The estimate is $750,000. He also had a state senator, Rene Garcia, on the school's payroll as a "government-relations expert." Among the recipients of Perez's generosity were many high state officials. The most prominent of them? Good guess! Rick Scott (you're getting good at this).
Reporter Michael Vasquez of the Miami Herald shares this tidbit: "When Perez needed a

---

* This includes another for-profit college, FastTrain, which was raided by the FBI in 2012, and whose owner was recently convicted for fraud, having accepted students without high school diplomas and bilking the government for millions in student loans and grants, an operation that featured aggressive recruiting tactics that included hiring strippers to work as recruiters while donning miniskirts and stiletto heels, "some hot mommas...the sluttiest girls you can find," as ordered by Alejandro Amor, the school's owner.

favor...he would charter a plane, invite a couple of politicians to join him and head to Tallahassee for a personal meeting with Gov. Rick Scott." [12]   Good buddies these guys.

So how did Perez funnel school money to politicians without making it too obvious? Answer: via his employees, directing them to make political contributions for which he would later illegally refund them (sometimes even backing opposing candidates running for the same office!). The man was a favorite darling of government officials, a political sugar daddy.   Grateful public servants that they are, with all that "support" Perez provided, Tallahassee legislators responded in kind, protecting and advancing the for-profit colleges industry via at least fifteen laws designed to lower quality standards, cut down on monitoring and supervision of the schools, and curtailing funds for state community colleges to hamper their competing programs, which are accredited and have produced good results at significantly lower prices.

But it doesn't seem that Mr. Scott and state legislators were too concerned about Perez's sleazy operation. In the words of Herald columnist Fred Grimm: "Lawmakers weren't bothered by an abysmal failure rate among his grads, or the high tuition, or the predatory loans foisted on his hapless students, or the dismal percentage of graduates who landed decent jobs. Not as long as they got their money." Grimm also charges that legislators used their power to curtail competition by "undermin[ing] respected nonprofit public institutions along with their constituents' best interests to keep a low-down operator happy." I would not find it astonishing if those lawmakers happen to have the lowest rates of insomnia in the state; they apparently sleep well at night—quite well.

As of this writing, Perez just recently pleaded guilty of illegally bundling more than $159,000 in campaign contributions (which is just part of the estimated $750,000 he dished out in political hand-outs). As you might expect, with his Tallahassee and South Florida connections, he got a wrist slap: two months of house arrest and probation, plus $59,000 for investigation costs, and a $50,000 charitable donation. But Perez has more trouble on the horizon, as he must face a criminal investigation into financial "irregularities" dealing with student loans.[12 & 13] In his defense, Perez says that he has been targeted. Couldn't happen to a nicer guy. By the way, during Scott's last run for governor his mom assured us that "Scotty is a good boy," so how could he associate with slime bags like Perez? Well, part of it is greed, of course, but it's also clear that Scotty lacks common sense, to the point of irrationality. Follow me to the next paragraph.

And from the files of the utterly unbelievable, we have the stupefying fact that after Rick Scott assumed the governorship, state environmental officials were told to refrain from using the terms "global warming" and "climate change" in official communications, emails, and reports. Even the word "sustainability" is discouraged. *What?* The agency entrusted to deal with the issue cannot call it by its name? How is this not a bad joke? Well, you see, Mr. Scott is among those who—ignoring the mounting evidence—still deny the existence of increasingly substantial environmental changes, such as rising ocean levels, that threaten our way of life (whether they are caused by human activity or by natural processes). He prefers to overlook the issue altogether, although when pressed he will refer to it as "nuisance flooding." This is particularly interesting, since Florida has been identified as one of the states most likely to be severely impacted by environmental threats in the not-too-distant future.

We know, of course, why Scott is so blind to the phenomenon, and it has to do with

16

business interests and budget considerations, as expenditures to combat the effects of climate change could run high. Legislation to attack the problem would not be popular with certain power brokers. So, let's pretend global warming and climate change do not really exist—not even as concepts—and let future governors deal with the consequences! [14] It's a proven formula: kick the can to the next generation; let them worry about it.

In a related issue, in 2016, parts of Florida's eastern coast have been suffering enormously from a gigantic toxic algae spread that is killing large numbers of fish, ruining beaches and the quality of life and business in affected townships. The main cause is agricultural waste from large farms, especially from Big Sugar, being dumped into Lake Okeechobee, which then works its way to the coastline via waterways. But Governor Scott and his Tallahassee cronies will not acknowledge the source of the problem because, well, by now you've already figured it out—those businesses contribute much mullah in political donations. Thus, Scott prefers to blame the Federal government for failing to provide the funds to increase the lake's capacity (to hold even more waste). Supposedly, Scott is becoming a bit desperate because he is entertaining a senate run in 2018 (God help us) and does not want to be remembered as "Governor Algae." However, his big problem is that he cannot antagonize the polluters because they will be helping finance his campaign! Now, that's a sticky one. Still, do not underestimate our man. He is more than capable of pulling off the high-wire act.

There is so much more that raises questions about Florida's governor and his cohorts that we could dedicate this entire book to reviewing the material. However, that is not the exclusive focus of this text, and so we should move on. Nevertheless, I'm not easily satisfied when it comes to discussing Rick Scott, so I find it irresistible to include at least one more item—this one dealing with the home insurance crisis in Florida—which, for those interested, I have placed in *appendix A* (Don't miss it; it's a deuce).

To close this segment (for real now), it should be noted that PolitiFact, the well-known fact-checking agency, has ranked 132 of Scott's statements, and two-thirds (66%) landed in the categories of half-truths, false, mostly false, and pants on fire. For the record, only 11% of his statements were scored as true (and 23% as mostly true).[15] With this statistical endorsement, I nominate Scott for the title of Florida's King of Bullshit. And I have no doubt the governor could compete at the national level in that category.

Speaking of bullshitters, it is only logical to allocate some space to the Democratic and Republican nominees of the 2016 presidential race. We'll start with the winning candidate, Donald Trump, unquestionably one of the most prolific bullshitters to run for the highest office in the land.

Donald Trump

Let me tell you, I'm a really smart guy. / The beauty of me is that I'm very rich.

I could stand in the middle of Fifth Avenue and shoot somebody; I wouldn't lose voters.

Saddam Hussein throws a little gas, everyone goes crazy. Oh, he's using gas!

–Donald Trump

You know that if Donald Trump wins we are going to have a Kardashian as president one day, right? It's the only logical step forward.

–Jimmy Kimmel

Those who went to bed early on November 8, 2016 woke up to the political shocker of the 21st Century. Underdog Donald Trump defeated heavily favored Hillary Clinton to close out one of the most contentious presidential races in U.S. history. In the process, "expert analysts" with their sophisticated polling systems got pie in the face. They never imagined that business mogul and television personality Donald Trump would beat all the odds and became the forty-fifth president of the United States. Ironically, Trump got less total votes but won the electoral votes, obtaining the presidency via a system that in 2012 he called "a disaster for a democracy." How do you like it now, Donald? For months the political pundits filled the public's ears with their predictions and "scientific" polls, all pointing to a Clinton victory, even a landslide triumph according to some. And lo and behold, it was all bullshit!

The same political analysts gave Trump a near-zero chance to win the Republican Party's nomination, and we all know how that turned out. How can they be so bad? And to think they get paid for that! In fact, Trump held the lead almost from the moment he announced his candidacy and dispatched opponents easily even with a foot in his mouth during most of the race for the nomination. That is utterly incomprehensible to many people, including this author. Who could have foreseen that this egotistical, offensive clown, devoid of any sense of propriety and as far from presidential as a person can be, would get to reside in the White House for at least four years. And no one but his most ardent supporters saw it coming—no one.

One of the most divisive figures ever in politics, Donald Trump managed to alienate large numbers of women, blacks, Hispanics, Muslims, immigrants, even the disabled with insults and derogatory remarks, a "strategy" many believed would cost him and the Republican Party dearly in the general elections (so much for that theory). Still, from the beginning, he had many people enthralled and ended up getting enough votes from estranged groups to win. WSJ columnist Monica Langley stated that Trump accomplished that by "playing to the Kardashian culture..." And in his own words: "I play to people's fantasies," and "a little hyperbole never hurts." Yes, as preposterous as it sounds, this rich, bombastic, tax-evading, lying con man, this bully, knew how to slip his crap past the bullshit filters of millions of voters and is now president.

Particularly dismaying is the cult that so quickly grew around Trump once he made clear his intentions to seek the presidency. Take this downright inconceivable survey result reported by The Miami Herald: "A Quinnipiac University survey...found that 45 percent of Trump supporters agreed with the statement, 'the American dream is dead...'" But when told the statement was made by Trump, 68 percent said they agreed."[16] Imagine that! If the Donald says it, well hell, it must be true. This cult-like adoration is why the tycoon, "reality TV" personality can make statements such as the one quoted above: "I could stand in the middle of Fifth Avenue and shoot somebody, and I wouldn't lose voters." What kind of bullshit is this? Comedian Conan O'Brien had this to say in one of his monologues: "A new study finds that Donald Trump's speeches are at a fifth-grade level. In other words, he's speaking two grades above his supporters." O'Brien may be right in pointing to Trump's wide appeal among the less educated, but let's not kid ourselves, a lot of well-informed, intelligent people also voted for Trump.

Even if often unable to articulate cohesive sentences and frequently resorting to simplistic language, innuendo, exaggeration, lies, and insults, Trump nevertheless saw himself as the best qualified candidate for president (and, obviously, many agreed). This is a man given to outlandish claims, such as his famous declaration that he will stem the immigrant tide from Mexico by building "a huge and beautiful" fence for which he will make Mexico pay (when Mexico's president commented that Trump is, essentially, full of it for making that claim, Trump retorted by saying, "Now the wall just got ten feet higher"); a candidate who claimed to have won a debate that he never attended; a science-challenged personality who claimed global warming is a Chinese hoax; a businessman who wants to fix the U.S. economy but bankrupted four businesses and is known to avoid paying bills, especially when the billing entity is a small business that can be bullied; an ultra-wealthy mogul who unconscionably preyed on aspiring business men and women by creating a bogus university that, essentially, turned out to be a rip off (more on this later).

However, sadly, it's worse than that. This is an individual who never served in the military—actually avoided the Vietnam War—and never served in an elected government position, but he still had the gull to belittle war heroes such as Arizona senator John McCain. This is a man who has bragged about sexually harassing women and fat-shamed a Miss Universe contestant. This is now the president of the United States, the man with control over the proverbial nuclear button, and yet in one of the Republican debates showed that he had no idea what makes up the United States' nuclear triad—the combined force of nuclear-armed bombers, submarines, and land-based missiles—that safeguards the nation and keeps our foes in check. That is beyond bullshit; it is outright terrifying.

Of particular concern is that one of Trump's strongest skills is lying—often. Yes, all politicians lie; it seems that it's part of the job description. But The Donald has turned the practice into an art. With his loudmouth rhetoric, he pulls people into his fact-free universe. From incorrect statistics about the United States' trade deficit with China and the numbers of undocumented Mexican immigrants coming into the country to the preposterous claim that "Hispanics love me," this tycoon-turned-politician cranks out the bullshit with prodigious, almost mechanical, efficiency. The influential magazine Politico, in a one-week survey determined that Trump's lying rate was one "inaccuracy" per five minutes of speech. Think about that. They state: "His remarks represent an *extraordinary* mix of inaccurate claims about domestic and foreign policy and personal and professional boasts that rarely measure up when checked against primary sources." As of October 2016, PolitiFact had tallied Trump's statements at 76 percent mostly or totally false. [17] That is even worse than Rick Scott's numbers!

Trump is no stranger to scandals, and since he's been under the political microscope, sordid details about some of his business dealings have emerged. Among these, we have the infamous Trump University scandal where thousands of students were duped with empty promises of a first-class education in real estate. The first thing the public learned is that Trump University was not a university at all, and that it operated illegally, without a New York state license. In effect, it was a classic bait and switch ploy, with the average sting running about $20,000 (some as high as $60,000). The National Review explains:

> ...free seminars were the first step in a bait and switch to induce prospective students to enroll in increasingly expensive seminars starting with the three-day $1495 seminar and ultimately one of respondents' advanced seminars such as the "Gold Elite" program costing $35,000. At the "free" 90-minute introductory seminars to which Trump University advertisements and solicitations invited prospective students...instructors engaged in a methodical, systematic series of misrepresentations designed to convince students to sign up for the three-day seminar at a cost of $1495. [18]

One of program's main attractions was the promise of a series of professional speakers and that "students would be "mentored" by "handpicked" real-estate experts, who would use Trump's own real-estate strategies." However, "none of the instructors was "handpicked" by Trump, many of them came from fields having nothing to do with real estate, and Trump "'never' reviewed any of the school's curricula or programming materials." The materials were actually outsourced to a third-party business geared to developing programs for various motivational speakers and timeshare rentals. According to the article, a university "playbook" was obtained that revealed the truth about the "university:" "The playbook says almost nothing about the guest speaker presentations....Instead, [it] focuses on the seminars' real purpose: to browbeat attendees into purchasing expensive Trump University course packages. To do that, instructors touted Trump's own promises." [19]

There is much more to this outrageous swindle, including "Trump's promises that the three-day seminar would include "access to 'private' or 'hard money' lenders and financing," that it would include a "year-long 'apprenticeship support' program," and that it would 'improve the credit scores' of students....." All of this was false. [20] It was a rip off, all bullshit, a calculated scam from the beginning, coldly designed to prey on people wishing to get ahead in life by starting their own businesses, some battling serious financial difficulties, even maxing out their credit cards to pay for the course. That Trump is willing to headhunt hapless people for personal gain is another indictment of the heartless, money-hungry tycoon.

It can't go without mention that the Trump University scandal had the Donald swimming in uncomfortably hot water, facing civil fraud lawsuits in New York and California. And here is an interesting morsel: The State of Florida announced that it was considering jumping in with the State of New York in a fraud probe targeting Trump U. and affiliates. Weeks before the announcement, Florida Attorney General Pam Bondi had asked Trump for a campaign donation, and he had not responded. However, only four days after the threatened participation of Florida in the New York fraud probe, Bondi's re-election officials received a $25,000 check. And guess what happened? *Miami Herald* columnist Fabiola Santiago tells us: "Bondi's office has a change of heart, finds insufficient grounds to proceed. No merit to the more than twenty complaints from Floridians against Trump University.... No need to join the New York lawsuit." [21]

Of course, that did not go unnoticed, and Bondi, concerned over the ink spill on her campaign, tried to justify her actions claiming she had only received one complaint against Trump U. However, the *Orlando Sentinel* found documents (later reviewed by AP) showing otherwise. Santiago explains: "The attorney general's office had received numerous complaints from people seeking help to get promised refunds for materials and personalized instruction that were never delivered by Trump Institute and/or Trump University, both under scrutiny in the New York trial." So the state attorney, the state's top dog in legal matters, the individual who is supposed to protect the people from scams such as Trump's, was, ahem, financially enticed to abandon the hunt, in the process abandoning the poor sucker's, the lambs who were fleeced by The Donald's shearing mill. This is not surprising of course. As Santiago points out: "Trump doesn't tire of boasting that he gives politicians money and receives favors from them." [22]

Trump was quite ready to throw his wolf pack of lawyers into a long-protracted fight overt Trump University, but something happened along the way: he became the next president of the United States. The scandal then became even louder, like a screaming ink stain on a clean white shirt, and shrewd Donald could not let that become the first blemish on his presidency, so only ten days after the elections he agreed to a $25 million settlement that will likely end this circus act. Ignoring the boos at the three-ring circus, Donald takes a bow, and the spotlight moves to another attraction. In fact, as of this writing, Trump's legal dogs are busy working to settle at least a few more of the large number of pending suits against him to keep him from having to testify in court and spare him additional embarrassment as president. But there is more, much more to be worried about.

Trump has shown to be clueless about national issues to a concerning degree and frequently resorted to simplistic answers and fabricated facts and accusations when asked challenging questions during the debates. He behaved, in effect, as a pompous ignoramus, but, as we saw all throughout his campaign, he is darn good at mounting personal attacks on his opponents, tapping into people's fears, and stirring up the extreme elements in the electorate. And that worked for him well enough to earn him the presidency. It's hard to argue with success.

It should also be noted that, for all the stink Donald Trump raised about Democrats during the race, he has never been especially loyal to any party. Trump was a Democrat until 1987 when he became a Republican for twelve years, switching to the Reform Party for three years until 2001, at which time he turned Democrat again, this time for eight years, until 2009, the year he became a Republican once more, this time only for about two years, when he decided to identify as independent from 2011 to 2012, at which point he returned to the Republican Party yet again. Not surprisingly, over the years Trump has made financial contributions to both parties, and while he supported Reagan and Romney, he picked Bill Clinton over both Bush presidents when asked which recent president was best. He's also donated almost a quarter million dollars to the Clinton Foundation and invited the Clintons to his wedding reception. Remarkably, he once wrote that Hillary would make "a great president," a woman he then declared to be completely harmful to the nation if she were to win the presidency. It seems clear that Trump will remain a Republican only as long as it is personally expedient (at least for the next four years). [23]

There is also evidence that, despite his claims, Mr. Trump is no conservative. As pointed out by William A. Gaston in the Wall Street Journal: "He backed the Obama administration's economic stimulus and the bailouts for the banks and the automobile industry. He supports higher taxes on the wealthy and the aggressive use of eminent domain. He has spoken approvingly of single-payer health insurance, tougher gun-control legislation and Planned Parenthood." Gaston also reveals that Trump has backed partial-birth abortion, and that his commitment to religious liberty has also been called into doubt. Trump's admiration for the despicable Russian ruler, Vladimir Putin, is also revelatory. That's hardly the record of a proclaimed conservative Republican. Gaston warns: "If I were a conservative, this litany would be enough to make me run screaming in the opposite direction." [24]

The WSJ summarized Donald Trump this way: "[He] is an opportunist, a huckster, and a demagogue; heedless and crude; bawling, blustery, and mean-spirited; emotional, insecure, and needless to say narcissistic...he is not interested in limited government or in constitutional restraints. He is obsessed with winning, regardless of the means. He believes in one-man rule. For every problem, he insists, there is a single, simple solution; He's so smart that he can fix it—details to come..." Short translation: the man is all about bullshit. There is also additional reason for concern, as the establishment in Washington is taking a cynical view: "Because Mr. Trump is a man without principles, we can do business with him. And besides, he's so clueless that he'll need us." [25] Yikes!

Trump's hypocrisy knows no bounds. During the presidential debates he consistently sounded his horn about bringing jobs back from China and other low-wage nations, even criticizing American businesses who took advantage of the starvation wages and relative lack of regulatory oversight their companies could enjoy in third-world nations. He has actually threatened the American automaker, Ford, with enormous penalizing taxes—should he become president—for having the audacity to build many of its cars in Mexico. In fact, he has been sufficiently insolent to declare that as president he would prohibit Ford from building a new facility in Mexico. But guess what? It has come to light that Trump himself has much of his clothing products made in both China and Mexico, not to mention his overseas hotel investments. Declares University of Michigan professor of economics and finance, Mark J. Perry: "When it comes to political hypocrisy, Donald Trump deserves a gold medal." [26]

Nevertheless, in spite of all we now know about Donald, a disturbingly high portion of the electorate did not seem to mind on November 8, 2016. His dubious background, his gargantuan ignorance, and the bullshit spewing out of his mouth had little detrimental effect on his campaign. And during the race for the nomination, he won a majority of states with barely a hiccup along the way. For instance, in Florida, none of the major newspapers endorsed Trump and were highly vocal in their criticism, and yet it didn't help Florida Senator Marco Rubio—one of many vanquished opponents—to have had the endorsement of not only renowned newspapers, but also governors, congress men and women, and other political leaders by a 30-1 margin. Trump pummeled Rubio in the primaries anyway, getting over one million votes and outscoring the junior senator in all but one Florida county. Amazing. And by the way, guess who is one of the few governors who endorsed The Donald? Why, Rick Scott of course! (surely you suspected this).

A final crumb or two about Donald Trump. This abysmally unqualified doofus has the unsavory distinction of appearing on the Howard Stern Show about a dozen times, visits during which the aspirant to the presidency of our nation discussed his sexual tendencies and preferences in ample detail with the repulsive shock jock (about whom I have dedicated a segment later in the book). [27] In fact, the sordid tycoon gave the sleaze king Stern permission to call his daughter Ivanka "a piece of ass." [28] Nice dad! And with less than one month before the elections, a 2005 audiovisual recording of Trump making lewd, sexist remarks that indicate he has used his celebrity power to sexually assault women surfaced, one more brushstroke on the lurid picture that has emerged about this controversial (that was a compassionate adjective) figure. For these assaults on decency alone, Trump does not deserve to reside in the same White House that shined with the likes of Lincoln, Roosevelt, Eisenhower, Reagan, and others who brought dignity and nobility to the office.

Let's consider this statement by Tony Schwartz, Donald Trump's ghostwriter for *Trump's Art of the Deal*, a person who got to know Trump very, very well:

> Lying is second nature to him. More than anyone else I have ever met, Donald Trump has the ability to convince himself that whatever he is saying at any given moment is true, or sort of true, or at least ought to be true. It's impossible to keep him focused on any topic. I feel a deep sense of remorse that I contributed to presenting Trump in a way that brought him wider attention and made him more appealing than he is. I genuinely believe that if Trump wins and gets the nuclear codes, there is an excellent possibility it will lead to the end of civilization.[29]

No doubt, a big factor behind the Trump phenomenon is the people's rejection of government, people fed up with the status quo and tired of crooked politicians, a clique of which Hillary Clinton is both a member and a symbol. It was an in-your-face rejection of corrupt Washington and all for which it stands, along with an unprecedented national debt, a faltering Affordable Care Act, the continuing loss of American jobs to third world countries, and lax enforcement of immigration laws. So, many voters pinched their noses and voted for change, even if Donald Trump made that choice nauseatingly difficult. Thus, for the sake of the nation and giving the new president a chance (which he has earned via free elections), we must now practice collective amnesia and try to forget a lot of what we saw and learned during the presidential race. It's the right thing to do, many now say, even if so unpleasant.

Actually, Trump has already begun to back off from his campaign rhetoric. All the talk about eliminating Obamacare, having Hillary Clinton prosecuted, building the wall on the Mexican border, and several other big claims and threats he made during the campaign were just classical bait-and-switch, promises made just to get elected—in other words, bullshit. Actually, this may turn out to be a good thing, as perhaps Trump will not be as radical as many feared. Only time will tell. Enough about The Donald.

Hillary Clinton

Don't let anybody tell you that it's corporations and businesses that create jobs.

My husband may have his faults, but he has never lied to me.

—Hillary Clinton

Donald Trump said he will not try and send Hillary Clinton to Jail. After hearing this, Bill Clinton said, "Hey, you promised."

—Conan O'Brien

Based on the preceding discussion, readers might suppose, not unreasonably, that this writer supported Hillary Clinton; but they would be wrong. Claiming that Clinton was the only hope standing between Trump's madness and the American people, her supporters correctly point out that, unlike The Donald, Hillary has the credentials, the experience in politics and intellect that her opponent sorely lacks. Among her more salient qualifications are an Ivy League law degree and having served as U.S. senator and Secretary of State (we could add First Lady as well). It would seem then, that with all we've learned about Trump, Clinton would have made an obvious choice in November. But was it really that obvious? Not to me. Let's look deeper into this.

One of the problems with Hillary Clinton is that she is the ultimate symbol of "the establishment," of Washington politics as usual, and as the election results indicate, voters are fed up with that. She is also seen as a Wall Street puppet who will sell her soul for a dollar. Those are two reasons Bernie Sanders gave her so much trouble in their bid for the Democratic Party nomination. Sanders continuously reminded electors about these points, especially her chummy relations with big corporations, hardly needing to attack her perilously exposed underside from the well-publicized email and Benghazi scandals. For readers with short memories, here is a review of those issues.

As then-Secretary of State, Clinton was accused of ignoring warnings of a possible attack on an American consulate in Libya that led to the deaths of several Americans in 2012, including ambassador Chris Stevens. Unconscionably, as the threat of attack became imminent, requests for additional security at the compound were denied by the State Department (in such a dangerous and unstable part of the world, no less!). This possible neglect of duty was compounded by the fact that when the State Department tried to respond to a 2014 request for Clinton's email records by a House committee investigating the Benghazi tragedy, no emails were available because Hillary had, "for convenience," used her private email accounts to conduct government business. That such a high-profile government official should have a completely empty work email record immediately raised eyebrows, fueling suspicion of a conspiracy to hide the truth about Benghazi, although it should be noted that a subsequent inquiry into the Benghazi affair appears to clear Clinton from the charge that she knew of the planned attacks.

Also of concern is that when Clinton left the job, she kept all her emails, even though she was obligated to turn them in under the Federal Records Act, and she delayed two years before giving up half of 60,000 emails that had resided on her server, claiming the rest were personal. Clinton repeatedly stated that she would cooperate with officials investigating the matter and answer all questions, prompting columnist Carl Hiaasen to observe, "...this promise is looking more and more like another shaded lie. Which investigators? Which questions? She refused to be interviewed by the inspector general or his staff while they worked on their report. A number of her top aides also declined to be questioned." [30] That eventually changed when the FBI got involved.

On July 5, 2016 the FBI announced the end of an investigation into the email controversy, concluding that Clinton had been recklessly careless by knowingly sending and receiving classified, *even top secret material* via several unprotected personal servers and multiple cell phones. Previously, Clinton had repeatedly denied that any classified material had ever been moved through those servers. She was caught in a lie—a big lie. Still, she caught a break when, even though she had clearly committed serious dereliction of duty, the FBI decided that prosecution was not warranted, on the grounds that she did not *intentionally* transact sensitive government material via the unsecured servers. Clinton's camp exhaled a sigh of relief as a potentially criminal act could now just be called "poor judgment." Whether a criminal act or not, the affair raises serious questions about Clinton's common sense and her valuing privacy and convenience over state security—really bad traits for a president.

Before the investigation Clinton had tried to wiggle out of the fracas, accepting responsibility for her oversights (but always denying handling classified information via her servers). What does that mean, exactly? What happens when we accept responsibility? Many of us would lose our jobs or get demoted in an organization for relatively small transgressions, but what were the consequences for Hillary? Was she even chastised by the administration? Of course not. This is serious stuff, folks. It is widely believed by cyber-espionage experts that her inadequately-secured email system was hacked by spy agencies from adversaries such as China and Russia, and possibly others, and the FBI admitted to the possibility (I suspect the FBI knew it happened but decided to avoid that hot potato). This negligence and the still lingering questions about by Benghazi put a visible dent on Clinton's political armor as the country wondered if she deserved a shot at the presidency. Let's talk about Hillary and money.

It is well known that the Clinton Foundation (founded by Bill) received "donations" from Wall Street powerhouses, such as Golden Sachs (from which she took $675,000 for three speeches), but also from Saudi Arabia, Morocco, and Oman—countries not known to be particularly friendly to women's rights—and even from Donald Trump.[31] Interestingly, the number of countries contributing to the foundation doubled from 2013 to 2014. Is it too cynical to suggest that this spike in contributing nations had nothing to do with Hillary becoming a presidential contender? I mean, we are being asked to accept that these are all well-meaning donations from foreign governments who care about the needy in the world. So, no one was trying to buy influence in the U.S. government, right? And besides, Hillary would not have allowed those "donations" to influence her in any way had she become president. Right? If you believe that, I have a sky lodge in the Everglades and a beach resort in Idaho I would like to sell you.

But that only refers to contributions to the Clinton Foundation and does not include money funneled to her campaigns via Super Pacs and donations from "individuals" related to large businesses and political organizations. In this regard, Clinton has not been shy about accepting money, regardless of the source. Beginning in 1999, when she first ran for the senate, Hillary received millions from "individuals" associated with the big names, with contributors including Emily's List ($907,510), Goldman Sachs ($831,523), Citigroup ($891,501), JPMorgan & Chase Co. ($801,380), Morgan Stanley ($765,242), DLA Piper ($852,873), and Time Warner ($603,170), just to name a few. [32] We are then expected to believe Hillary's assurances that she would not be influenced by these organizations when developing economic policies as president. One word for you Mrs. Clinton: Bullshit.

For readers old enough, try to think back to the time when then President Bill Clinton's little fling with White House intern Monica Lewinsky broke out and Hillary went public to dismiss the affair, which, in a 1998 segment of NBC's The Today Show, she blamed the whole incident on Bill's political enemies, calling it a right-wing conspiracy. Now, here is a multiple choice question: Why did Hillary Clinton go on national TV to deny Bill's affair and to blame his enemies for fabricating a lie? Let's try multiple choice: A) Hillary lacks common sense and/or is plain dumb to think the American public would buy that story; B) Bill lied to her so well that she ate up his claim of innocence hook, line, and sinker, thus showing how naive she is, especially given his history of womanizing (however, please see the second quotation at the top of this section); C) Hillary is a liar; D) Both A and C. Which of these (or a combination of these) is okay for a person who sought the presidency of our country?

Even with the brief coverage I've given her, it is no wonder that as early as June 2016 62% of Americans found Hillary Clinton "not honest and trustworthy," and only 33% believed she says what she means. [33] By July, the percent of those distrusting her was at 67%, and by August, an NBC poll showed that only 11% of voters viewed her as honest and trustworthy. I have no doubt that this negative perception cost her dearly on election day. Hillary is a politician through and through, meaning she can serve you a bullshit cocktail at any time and without batting an eye. Furthermore, she likes Washington, loves Wall Street, has a chip on her shoulder, a personal agenda, something to prove, and thirsts for power.

So, Trump or Hillary? That was the nightmare question voters faced on November 8, 2016. As reported by Doyle McManus of the Los Angeles Times: "They're the least-popular candidates ever to win their parties' nominations. Both are viewed unfavorably by a majority of voters—the first time that has happened in the history of modern polling. Both are running as the lesser of two evils." [34] In effect, and regrettably, a large segment of the electorate did not vote *for* a candidate, but *against* the other.

And those who considered the Libertarian candidate, Gary Johnson, as an alternative (as I did), were disappointed to learn that not only was he completely in the dark when asked about the situation in Syria—as he had no idea what Aleppo, a rebel-held city suffering unimaginable suffering and brutal bombings by its own government, stood for—he could not even come up with the name of a single foreign leader he admired. He probably doesn't know any. Yet, this clueless man had the stupefying audacity to ask voters to trust him to lead the nation! What kind of bullshit is that?

Eyes closed now, I toss a dart at the politician dart board to put one more under *the bullshit microscope*. It doesn't matter where it lands; it is guaranteed to strike the image of a corrupt individual. So, eyes closed, fling the dart, and...pop! Nancy Pelosi!

Nancy Pelosi

We have to pass the bill to find out what's in it.

—Nancy Pelosi

Nancy Pelosi is Minority Leader of the U.S. House of Representatives and served as the Speaker of the House for four years (2007-11), the only woman to hold the position. She represents California's 12th congressional district (mostly in the city of San Francisco) and is among the richest members of Congress (a very bad sign).

Pelosi is known for her penchant to take advantage of her influential position. One example is her famed use of the U.S. Air Force for her personal travels, a shenanigan some call "Air Pelosi." Pelosi flew in Air Force aircraft 47 times from April 2009 to January 2010 and 43 times from January 1 to October of 2010.[35] Her defense was that the practice was instituted by President Bush for security reasons after the 9/11 attacks, since her position placed her as third in line for presidential succession (a terrifying thought!).[36] However, while this excuse may sound reasonable, the record shows "Pelosi not only receiving special treatment on military flights (chocolate covered strawberries for her birthday, for example), but also ferrying her family back and forth on military aircraft, including her husband, daughter, granddaughters and son-in-law."[37]

Mrs. Pelosi has been frequently criticized for using her clout to benefit friends and wealthy contributors to the Democratic Party. A case often cited is her steering over one billion dollars in subsidies to a transportation project in San Francisco that resulted in sizeable financial benefits for Salesforce, a cloud computing company belonging to a big-time political contributor and in which her husband has made substantial investments. According to L. Markay of the *Washington Free Beacon*,

> "Pelosi...worked for more than a decade to steer taxpayer funds to a light rail project in San Francisco's Mission Bay neighborhood, where Salesforce had planned a new campus. Experts say the project boosted the value of Mission Bay real estate. The company's CEO...is a high-dollar Democratic donor. Pelosi and her leadership PAC are among the recipients of his generous campaign contributions. Pelosi's husband is also a major Salesforce investor." [38]

Nancy's penchant for abuse of power was also exposed during the insider trading scandal that hit the airwaves in November 2011 triggered by author Peter Schweizer's book *Throw Them All Out* (more about this in the next section). Schweizer had been particularly interested in learning why some members of Congress managed to grow their wealth so markedly after getting into office and how they became particularly skilled at timing the ups and downs of stocks. Apparently, the CBS's *60 Minutes* team of correspondents also wanted to know, as they too covered the scandal, which greatly expanded public awareness of the issue. The watchdog agency, *Judicial Watch*, explains one of the instances involving Pelosi:

> As detailed by Bloomberg, "Pelosi and her husband, Paul, with a net worth estimated at $40 million, bought shares in the initial public offering of credit-card company Visa Inc. in 2008, when Pelosi was speaker of the House... They bought the shares just before legislation died that would have limited the fees credit-card issuers could charge retailers. The shares more than doubled in the next two months."[39]

However, Pelosi was not the only prominent politician implicated (It would be naive not to expect more dirty hands inside the pot). Then Speaker of the House, John Boehner, was also exposed, and both avoided interviews with *60 Minutes'* correspondent Steve Kroft. "Nobody would talk to us," he said, recalling his frustration in trying to reach members of Congress. But Kroft was not about to give up the chase. Like a determined bloodhound on a fresh trail, he pursued his prey, relentlessly, and finally cornered Pelosi and Boehner during press conferences where, predictably, Pelosi tried to squirm out of answering the questions, offering evasive answers (read, bullshit) and redirecting the issue towards unrelated points.

Meanwhile, Boehner denied any decision-making regarding his trading of health care stocks while Congress was debating legislation that would affect the industry. In his words: "I have not made any decisions on day-to-day trading activities of my account.... I do not do it, haven't done it and wouldn't do it."[40] Notice the slippery nature of the statement, which aims to qualify the kind of trading (day-to-day) and the account involved (my account). You have to wonder what happened when his trading wasn't day-to-day or if an account under someone else's name was used. Kroft's ears must have been clogging from the bullshit coming from Pelosi and Boehner.

That two House Speakers have been implicated in insider trading activities is probably shocking to many people (but not me, and I suspect quite a few Americans). The illegal practice is a serious problem in Washington. I mean, this is criminal activity folks. We'll expand our discussion on this troubling issue some more a little later in the chapter, but first, let's cover one more political figure.

This time I will not cover my eyes when tossing the dart; I will aim directly to...drum roll please...Fidel Castro. Yes, I cheated by not following my script of blind selections, but this one became a must do, the result of events unfolding just before I was ready to release the book.

Fidel Castro

"He ran Cuba for almost 50 years. And political analysts are now debating what kind of changes the Cuban people will hope for. I'm gonna guess: term limits."
—Jay Leno

I had no plans to include Fidel Castro in this tome, but just before the manuscript was ready for publication, Fidel died—age 90—and, living in Miami, the epicenter of everything Cuban, I had to endure nearly ten days of unrelenting television and newspaper coverage of his life, "accomplishments," and the funeral procession that paraded his ashes from one end of Cuba to the other. It was a heavy dose of the same bullshit, the distorted, sanitized story of a revolutionary hero who deposed a hated tyrant, stood up to the mighty USA, brought relief to the poor, boosted literacy, and introduced free healthcare for everyone. While his opponents did get some media coverage, it was paltry in comparison. Thus, witnessing the rise of the old Castro myth—again—it would be a betrayal of my ancestors and the many who fought tirelessly against a ruthless dictator not to try to set the record straight.

28

Fidel Castro was, above all else, a power-hungry tyrant and murderer. There aren't enough lipstick and perfume bottles in France to cover up that truth despite the best efforts of that unrepentant legion of socialist admirers who insist on romanticizing the bloodthirsty despot's story. I was still living on the island when in his first year in power Castro went about the business of eradicating his enemies and anyone he suspected could give him serious opposition. He accomplished this via a horrifying string of executions. While the government-organized mobs screamed "Paredon! Paredon!" (the execution wall), the accused underwent quick, sham trials that usually ended in death sentences (the "lucky ones" sentenced to 20-30 years imprisonment). The convicted were then almost immediately walked to the "paredon" where they were executed by firing squad. On and on, day after day, this continued, the blood of the unfortunate ones accumulating on the dirt at the foot of the paredon, along with the bitter tears of mothers, fathers, wives, and children.

Fidel's partner in crime, the much exalted Che Guevara (another darling of the international left whose image persistently appears on t-shirts still popular among the ignorant) oversaw many of the executions, sometimes placing a bullet into the pleading victim's head himself. Over time, dozens became hundreds, and hundreds became thousands. It did not take very long for the early-days euphoria to transform into terror.

There is so much that can be said about Castro and the misery he brought to his people that we could easily fill a thick book with small print. So, for brevity's sake, and since this is not a book about Fidel, I'll recap what I know to be factual, with a little help from Carlos Eire, author and T.L. Riggs Professor of History and Religious Studies at Yale University who wrote a sobering article for the Washington Post on November 26, 2016, one day after Castro's death.

● As already stated, Castro employed firing squads to murder thousands of his own people, and these sometimes included men who fought in the mountains side-by-side with him, those who began to resist the dictator's drift towards a highly repressive system of government. One of them, Camilo Cienfuegos, a beloved "comandante," a favorite with the people (more loved than Fidel in those days, many say), was "lost in an accident," when his plane disappeared off the north coast of the island. The not-so-well kept secret is that Castro had the plane shot down.

● He embraced communism and made Cuba a slave-state of the Soviet Union, maintaining the nation perennially on a war-footing, in constant fear of the U.S., which which he blamed for everything that ailed the nation. This tactic that served him well for decades.

● He sponsored terrorism in Latin America and sent Cuban soldiers to die in Africa as proxies for Russian troops.

● He allowed—actually encouraged—the Soviet Union to install nuclear missiles in Cuba, and during the Cuban Missile Crisis of 1962 actually egged Russian leader Nikita Khrushchev to *initiate a pre-emptive nuclear strike on the United States* that, fortunately, never took place.

● He cracked down on all forms of dissent and built concentration camps and prisons that he filled with those daring to oppose him, alongside others he deemed undesirable. These were tenebrous places where beatings and torture were common. On a percentage basis, Castro incarcerated more of his own people than many other dictators, including Stalin.

• His "wonderful revolution" has so far pushed 20 percent of his people into exile, with many unfortunate ones dying at sea in their desperate efforts to flee Castro's "utopia." It should be noted that no Cubans have died, or have even been seen, going in the opposite direction, trying to reach Cuban shores.

• He outlawed private businesses and labor unions, in the process eradicating Cuba's large middle class, enslaving a vibrant nation, and devastating Latin America's third largest economy, all while he accumulated personal wealth for himself and his henchmen.

• He persecuted gays and exalted his atheist communist state over God, enfeebling religion.

• He eliminated elections and censored all means of expression and communication.

• He instituted an omnipresent surveillance mechanism where neighbors spy on neighbors and report them to authorities for the smallest of infractions or perceived anti-government sentiments. In fact, in Cuba you can be jailed for just seeming to be a potential threat—peligrosidad (dangerousness) they call it. Just ponder that for a minute or two. In such an idyllic nation, you wonder why; what did Castro, and now his brother, have to worry about?

• His vaunted schools were (and still are), above all else, indoctrination centers where students were taught the superiority of communism over democratic systems and to worship Fidel.

• His admired health-care system consisted of two levels: one with inferior medical care for the majority of Cubans (lacking drugs and even sheets for hospital beds) and the other with first-class physicians and facilities for himself and other high-ranking government officials.

• Due to his failing economy, he had to allow the country's infrastructure and once immaculately-maintained buildings to crumble. After a few decades, the capital city of Havana, once hailed as the "Paris of the Americas," was in ruins, with some neighborhoods reminiscent of the poorest quarters in Haiti, the most wretched state in the Americas. Essentially, the country became suspended in time, 1959, paralyzed, except for the more desirable locations on the island where the communist government incentivized international investors (those capitalist pigs) to build modern resorts on Cuban beaches, places where today foreigners enjoy privileges denied to the native population. In effect, the Cuban people became second-class citizens.

• While other dictators were internationally condemned and some made to pay for their crimes and injustices, Castro was never convicted. Instead, he basked in the adulation of many world leaders who preferred to view him as a Latin American Robin Hood, shamefully looking the other way while the Cuban people languished under the most oppressive, homicidal government in the history of the western hemisphere.

In Eire's words: "In sum, Fidel Castro was the spitting image of Big Brother in George Orwell's novel '1984.'"

And then I, along with many other Cuban exiles, especially those who experienced the nightmare directly, must continue to treat our acid indigestion every time we hear media apologists exalting the Cuban revolution and its amazing accomplishments, those who call Castro a liberator, the father of the revolution, a hero, a symbol of freedom for the world's oppressed and exploited. We have to continually remove from our ears the stinking bullshit of those morally-challenged propagandists.

There. That needed to be said. Now let's get back to American politics.

Insider Trading in Congress

It could probably be shown by facts and figures that there is no distinctly American criminal class except Congress.

—Mark Twain

The Pelosi and Boehner cases discussed earlier in the chapter are only two examples of a long-standing problem of insider trading in Congress, and Washington has shamelessly pushed the issue under the rug for decades. In 2011, best-selling author and President of the Government Accountability Institute Peter Schweizer, published *Throw Them All Out: How Politicians and Their Friends Get Rich off Insider Stock Tips, Land Deals, and Cronyism That Would Send the Rest of Us to Prison*. As mentioned earlier, and as the book's title suggests, Schweizer went after politicians he believed had dirty hands in insider trading transactions. This led to an award-winning CBS *60 Minutes* investigation and report.

The book's success and *60 Minutes'* report rattled Washington, leading to President Obama mentioning the troubling issue in his 2012 State of the Union Address, which led to the passing of a bill to tackle the problem. Members of Congress—including Pelosi and Boehner—knew it would be political suicide to vote against the bill, and so in an extremely rare bipartisan show of solidarity, they passed it by an overwhelming vote (Senate: 417-2; House 96-3).[41] All seemed well with the STOCK Act, as it was called. However, privately, members of Congress seemingly were not happy with the bill's provisions. I wonder why?

Consequently, in 2013, Congress quietly moved to disembowel the bill, eliminating a pivotal stipulation that called for the online publishing of financial disclosure records of federal officials (publicly available) in an effort to enhance transparency. In effect, politicians did not want to make it too easy for the public to access the information.

Further proof of Congress' hypocritical stance came when they moved to block a major SEC investigation of insider trading. As reported by Lee Fang of *The Intercept*:

> The SEC investigation focused on how Brian Sutter, then a staffer for the House Ways and Means Committee, allegedly passed along information about an upcoming Medicare decision to a lobbyist, who then shared the tip with other firms. Leading hedge funds used the insider tip to trade on health insurance stocks that were affected by the soon-to-be announced Medicare decision.[42]

Fang adds that House attorneys "claimed that a SEC investigation...should be blocked on principle, because lawmakers and their staff are constitutionally protected from such inquiries given the nature of their work." They further argued that "the insider trading probe violated the separation of powers between the legislative and executive branch." [43] No, I'm not making this up. On the 1-10 bullshit scale, this hollow argument rates a solid 9.5.

So, if you ever wondered why so many members of Congress end their service wealthier than when they first went to Washington, you have part of the answer. Not surprisingly, those now in office do not want to see the gravy train stop.

Pork and Bullshit

The owners of this country know the truth: It's called the American dream because you have to be asleep to believe it.

—George Carlin

"Can any of you seriously say the Bill of Rights could get through Congress today? It wouldn't even get out of committee."

— F. Lee Bailey

Pork barrel is nothing new in politics, but it seems politicians are forever looking for new ways to add the fat to government budgets as they seek to entrench themselves in office. In recent years, with federal, state, and local government budgets under enormous pressure to contain expenditures, pork nevertheless found its way into financial plans at all levels of government. Some of it was particularly outrageous, as in the case of IMG Academy in Bradenton, Florida, which managed to suck $5 million from Florida's taxpayers in 2014. The academy is a private training center for professional athletes that includes a boarding school specifically designed for aspiring tennis, golf and baseball players. In the words of Miami Herald columnist Carl Hiassen, "At a time when some public school teachers don't have enough textbooks for all their students, the idea of subsidizing a for-profit campus like IMG is obscene." [44] The next year brought more, of course.

For the 2015 budget, the legislature allocated a much restrained $50,000 for the academy, but just before the budget was finalized it "mysteriously ballooned to $2,050,000" No rationale was offered for the surprise $2 million, but, according to Hiassen, it is known that the school has a major supporter in the legislature—House Speaker Steve Crisafulli, who defended the appropriation, calling it an "'opportunity for more choice in education.'" Hiassen comments: "Really? IMG might be a fabulous 'choice' if you can afford $70,000-a-year in tuition and your kid can whack a tennis ball 100 mph." To his credit (and under the magnifying lens of his critics), Governor Scott vetoed the handout.[45]

At the federal level we've seen ridiculous pork projects that would make good jokes if it wasn't that taxpayer money was involved. For some examples, let us look back at 2010 during Obama's first term: How about $200,000 for a tattoo removal project in California? $500,000 to maintain a WW I statue in France? $3.8 million to save part of old Tiger Stadium in Detroit, just for the memories? $9.7 million to save Hawaiian sea turtles, seals and crustaceans? A $15 million contribution to the International Fund for Ireland (IFI) to "promote economic and social advance and to encourage contact, dialogue and reconciliation between nationalists and unionists throughout Ireland"? [46] Think these are bad? Here is one for the history books.

A $465 million siphoning of citizens' pockets to continue development of the F-136 engine as an alternative engine in the Joint Strike Fighter program. Already over budget by $55 billion, Congress kept funding the project even though they knew the engine would never be used. The funds were allocated "despite the fact that the winning engine had already prevailed in half a dozen public and private competitions...." In addition, years before, "the Air Force and two independent panels concluded that the second engine [was] 'not necessary and not affordable' and that the professed savings from competition "'will never be achieved.'" The article concludes with the comment: "No wonder that all 435 representatives and 100 senators refused to be identified with this massive waste of tax dollars." [47]   All this waste of our money, and yet, woe onto you should you try to slip an undocumented contribution to your church or make a mistake in your IRS return!

A close second in the waste category is the F-35 fighter. Riddled with problems and barely working, the Department of Defense still considers it the "next generation" jet and has already paid over $400 billion (and counting, as Congress seems willing to pour more billions into the project). [48]   I mean, what's another few billion when you've already thrown hundreds of billions into the hole?

These and more inexcusable expenditures during a time of unprecedented expansion of the national debt! And then we have to hear the politicos' bullshit about how hard they're working to control expenses, passing the blame when possible to the other party. So, carry on good citizens, keep voting and putting those irresponsible bastards in office so they can continue to plunder government coffers, wasting our money and amassing personal wealth.

Globalization — More Bullshit

Capitalism has defeated communism. It is now well on its way to defeating democracy.

— David Korten

"Facts do not cease to exist because they are ignored..."
—Aldous Huxley

The concept of globalization was sold to the American people as beneficial (much as trade agreements are invariably advertised). Here is a definition: "Globalization is the *integration* of national economies through trade, investment, capital flow, labor migration, and technology." The key word in the definition is "integration." And some may ask, Why would any economically developed nation would want to *integrate* with a lesser developed one?

The answer is rather obvious if you look at it from the perspective of large corporations. There is nothing sweeter to the bottom line than being able to exploit foreign workers for, say .75 cents an hour versus paying Americans at least a minimum wage salary (plus benefits in many cases). Moving entire manufacturing divisions out of an economically advanced country often brings additional perks in the form of reduced tax liabilities (or none at all). So why would big companies not want globalization? What's not to like?

The same question would be answered quite differently by the many workers who lose their jobs when factories close shop and move to China, India, Malaysia, and a host of other countries where labor is cheap and restrictions on companies are minimal. Think of the labor laws, employee rights, environmental protection regulations, and other such social advances that took many years to become a part of developed nations, societies that learned to value individual rights and the basic human need to live a decent life. Unfortunately, those cost money, and businesses, especially the large corporations, do not like the effect those social advances have on their profits.

Regrettably, globalization results in the accelerated transfer of jobs from developed nations to undeveloped (or less developed) countries because it is difficult for companies based in economically stronger states to compete with corporations benefitting from the lower costs of operating in the third-world. Consequently, it should not come as a surprise that "the percentage of US citizens holding jobs started dropping about the time China joined the World Trade Organization in 2001." [49]

One of the problems with this corporate flight (other than the obvious economic harm done to workers) is that the tax base in countries losing jobs, such as the United States, is reduced: the less people employed, the less taxes the government collects. This has contributed, along with high oil prices (at least until recently), increased unemployment payments, and other factors, to higher U.S. government spending. And because the dollar is the world's reserve currency, we can continue to run deficits for years, which is not bound to end well. Gail Tverberg, Fellow of the Casualty Actuarial Society and author of *Our Finite World*, explains the unsavory consequences: "...the result is that the US can run deficits year after year, and the rest of the world will take their surpluses and use it to buy U.S. debt. With this arrangement, the rest of the world funds the United States' continued overspending." [50]

There are other serious problems with globalization, but this is not a book, or even a chapter, about the concept, so I must keep what follows brief. Tverberg makes several other observations about globalization, including the tendency for countries to devalue their currency to gain a competitive advantage via the lower prices of their goods. But this "race to the bottom" can have dire consequences, one of which is the corresponding high prices of imports (due to the debased currency), the creation of asset bubbles (artificially high stock market prices and bond prices), which could lead to investment crashes.

Furthermore, globalization leads to dependence. Because certain goods can be bought cheaply outside of the country, nations may decide to stop producing those goods. This is particularly dangerous if those commodities are essential, such as food or highly specialized components for military use. An interruption of these vital imports as a consequence of an unexpected change in leadership or government practices in nations upon which another relies could be dangerously destabilizing, even a threat to the national security of the dependent state. There are already concerns that the United States has become too dependent on China, including dependence on what are known as rare earth minerals (which are critical to high-tech devices from cell phones to fighter planes), which the U.S. essentially stopped mining. Another example is shipbuilding, where just about all ships are now made in China.

In fact, the 2015 sinking of the cargo ship "El Faro" in the Caribbean could be partly blamed on globalization. The sinking was not just the consequence of the captain daring to take the ship through the outer reaches of a hurricane, but also the result of keeping a very old craft in operation, which was due to current laws requiring that ships running the route between Jacksonville and Puerto Rico (and I assume other routes as well) be U.S. made vessels. The problem is that no such ships are built in the United States anymore—they are all made in China.

I hope this brief discussion has been sufficient to show that globalization is bullshit. The U.S. government (whose officials benefit from financial contributions by big businesses who see advantages in globalization) sold this pile of crap to the American public, claiming that it would be extremely beneficial, such as bringing us low-cost lawn mowers, prefab furniture, hardware, pencils, toys, and myriad other products (many so poorly made they're not worth the savings). The bottom line is this: there has been a massive transfer of wealth to other countries. Worse, it has also been a transfer of wealth to our enemies, especially China.

Let us not forget that China is not our friend. Consider the revelations made in a January 2016 *60 Minutes* report about the enormous amount of espionage the Chinese are conducting to plunder the technological and intellectual wealth of U.S. companies. The Justice Department has said that "the scale of China's corporate espionage is so vast, it constitutes a national security emergency, with China targeting virtually every sector of the U.S. economy, and costing American companies hundreds of billions of dollars in losses—and more than two million jobs." As John Carlin, the Assistant Attorney General of National Security asserts, the Chinese do not seek to beat us at innovation, research, or development; they simply want to steal it all; they want to get to our most valued, cutting-edge corporate know-how, and they are doing it. They are massively invested in it. This all-out attack on the American economy has been called 'The Great Brain Robbery' of America." [51]

The journalistic segment highlighted a U.S. company, American Superconductor, that spent millions developing sophisticated gadgetry and computer software for wind turbines, which the Chinese stole from them, and then proceeded to put in their turbines and sell them worldwide, including to the State of Massachusetts (paid with government funds) where the victimized company is located! The Chinese are also using this stolen technology in turbines installed all over China. American Superconductor almost went broke, losing over a billion dollars in market share and having to let go 600 out of 900 American workers. [52] This from "our friends in the Pacific." Unbelievable.

Adding to the threat is the flexing of our "economic partner's" newfound financial muscle (largely thanks to us) and its quickly-modernizing military to challenge the United States in Asia and other parts of the world, even in space. China has already begun to ratchet up its bullying of neighboring states (e.g. The Philippines, Japan, Taiwan, Vietnam), forcing the United States to maintain high levels of military spending to counter the growing threat in the Pacific. It is disheartening that through the farce of globalization and its inaction in the face of blatant Chinese espionage and to satisfy giant, avaricious corporations, our government has helped finance the rapid strengthening of the Colossus of the East. In effect, we have bankrolled the creation of a threat to ourselves. This is dangerous and shortsighted; this is harmful bullshit.

Democracy in America — Even More Bullshit

When one hundred million people don't vote, the nation is not bitterly divided. The nation mostly doesn't give a shit.

— Matt Taibbi, Rolling Stone writer

The best argument against democracy is a five-minute talk with the average voter.

—Winston Churchill

When you find yourself on the side of the majority, it is time to reform.

—Mark Twain

It's interesting, rather amusing actually, how we spend so much effort in predicting the winners of American elections. Political analysts devote a significant part of their professional lives to the pursuit, and voters dedicate countless hours to listen to what those "experts" and their "scientific" polls have to say. The results of these always-premature and unreliable surveys are over analyzed and debated, and some kind of meaning, usually communicated via baseless prophecies from political pundits, is extracted from them. Issues of the day are tossed around and argued, sometimes quite heatedly. We exalt the "democratic" system and emphasize the duty of citizens to vote, and we teach that to our children. And yet, for the most part, none of it matters. Let's make it brutally simple: the candidate with the most money is going to win (most of the time).

You see, we do not live in a democracy; we live in an oligarchy, that is, government by a few. And those privileged few have deep pockets—very deep. So, if you want to know who is going to win a race for public office, spare yourself the trouble of sifting through all the political bullshit we get from television and other news sources and just follow the money. Think I'm exaggerating? I'll make it brief and simple. Here are some uncomplicated but highly revelatory figures about the 2014 midterm races: [53]

- 94 percent of biggest spenders in races for the House of Representatives won.
- 82 percent of biggest spenders in races for the Senate won.

There. For those who still believe American voters choose their leaders based on candidates' positions on important issues, their values, perceived integrity and such nostalgic factors, those numbers are a wakeup call—and a loud one. It speaks volumes not just about the power of money, but about the ease with which citizen Joe and citizen Jane are manipulated by those who can afford it. Sad to say, we are not smart enough, informed enough, and possibly do not care enough, to see through the smoke screens and make good choices (assuming there are good choices to make!). Tragically, the money that buys our votes oftentimes comes from powerful industries that—I hate to break it to the naive among us—do not have our best interest in mind. The rich buy their puppets and propel them into office in an avalanche of dollars. Those dollars, of course, are *an investment*, since these elected officials will be creating and passing bills designed to profit their sponsors and, when feasible, stifle their competitors.

Unpardonably, in 2010 the U.S. Supreme Court, as part of the Citizens United decision, voted to institutionalize this travesty by ruling that corporations are people, thus opening the door for unrestrained political contributions by corporate giants. The argument is that corporations have the right to make political expenditures because political spending is protected by the First Amendment right to free speech. That decision screams—bullshit!

The creation of so-called Super PACs has only added to the problem. Although in theory these political money machines cannot contribute directly to a candidate's campaign, they can spend all the money they want running their own propaganda in support of a contender (or several), consequently having the potential for a huge impact on the result of an election. And while the majority of contributions to Super PACs (at least for the moment) are mostly from wealthy, private individuals, we don't need to ask who owns those big companies that stand to benefit from preferential legislation from friendly elected officials—do we?

In effect, our system of electing government officials is a farce, a charade. And for all the noise we make these days about not trusting politicians, especially those candidates with substantial financial backing from special interests, we still keep voting them in. In fact, we vote them in even when they have violated laws and shown clear lack of integrity, as we have seen with Florida Governor Rick Scott, among several (and, think about it, whoever we decide to make president in November 2016). Examples of this cultural illness abound, but let's just look at one more.

Let's take U.S. Rep. Alcee Hastings of Florida, an ex-federal judge who was charged with bribery in 1983 (acquitted), later impeached by the House of Representatives and then fired from his post as federal judge by the Senate. You'd think his political career would have been kaput after that, right? No, no, no—not by a long stretch. In fact, with incomprehensible shamelessness he ran for office and was immediately *rewarded* by voters, electing him to Congress in 1992. And, disturbingly, he has hung on to his job since then and is aiming for reelection in 2016. How 'bout them apples? Is our collective olfactory sense so stunted that we can't smell the bullshit? In the famous 1960s protest song, *Where have all the flowers gone?* artists Peter, Paul and Mary ask: "When will they ever learn?" It's a good question for our times. When, indeed.

Now, here is a shocker I've been saving for last. As unbelievable as this is going to sound, it is, sadly, true: Congress men and women spend more hours in a work day soliciting money than conducting government business, and it is *their first responsibility*. Yes, you read that right. Running the country, doing what the voters mandated them to do is secondary, and to some possibly just an afterthought.

Florida congressman David Jolly, who was first elected to congress in 2014, and who is extremely disappointed with what he learned as a rookie congressman, explained the process in a *60 Minutes* report with correspondent Norah O'Donnell that aired on April 24, 2016. It's important to give the issue some space in this section so that readers can really understand what is going on in Washington. Here is part of the transcript:

> Rep. David Jolly: We sat behind closed doors at one of the party headquarter back rooms in front of a white board where the equation was drawn out. You have six months until the election. Break that down to having to raise $2 million in the next six months.

And your job, new member of Congress, is to raise $18,000 a day. *Your first responsibility* is to make sure you hit $18,000 a day.

Norah O'Donnell: Your first responsibility—
Rep. David Jolly: My first responsibility

Norah O'Donnell: --as a congressman?
Rep. David Jolly: --as a sitting member of Congress.

Norah O'Donnell: How were you supposed to raise $18,000 a day?

Rep. David Jolly: Simply by calling people, cold-calling a list that fundraisers put in front of you, you're presented with their biography. So please call John. He's married to Sally. His daughter, Emma, just graduated from high school. They gave $18,000 last year to different candidates. They can give you $1,000 too if you ask them to. And they put you on the phone. And it's a script. There are actually scripts for calls. We got our hands on one distributed by the National Republican Congressional Committee to help GOP members invite donors to attend their annual fundraising dinner in March.

It has this useful diagram. If the donor answers the phone, the caller should plug the "unique opportunity to come together with House Republican leadership." If they get turned down, they should remind the donor that "the NRCC did a great deal to help maintain...the majority in 2014." And if they get a yes, there's even an instruction for the caller to "pause and let the donor speak."

It must have worked. That NRCC dinner raised more than $20 million -- breaking records. It was attended by members of Congress, major donors and lobbyists....But one successful fundraiser does not let Congress members off the hook. The phone calls asking for money never stop.

Rep. David Jolly: The House schedule is actually arranged, in some ways, around fundraising.

Norah O'Donnell: You're telling me the whole schedule of how work gets done is scheduled around fundraising?

Rep. David Jolly: That's right. You never see a committee working through lunch because those are your fundraising times. And then in between afternoon votes and evening votes, that's when you can see Democrats walking down this street, Republicans walking down that street to spend time on the phone making phone calls. By law, members of Congress cannot make fundraising calls from their offices. So both parties have set up "call centers" just a few blocks away...

Norah O'Donnell: So can I go in there?

Rep. David Jolly: I don't think they would let either one of us in here, at this point. Remember, I stopped paying my dues.

What Jolly means is that in addition to raising money for their own campaigns, members are supposed to raise thousands of dollars for their parties. That's their dues. If Republican members don't pay up, they can't use the party's call suites...

Later in the interview:

Rep. David Jolly: It is a cult-like boiler room on Capitol Hill where sitting members of Congress, frankly I believe, are compromising the dignity of the office they hold by sitting in these sweatshop phone booths calling people asking them for money. And their only goal is to get $500 or $1,000 or $2,000 out of the person on the other end of the line. It's shameful. It's beneath the dignity of the office that our voters in our communities entrust us to serve.

Norah O'Donnell: What has your party said about how members of Congress should raise money?

Rep. Rick Nolan: Well, both parties have told newly elected members of the Congress that they should spend 30 hours a week in the Republican and Democratic call centers across the street from the Congress, dialing for dollars.

Norah O'Donnell: Thirty hours a week?

Rep. Rick Nolan: Thirty hours is what they tell you you should spend. And it's discouraging good people from running for public office. I could give you names of people who've said, "You know, I'd like to go to Washington and help fix problems, but I don't want to go to Washington and become a mid-level telemarketer, dialing for dollars, for crying out loud."

Norah O'Donnell: You're saying members of Congress are becoming like telemarketers?

Rep. Rick Nolan: Well, 30 hours a week, that's a lot of telemarketing. Probably more than most telemarketers do.

The Republican House Campaign Committee would not tell us whether it recommends a specific amount of call time. The Democratic Congressional Campaign Committee claims it currently does not. But in 2013, at an orientation meeting, new Democratic members were shown a model schedule. It was later published by the Huffington Post.

It suggested representatives should spend four hours a day on calls and just two hours a day on the business of Congress - committee meetings and time on the House floor.

In Norah O'Donnell's words: "That's more time calling and asking for money than constituent work or floor work in Congress." [54] There is much more to the interview (I recommend that you visit the website—see endnote 53 for the address), but this should suffice to leave at least a few readers in a near-catatonic state.

Assuming the reader has recovered from the jolt of the preceding revelations, I move to add one more stunner, and it deals with a recent book by magazine writer Robert Atkinson: *The Confessions of Congressman X: A Disturbing and Shockingly Frank Tell-All of Vanity, Greed and Deceit.* According to Amber Phillips of *The Washington Post,* the lawmaker—Congressman X—who understandably wants to remain anonymous, told Atkinson about the greed, power-obsessed mentality in congress where so many—himself included—respond, not to their constituents, but only to money-wielding lobbyists and super PACSs. In his words: "The average man on the street actually thinks he influences how I vote. Unless it's a hot-button issue, his thoughts are generally meaningless. I'll politely listen, but I follow the money." He adds: "I flatter constituents with birthday greetings on gold-embossed congressional stationery....It's all crock, but happy people mean more votes at the polls. And that's what it's all about." [55] Think about that next time you head to the polls to fulfill your citizen duties.

In conclusion, our representative democracy exists only in principle. Politicians are for sale like a commodity; it's all about money. The levels of corruption are taking dishonesty to unprecedented heights and leadership to new lows. Donald Trump himself put it best: "When I want something, I get it. When I call, they kiss my ass. It's true."

The statesmen of yore—the Lincolns, Roosevelts, and Eisenhowers—are nowhere to be found. The opportunists, money grabbers, and clowns now run the circus. Together now: This is bullshit!

Bullshit in Political Language — Lies and Euphemism

> *"First get your facts; then you can distort them at your leisure."*
> — Mark Twain

> *Do not confuse us with the facts; our minds are already made up!*
>
> — Earl Landgrebe

In his influential essay "Politics and the English Language," famed British writer George Orwell states that political language "is designed to make lies sound truthful and murder respectable, and to give an appearance of solidity to pure wind." He also declared that "political speech and writing are generally in defense of the indefensible," and hence must often rely on euphemism, canned phrases, and an inflated prose. In effect, he believed that politicians do not choose words to convey meaning, but instead to cloud issues and minds. "But if thought can corrupt language..." Orwell said, "language can also corrupt thought." Later in the essay he warns: "This invasion of one's mind by ready-made phrases...can only be prevented if one is constantly on guard against them, and every such phrase anaesthetizes a portion of one's brain."

Orwell provides examples of political euphemism during World War II:

> Defenseless villages are bombarded from the air, the inhabitants driven out into the countryside, the cattle machine-gunned, the huts set on fire...: this is called pacification. Millions of peasants are robbed of their farms and sent trudging along the roads with no more than they can carry: this is called transfer of population or rectification of frontiers. People are imprisoned for years without trial, or shot in the back of the neck or sent to die of scurvy in Arctic lumber camps: this is called elimination of unreliable elements. [56]

In Orwell's celebrated political novel, *1984*, the use of language as a tool of control by the government is a major theme, and *euphemism* is central. For example, in Big Brother's police state of Oceania, where the story unfolds, the Ministry of Peace is the government agency that directs wars; the Ministry of Truth is the bureau where government lies and propaganda originate and history is changed; the Ministry of Plenty is the office that controls rationing of goods and keeps the population in a constant state of scarcity; and the Ministry of Love is where citizens and "enemies of the state" are tortured and sentenced. While the discrepancy between name and function of Big Brother's government agencies may seem exaggerated, we are not that far removed today. The tactic is very much alive.

For instance, it is in the departments of justice of many nations that the greatest injustices are committed, and it is in totalitarian countries that deny the most basic rights that we find names similar to those Orwell created. For example, before it was liberated from behind the Iron Curtain, East Germany was called "The German Democratic Republic," and today North Korea, the most extreme totalitarian regime in the history of the planet, calls itself "The Democratic People's Republic of Korea." The Soviet Union called itself "Union of Soviet Socialist Republics (USSR)," a "union" of so-called "republics" maintained by brute force. China's title is "People's Republic of China," as if the people had any say in the affairs of the country. Of course, we all know how ridiculous the names are, for none of these nations are (or were) democracies, and they stretch the concept of a republic to the breaking point. It is, quite simply, bullshit.

Let's now examine some examples of deceitful political language specifically in the United States. An unbelievable, and shameful, use of euphemism by government took place after the 2009 Fort Hood Massacre (Texas) where a U.S. Army Major, Nidal Malik Hasan, of Middle Eastern lineage, went on a shooting rampage that killed thirteen and wounded thirty-two. Hasan was known to have been in contact with a Yemen radical, imam Anwar al-Awlaki, who had already been declared a security threat to the nation. Yet, the Obama Administration, aiming to avoid upsetting Islamic people and governments, refused to call the incident an act of terrorism or that the action was provoked by militant Islamic religious passions. Instead, it called the massacre (be sure you are sitting down for this) a case of "*workplace violence*." [57] Disgusting. Seven years later, on June 12, 2016, when the largest ever shooting massacre in U.S. history took place in Orlando, Florida, again the Administration refused to call it a case of radical Islamist terror, even though the assailant declared his alliance to ISIS just before he started the carnage! Obama called it "an act of terror and hate," again avoiding the blunt truth of the matter.

This leads us to thinking about the term "rogue states," itself a euphemism, which is now sometimes further softened by the word "outliers." Think about it. Nations that sponsor or support terrorism could, when the government finds it expedient, simply be referred to as "outliers." Just how much can you cloud things up? How tame that sounds! Another euphemism quite popular in White House parlance (not exclusive to any administration) is "advisers." As in, "The United States will be sending another 500 advisers to Iraq," which really means troops, but the administration has promised not to put "boots on the ground" (which is another euphemism), so we send more and more advisers. It would not be surprising, at least in some instances, if the number of "advisers" exceeds the number of military personnel being advised.

We also now have phrases such as "kinetic military action" and "overseas contingency operations." Say what? What on God's Earth do those mean? Well, "kinetic military action" refers to the use of lethal force by the armed forces. What a nice phrase. I remember the term kinetic energy from science class in high school, but never in association with anything deadly. And what about "overseas contingency operations"? That refers to the act of responding to crises outside of the country, which could be a quick, unplanned attack on a terrorist group or providing humanitarian assistance to a nation in the Middle East, or other unforeseen events. It should be noted that the Department of Defense is allowed to maintain a separate fund (really a slush fund) outside the national budget to finance these operations (read: unsupervised use of taxpayer's money).

Euphemistic political jargon includes other deceptive terms such as "investments" to cover for "government spending," and the term "targeted measures" may refer to government spending, taxation, or a combination of both. Taxes are also hidden behind phrases like "revenue enhancement," "shared sacrifices," and "a balanced approach."[58]

As a final example of this abuse of language, I offer the title of a proposed 2016 amendment to the Florida constitution that was heavily promoted by the state's utility companies for the purpose of protecting their interests and wiping out competition by users and providers of solar power: "*Rights of Electricity Consumers Regarding Solar Energy Choice*." Beautiful words, aren't they? "Rights." "Solar Energy." "Choice." Who wouldn't vote for that? Well, the big utilities bet $20 million that their deception would work. However, a number of state newspapers such as The Miami Herald and the Tampa Bay Times blew the whistle, with various writers devoting much ink to warn voters. For example, columnist Daniel Ruth of the Tampa Bay Times explains to readers that the amendment would let the big power companies

> to impose new fees on solar customers to recoup the loss of revenue when solar customers don't buy their power, thus undermining the economic value of implementing a solar power panel system. The amendment also restricts the ability of solar power users to sell off excess electricity in the marketplace, which always has been one of the key selling points to encourage more people to install solar panels. [59]

In effect, the "sunshine amendment" wanted to block out the light. What an amazing display of bullshit—mean, self-serving, harmful bullshit. But this time it didn't work. With the help of newspapers and various concerned citizens groups, the voters were able to see through the smoke screen and defeated the proposal at the polls.

Nevertheless, adept as they are in the game of deception, politicians do not have a monopoly on linguistic bullshit. We find that the media not only parrots political euphemisms, they also construct their own, leading the way into an extreme atmosphere of political correctness that threatens to divorce any word, any concept that could make a group—any group—uncomfortable, from its real meaning. Let's briefly explore this.

Political Correctness and Euphemism in the Media

Political Correctness is a doctrine, recently fostered by a delusional, illogical minority and promoted by a sick mainstream media, which holds forth the proposition that it is entirely possible to pick up a piece of shit by the clean end!

—Harry S. Truman

She is not a "Two-bit hooker" -- She is a "Low-cost provider."

—Anonymous

Just pick up a newspaper (or, for the younger set, read news from the Internet) or watch the evening news, and we are instantly enrolled in a course on political correctness and euphemistic language. We are bombarded with it daily, so it's not surprising that we are rarely conscious of it anymore. The late comedian, George Carlin, was a master at bringing the issue to our attention. In his words (approximately): "The CIA no longer kills people; they neutralize them...we don't have constipation anymore, we have occasional irregularity...we now measure radiation in 'sunshine units'...we no longer have poor people; we have the economically disadvantaged...." Regarding death, he says:

> No one can simply just 'die' these days. Thanks to our fear of death...I won't have to die—I'll 'pass away.' Or I'll 'expire,' like a magazine subscription. If it happens in the hospital they'll call it a 'terminal episode.' The insurance company will refer to it as 'negative patient care outcome.' And if it's the result of malpractice, they'll say it was a 'therapeutic misadventure.'

Carlin has been dead (or should I say, departed this world) since 2008, but even he would have been taken aback by the continued development of this kind of speech. A minor fuss in the media in July 2015 highlights the problem. It regards a "biased-free language guide" developed by students and staff at the University of New Hampshire in 2013 and posted in a UNH website as a resource, part of "the university's efforts to create an inclusive, diverse and equitable community." The outrage over the guide started when someone noted it included the advice to stop using the classification "American" to refer to people from the United States because it ignores people from South America. The guide then takes social euphemism to new heights. Consider the following suggestions: Replace the terms "older people, elders, seniors, senior citizens" with "people of advanced age." Eliminate the label "rich" by replacing it with "person of material wealth." Its opposite, "poor," would best be changed to "person who lacks advantages that others have." Overweight individuals should now be called "people of size." [60]

The guide also designates the term "illegal alien" as problematic. It accepts "undocumented immigrant," but recommends "person seeking asylum," or "refugee" as better alternatives. In addition, the label "foreigners" should be avoided in favor of "international people." Finally, since black people are now normally called "African-Americans," Caucasians, or whites, should be called "European-Americans." [61]

That is the same kind of thinking that has brought us the term "differently-abled" to cover for the now objectionable word "disabled." Is that really necessary? It is also now common to use the word "special" to refer to individuals suffering from a mental handicap. We sometimes call these unfortunate individuals disabled or intellectually challenged, but those apparently do not blur the issue enough, so now we call them "special." No doubt, it would be inconsiderate, callous to label the mentally handicapped with derogatory words such as stupid or retarded, but to go as far as calling them special subverts the most common understanding of the word as someone or something exceptional, extraordinary in the positive sense of those words. We could engage in an argument about the semantics, but let's not kid ourselves, we are dealing with extreme euphemism here.

Even if the reader believes that it is kind and appropriate to use the softer definitions in cases of physical and mental disabilities, we have plenty of other euphemisms to choose from that the media disseminates like snow over us every day. How about "escort service" for prostitution, or "adult entertainment" for pornography? Or how about "pregnancy termination" for abortion as well as the self-assigned titles of "pro-choice" for pro-abortion and "pro-life" for anti-abortion activists? We also have "gaming" for gambling, "freedom fighters" for rebels or even terrorists, "armed intervention" for a military attack, "between jobs" for unemployed, "ethnic cleansing" for getting rid of people from different racial or cultural backgrounds, and "collateral damage" for killing or hurting innocent people during a military attack. Not enough? Here are a few more.

We have "mistakes" for crimes (and how often have we heard the phrase "mistakes were made" to avoid personal responsibility), "negative cash flow" for broke, "executive assistant" for secretary, "academy" for school, "caretaker or custodian" for janitor, "unmotivated" for lazy, and "adult" for crude or obscene language and licentious entertainment material. Thus, the possibilities for new euphemisms are virtually endless. I even like to come up with some of my own. Here is one.

Let's say you walk into a store and a toddler has thrown herself on the floor, screaming and kicking because she can't have a toy she wants. Normally we would say the child is having a tantrum, but some people today may object to that word, insisting it is insensitive toward the child's undeveloped ability to understand the meaning of the word "*no*", so we should call it an "energetic display of assertiveness." Or, let's say a colleague consistently whines and ridicules everyone's ideas at the office meetings. You and I might call him *a pain in the ass*, but in today's culture we would be best advised to make another choice, so I suggest we opt for saying that the individual has an "affinity for provocative conduct," or that he has a "low tolerance level and a highly-developed proclivity for challenging new ideas." Try to think of a few yourself; it's fun!

Unfortunately, the ridiculousness of today's political correctness has crept into nearly every phase of our lives and into every field. Here is one example of how it is affecting show business: the need to avoid any suggestion of offensiveness has led performers such as Jerry Seinfeld and Chris Rock to state that they do not want to perform in college campuses anymore. Critic Ken Tucker helps explain why in his complaint:

> ...between liberal political-correctness and conservative sensitivity or rage at the expression of any liberal opinion, we're grooming generations of college grads, many of whom will be intolerant of listening to any opinion other than the mannerly, assiduously inoffensive ones they're taught it's safe to hold.[62]

It may eventually become impossible to hold an honest conversation about anything, at least in public. It may become an absolute necessity to meticulously euphemize the dialogue to try to communicate an idea without bringing offense to somebody. I think we are almost there already. However, it is quite interesting to note that profanity, which is still offensive to a considerable segment of the population, is more "in" than ever, increasingly well accepted in myriad social settings and by celebrities in the world of entertainment. In fact, the reader would not be amiss if he or she were to point out that my liberal use of the word bullshit in this tome is an example of such social acceptance. I offer my sincere apologies to those offended, but I honestly cannot find a word in the English language that communicates so many of the notions I'm writing about as well as bullshit can. (Please refer to the introduction where I unabashedly authorize myself to expand the word's meaning and to use it liberally here, based on its incomparable power to encompass so many of the issues, scandals, and disappointing revelations here presented).

The tentacles of political correctness reach in many directions, too many to cover them all, but here is a representative example from the field of education that shows how the problem permeates our lives today and to what ridiculous extents it can go. In December 2015, the University of Tennessee at Knoxville warned both faculty and students to "ensure your holiday party is not a Christmas party in disguise." [63]   This modern idea that celebrating Christmas is insensitive towards those of other religions as well as atheists contaminates many organizations today, as I witnessed at the Federal Reserve Bank during the later years of my employment. This surrender to the irrational forces of extreme political correctness, some of them individuals with nothing better to do in their otherwise uneventful lives, does not appear reversible any time soon.

At the elementary school level, we have the case of Aiden Steward, a nine-year-old from Texas who was suspended for, well, hang on to your seat while I let Glenn Garvin's opinion column in *The Miami Herald* tell the story. The punishment came because little Aiden "...after watching the *Lord of the Rings* movies, tried to make a classmate disappear with a magic ring." Garvin cynically adds: "A hard-bitten repeat offender, Aiden had already been suspended earlier in the year for showing up at school with *The Big Book of Knowledge*." [64]

If your mouth is not yet open wide enough, this little story from a newspaper column aptly titled, "It's a mad, mad, mad, mad world!" might just complete the job:

> Administrators at a high school in Summerville, South Carolina, locked down the campus and called the cops after a 16-year-old student turned in a short story in which he bought a gun to shoot a runaway dinosaur. [65]

You can pair that tale up with the case of Kody Smith, the Colorado Springs second-grader who, while participating in a class exercise to use the imagination to find shapes in clouds, reported seeing a gun-shaped cloud. Result: the school filed a behavior report on Kody. There you have it. It's a terrible thing that common sense is so *uncommon* today, at a premium in, of all places, schools.

Finally, it should be mentioned that sometimes our actions and word selection is dictated by possible legal consequences, as we could potentially be sued for any number of technicalities if we make the wrong choice, something I see as symptomatic of the wildly litigious times in which we live. That said, this is a good point to turn our attention to the justice system in the United States.

The Criminal Justice System

Did you know that medical researchers now prefer to experiment on lawyers instead of rats? Why? Actually, there are three reasons: 1) Lawyers are more abundant; 2) the researchers don't get quite as emotionally attached to them; and 3) well, there are some things a rat just won't do.

—An old favorite gag

I was hesitant to discuss the justice system, in particular the criminal justice branch, because the discourse could get lengthy and tricky, but it's a must do. I will keep it simple by going to the heart of the matter. Forget the laws themselves, which can be utterly absurd if not plain unfair. Let's talk about lawyers who, after all, are at the core of the system. In particular, prosecuting attorneys who frequently work their tails off to convict accused individuals they know to be innocent—based on the evidence, or its insufficiency—callously sending many to jail, some for a lifetime, and even to the execution chamber, just so they can pad their record of convictions and add another feather to their prosecutor cap. All too frequently, convictions rely on a coerced confession where police use extreme psychological pressure, lies, and coercion to get the suspect—oftentimes young, confused, and afraid—to "confess" to the charges after countless hours of intensive, intimidating, and exhausting interrogation.

Just how casual prosecutors can be when it comes to taking away other people's freedom was illustrated when the Miami-Dade State Attorney's Office wondered why it was such a big deal when DNA evidence made it necessary for them to free a man jailed for a rape he did not commit. In the words of prosecutor Kathleen Hoague: "This happens all the time. You know, OK? This is not the first time this has happened, and it won't be the last." [66] Nice. No outrage, no dismay, no apology. Simply, "Oh well, shit happens."

In contrast, but almost as bad, defense attorneys will employ every conceivable trick to prove their client's innocence, even when, based on overwhelming evidence, they know the accused as guilty as a bear caught with his paws in the honey jar. Think about O.J. Simpson's 1995 trial and the revolting "not guilty" verdict. High-priced trial lawyers got him off from two counts of murder. Talk about bullshit. These elite lawyers work almost exclusively for the wealthy and are particularly adept at keeping their clients from having to walk the plank, or at least finding ways to get them a reduced sentence, or, way too often, a laughable slap on the wrist. This is not the case with the poor suckers who must rely on court-appointed attorneys who could be good or bad but tend to be relatively inexperienced in criminal trials. All this is called "justice."

And what about the jury system? Just how confident would you feel standing trial for a crime you did not commit? It's outright frightening that the destiny of so many people has been, and continues to be, decided by totally inept or indifferent, and sometimes biased, individuals. Even worse, many people selected for jury duty don't even want to be there, and some are willing to expedite the deliberations just so that they can go home, the defendant's fate be damned. I've seen this first hand, and found it extremely unsettling and disappointing. Besides, even if well-meaning and committed to the task, how competent, really, can a group of "your peers" possibly be? How clearly could they see through the smoke screens thrown at them by those shrewd lawyers? The famous American poet, Robert Frost, once said: "A jury consists of twelve persons chosen to decide who has the better lawyer." He was right on target.

In conclusion, and tragically, the jury system in the United States, as fair and well-intentioned as it appears on principle, can be tremendously flawed and often results in wrong convictions (which unfortunately can result in executions of innocent individuals) and acquittals that are true travesties of justice. Succinctly, the system often works on bullshit—really foul bullshit.

All right, that's enough for the justice system and politics in general, which we can summarize with the words of columnist Michael Gerson of the Washington Post. "This is the American emergency: an acute shortage of public integrity at the highest level of our politics." [67] Bull's-eye! And I needed a whole chapter to make that point. Okay, let's leave politics behind and open a new section to explore another social sphere where bullshit reigns supreme—the corporate world.

Chapter 2

Corporate Bullshit

Nothing is illegal if one hundred businessmen decide to do it.
—Andrew Young

Corporations have neither bodies to be punished, nor souls to be condemned, they therefore do as they like.
—E. Edward Thurlow

Another sphere chockfull of bullshit is the corporate scene, and the consequences are as serious as with politics. From the abuses of Big Pharma and insurance companies to the incomprehensible billing and deceptive advertising, corporate bullshit, which can reach the criminal level, is abundant and essentially unstoppable. Let's look into that.

Drug Companies and their Bullshit

Early in 2016, I purchased several creams and ointments my dermatologist prescribed for some annoying, but not serious, skin conditions. One of the creams, according to the drugstore, would have cost me over $700 (for about 1.6 ounces) had I not had insurance (That number is not a typo). Another balm would have further depleted my wallet of more than $250. And my life was not even threatened by these conditions! You have to wonder just what on earth is inside those tubes—gold? With the price of the precious metal at about $1,300 an ounce, my more expensive ointment could have easily been one-third gold. Also, while I waited for my prescriptions, I overheard the pharmacy clerk quote a drug price of $820 to another shocked customer. Can such prices be truly justified? I don't think so.

Consider drug companies and their defense of astronomical prices that make some life-saving medicines inaccessible to many patients in the United States. Their central argument—which is absolute bullshit—is that drug prices reflect the enormous expenses the companies incur in research and development. Never mind that the same drug may sell for one-half or one-third the cost (often far less) in Canada, Europe, or South America. Even more outrageous and indefensible is that once in the market, after all the research and development costs have been absorbed, the prices of some drugs inexplicably continue to rise—dramatically.

A recent scandal dealing with the emergency device EpiPen illustrates the problem. This is a life-saving injection tool designed to counteract severe allergic reactions, the kind that can bring quick shock and death to victims. In 2009, the cost for a two-pen set was $100, but by 2016, it had increased six-fold to $600. This device is not new, dating back to 1977, and it is relatively inexpensive to manufacture, with the drug, epinephrine, costing $2 and the injectors under $50. So, what happened?

The story is revelatory of capitalism's dark side. The device's maker, Mylan, bought the manufacturer in 2007, when the EpiPen sold for $57. Later, a major competing product, Auvi-Q, was recalled, opening up the route to market dominance for EpiPen. Price escalation took off, and here we are at the $600 mark. "Coincidentally," the huge price leap took place concurrently with obscene financial compensation increases for Mylan executives. According to a Miami Herald editorial:

> Heather Resch—the daughter of Democratic Sen. Joe Manchin of West Virginia—was president in 2007 and has since become chief executive. She went from making $2.4 million nine years ago to $18.9 million last year. Other company executives enjoyed similarly gargantuan hikes in compensation.[1]

The article goes on to reveal that the EpiPen outrage "is only the latest example of price-gouging by pharmaceutical providers," explaining that in 2014 ten *generic* drugs, used for a variety of ailments such as asthma, high blood pressure, and high cholesterol, underwent price jumps between 420 percent and 8,000 percent! Big Pharma cannot crank out enough excuses for this blatant abuse (I would call it criminal actions), citing development costs and blaming high-deductible insurance plans that make their products unaffordable to consumers. Let's call it what it is: bullshit!

This disturbing issue becomes particularly severe—and heartbreaking—with cancer therapies. A notable example is the drug Gleevec, from Novartis. It has been called "possibly the greatest cancer drug ever invented." It cost $24,000 a year when it was introduced in 2001, which is expensive enough, but by 2014 the price was $90,000; that is four times the original price! In fact, many cancer drugs today cost about $100,000 per year, and most sick people do not have the resources to afford these life-extending drugs. Leukemia specialist Dr. Hagop Kantarjian of the University of Texas MD Anderson Cancer Center, puts it this way: "They are making prices unreasonable, unsustainable and, in my opinion, immoral." [2] And what could be more telling than the words of Pfizer Inc. executive Peter Rost in a candid interview: "I'm most troubled by the fact that we stick it to the people who can afford it the least." Is it any wonder that, despite its *potential* to bring economic progress and add wealth to a nation, capitalism is, and has been, a dirty word for many? Shameful.

Meanwhile, giant Johnson & Johnson will not be outdone. Based on the work of investigative journalist Steven Brill, the pharmaceutical colossus pulled in billions of dollars from the "off label" marketing of Risperdal, an antipsychotic medication. Showering doctors with gifts and so-called consulting fees, the Pharma behemoth managed to pump the drug into children and elderly patients even though the drug's FDA approval limited its use to adult schizophrenics. Documentation showing that the drug's side effects included "an excess number of deaths" among older patients and "the bizarre development of sometimes massive breasts by more than 5 percent of boys..." did not stop the drug maker until the Justice Department slapped them with criminal fines and other penalties adding to about $2.5 billion (however, they have made $18 billion from their poison, so no doubt they can look at the fine as a cost of doing business, a good return on investment).

The use of Risperdal and other psychotropics in Florida became a scandal (but then again, it's Florida), with kids in state-run foster homes pumped full of the stuff to keep them calm and manageable. Not surprisingly, there were deaths from this abuse and laws were passed, but who really cared when there was money to be made. As reported in the Miami Herald:

> "In 2011, the Palm Beach Post found that despite these scandals the state had purchased 326,081 tablets of Risperdal and other adult antipsychotic drugs over a two-year period to manage kids in state-run juvenile lockups. The Post found that psychiatrists prescribing off-label uses of these very profitable antipsychotics had been greased by drug manufactures with about $250,000 in gifts and speaking fees." The article concludes: "So drug companies milk the state for the kids' Medicaid money, psychiatrists get their goodies and state institutions are able to warehouse zombie kids." [3]

It was a winning combination for the pharmaceuticals, unethical psychiatrists, and the state. How could mere laws and a disgusted public do anything to stop such a powerful gang? Who can amass such power that allows them to make their own rules and be almost legally untouchable? Well, I can only think of one other kind of business entity with that much control: insurance companies. So, let's talk about insurers.

Bullshit in Health Insurance

Customer abuse is the specialty of the insurance business, particularly health insurance. Healthcare in our country is such a fiasco that I find it difficult to decide where to begin (and end). I also must keep it reasonable in length lest the issues plaguing this convoluted industry lead to twenty pages or more. Let's see what I can do while keeping it brief.

Through years of smart manipulation of the legal system and greasing plenty of politicians, insurance companies succeeded in corralling doctors, hospitals, and other medical services providers like helpless farm animals into their pens. You could also make the analogy of the insurance industry spider trapping them all in its large web. Truly independent practitioners at one time, most doctors now essentially work for the insurance companies. Physicians who are not in some kind of insurance-controlled network have virtually vanished. Today doctor's compensation is determined by the insurers who tell them what they can charge for visits, surgical procedures, and other services. In effect, for doctors to make the same revenue as they would have several decades ago (adjusted for inflation, of course), they must now treat more patients—many more. That is why in the past you could receive highly personalized attention from your physician while today most doctor's offices line up their patients in several rooms as the doctor hops from one room to the next, spending barely enough time with each individual. It's not what they want to do; it's what they're forced to do.

The system of cost controls that the convoluted insurance-dominated system has created is largely responsible for why we now have PA's (Physician Assistants) performing routine exams and consultations. While these individuals may be highly trained, they are not doctors, and you could argue for their effectiveness until your mouth dries up, but I will not be convinced that this is not diluting our quality of care. This questionable practice has been increasing, and we should not be surprised if in the not-too-distant future we find these assistants performing some minor surgeries (and God knows what else if that proves successful in the eyes of insurers).

Meanwhile, hospitals are also squeezed by the insurance companies. The insurer determines what they are willing to pay for a hysterectomy, a visit to the ER, or a Band-Aid. Hospitals are never happy with those rates, and so a game ensues, in which hospitals charge five or ten times the cost of the service to try to get as much as they can. However, powerful as they are, insurers will laugh off the extra charges, paying only what they want to pay, which leads the hospitals to extract some dollars from a much easier prey—the patient. Most insured customers can survive this, as a large portion of the balance is usually "forgiven," but beware if you are uninsured or out of network. The hospital can slam you with the full inflated price they use in their game with insurers, but you do not have the insurers' clout to laugh it off and pay what you think is reasonable. No can do.

I can't resist adding a little anecdote that reveals a lot about the outrageous situation in healthcare. It deals with a Mr. Ryan Grassley of Salt Lake City who discovered a puzzling charge on the hospital bill from his son's birth via cesarean section. It was a small charge, $39.95. And what was it for? It was for "skin to skin" contact with the baby. Pressed for an answer, the hospital explained that "the fee technically wasn't for Grassley to hold his baby, but to have an additional nurse in the recovery room for C-section patients to ensure the mother and baby were safe...." [4] Sounds fishy to me; what hospital is going to charge less than what they normally charge for an aspirin to have an extra nurse at hand? Things are getting strange in this field—and ridiculous.

Attorney Steven I. Weissman got an insider's view of the healthcare system when he became interim president of Palm Springs General Hospital in South Florida, and what he learned made him sick (not a bad pun, right?). At the core of the problem, he claims, is that the industry has eliminated competition by doing away with real prices: "Ask the price of anything and you invariably receive the same answer: 'What insurance do you have?'" Weissman insists that the complexity of healthcare, along with insurance networks, could be virtually eliminated with a system of real prices, assuring us that price competition would "make costs plummet." He finds it disturbing that "the law permits a provider to prey like a wolf on a wounded human" who needs life-saving care, sometimes adjusting prices by over 1,000 percent. In essence, we have a system of predatory pricing. [5]

Tragically, the well-meaning regulations of the Affordable Care Act make matters worse. The Act requires insurers to use about 80% of premiums on patient care, which sounds like a good provision. However, according to Weissman, this has "enshrined higher medical costs as the only means for the insurance industry to keep growing profits. He explains:

> The higher medical bills climb, the higher premiums rise and the higher the insurance industry's 20 percent share goes. Insurers, on whom the system relies to negotiate deals with providers, actually benefit from higher costs, while consumers can't protect themselves because of the lack of real prices. Nobody is watching the store. [6]

Weissman further explains that what providers call the "list price" is fraudulent—total bullshit. The list is supposed to show their "usual and customary charges," but these are normally inflated by 300 percent or more, and, unconscionably, those are the prices with which the uninsured and out-of-network patients get slammed. Callous.

The reader must be wondering, well, why don't we straighten out this price abuse that promises to go a long way in solving the insurance crisis? Not that simple, Weissman tells us, because *the industry spends more on lobbying than the defense, aerospace, and the oil and gas industries combined.*[7] How'bout them apples? Go ahead, write to your local congressperson and see what you can get done (but don't forget to include a fat check, I mean, a generous donation). Many politicians ride on the big insurers' pockets, and John and Jane Public cannot compete. We are screwed. One last thing about insurance.

A *60 Minutes* segment from 2015 highlighted the current situation with cases of mental illness where insurance companies routinely override doctors' evaluations that call for continued in-hospital treatment. Using company representatives and their own medical staffs—who never see the patients themselves—insurers justify the release of seriously impaired individuals and/or move them to outpatient care against the protests of the patients' psychiatrists who have had direct contact with the patients and managed their course of treatment while in the hospital. This includes individuals who, in the opinion of their doctors, could resort to suicide or even become a threat to others.

The exposé tells about company reps pestering physicians caring for these patients, with frequent calls asking about patients' conditions and pushing for their release. The company-paid doctors then have the final say, and most of them boast denial rates of over 90%, with some reaching 100% ! (translation: insurers' doctors, who never actually see the patients, are always right, and the psychiatrists who diagnose and treat the sick on-site are always wrong). The result is that quite often the mentally ill cannot complete a course of therapy that requires them to be institutionalized, and many go on to relapse, sometimes with fatal consequences. According to the report, the process goes something like this:

> ...after a patient is admitted, an insurance company representative starts calling the doctor every day, or every few days. If that representative decides that the patient is ready for a lower level of care, then the case is referred to an insurance company physician who reads the file, calls the doctor and renders a judgment. We have found in these chronic, expensive cases that judgment is most often a denial. How often the results are tragic, no one can say. But we have found examples.[8]

In the words of one of the caring physicians, "the insurers call it 'managed *care*,' but it's really managed *cost*." In other words, greed and stinginess wrapped in corporate bullshit. This mode of operation is used by insurers across the healthcare landscape, denying life-saving (but expensive) cutting-edge treatments, refusing to pay for medications prescribed by doctors (my family and I have experienced this), often forcing patients to use cheaper and possibly less effective alternatives, and so on. The game is to collect those premiums and give customers the least possible in return. And who else comes to mind when we think of corporate greed? Why, financial institutions, of course! Let's get to the heart of the matter with those moneychangers.

Financial Institutions: The Bullshit Masters

Insatiable corporate greed often leads to criminal conduct, and this is best exemplified by the misconduct of many financial firms that led to the economic crisis and ensuing recession of the first decade of the 21st century. That calamity brought the collapse, or near-collapse, of large financial institutions that required the massive assistance of government at the expense of the tax payers who saw their collective wealth drop by *trillions* of dollars. The ensuing slowdown in the economy that began in 2008 hit businesses and consumers hard, with high rates of unemployment, which led world governments to the controversial decision to bail out banks and large companies, such as the General Motors bailout of 2009-13. Real estate suffered enormously, with foreclosures and evictions reaching record heights. Big names in finance such as Lehman Brothers, which filed an unprecedented bankruptcy, were devastated. Merrill Lynch, AIG, Freddie Mac, Fannie Mae, HBOS, Royal Bank of Scotland, Bradford & Bingley, and others were ready for total failure as well and had to be rescued— meaning, you and I paid for the money floaters that kept the institutions from drowning.

Plenty of blame has been tossed around for the monetary catastrophe, and while there is some disagreement about what prompted the debacle, it is generally accepted that the leading causes included

> widespread failures in financial regulation and supervision, dramatic failures of corporate governance and risk management at many systemically important financial institutions, a combination of excessive borrowing, risky investments, and lack of transparency by financial institutions, ill preparation and inconsistent action by government that added to the uncertainty and panic, a systemic breakdown in accountability and ethics, collapsing mortgage-lending standards...[9]

There is little debate that the breakdown was triggered by a combination of factors that included financial institutions encouraging home ownership among people who could not afford it, making many easy-to-qualify for loans to keep fanning the flames of an overheated real estate market, and exaggerating the value of "bundled subprime mortgages based on the theory that housing prices would continue to escalate, questionable trading practices on behalf of both buyers and sellers...and a lack of adequate capital holdings from banks and insurance companies to back the financial commitments they were making." [10] Author Gordon White explains that "ten million jobs were lost, and the banks received $11 trillion in bailouts." And he adds something that will anger you:

> It is worth noting that the total mortgage debt of the United States at the time was approximately $9 trillion. It would have been cheaper for the taxpayers to pay off every single mortgage in the country and let the banks who placed dodgy bets fail. Go ahead and let that sink in."[11]

Let's unpack this. The banks screwed the American people in *three* ways:

1) By engaging in irresponsible lending practices that saw them issuing interest-only second mortgages to people who could not afford them to pay for properties that were overvalued, and by their rolling the dice Las Vegas style, packaging riskier and riskier securities backed by those dangerous, likely-to-default mortgages they were so loosely giving out.

2) When the shit hit the fan, many of these financial giants had to be "saved" by the taxpayers because they were deemed "too big to fail," which *supposedly* meant we would all be worse off if they did—*supposedly*.

3) The third way in which the people got screwed is often overlooked: after creating the whole mess and getting saved by the taxpayers, these colossal entities then went after the properties where the now poor, unemployed suckers indebted by the same suspect mortgages the banks issued were living, foreclosing on their homes and putting them on the streets!

In effect, the banks created the chaos, then got bailed out at the expense of the people, and then turned around and took away the homes from the people, the now-jobless who could not pay the inflated mortgages (many having lost their jobs as a consequence of the catastrophe the banks created in the first place) and whose taxes helped "save" them from bankruptcy. White puts it tersely: "It was a win-win." [12] For the banks.

If we further simplified all of this discussion about the economic crisis, we could say that in their insatiable quest for excess profits, financial institutions, including some of the most recognized and respected names in the industry, bullshitted the nation—make that, the world—into a fiscal disaster from which we are still trying to recover. And this collection of bastards still ask you to trust them with your money—every day.

For those still willing to trust banks, perhaps thinking that they learned their lesson, here is a sobering reminder. In September 2016, Wells Fargo was slapped with $185 million in fines for opening false bank accounts without their customers' permission between 2011 and 2015. Aiming to meet what ex-employees charge were unreasonable sales targets, Wells fargo staff were opening unauthorized bank and credit card accounts (1.5 million and 565,443 accounts respectively) that generated additional money for the bank via annual fees, insufficient funds penalties, interest charges, and overdraft protection fees. As of September 2016, the financial giant had fired over 5,300 employees. [13] But we should ask, how could such a devious scheme go on for several years without the knowledge of bank administrators?

The short answer is, of course they knew what was going on. Many employees have come forward charging it was common practice for supervisors to pressure them into meeting unrealistic sales quotas whether via legal or illegal practices. Furthermore, while Wells Fargo's investigation goes back only to 2011, it seems clear the problem existed before that time. A teller, Denny Russo, who started his job at a California branch in April 2010, states that "the sales machine was well under way then," asserting that Wells Fargo's senior executives lied about their being unaware of the problem: "The part that really upsets me the most is these directives absolutely came from upper management," he said. [14] Other ex-employees allege that the scheme was already in place as early as 2007, which would double the period Wells Fargo has acknowledged.

So, how many readers actually believe that such a large-scale conspiracy could have been carried out by at least 5,300 dishonest employees without the knowledge of the bank's big wigs? A show of hands, please. Don't see any. Good. Let's move on and see how else corporations mistreat their customers.

Bullshit in Customer Service

It is a common practice now for companies to subject customers to meaningless corporate jargon—a refined form of bullshitting intended to sock it to the customer while making it seem they are being highly regarded or being given a better product or service. As many of us have come to learn, frequently used business phrases such as "*Your call is important to us,*" "*To serve you better,*" and "*For your protection*" mean nothing remotely similar to what the words imply. Here is a suggested translation of "*Your call is important to us*":

> Due to vicious staff reductions to cut our costs to the bone, we are going to put you on hold for a long time and then connect you to a low-paid clerk sitting on a desk halfway around the world who can hardly speak your language and who will likely not provide any useful answers to your questions.*

We encounter those irritating, deceiving phrases almost every day. We can't escape them. Call almost any business office today, and you will be immediately subjected to the torturing phrases, now nearly always in the form of robo-bullshit. You won't even get to talk to a human (at least not right away) and call them on their bullshit, so you'll have to put up with the prerecorded spiel if you want to get anything done. "Listen closely, for our options have changed..." This is repeated every time you call certain organizations, for years! Just how often do options need to be changed? And I don't know about you, but whenever I call a company with any kind of issue (which is why ninety-five percent of us call anyway) I never, *ever* find resolution with the automated system; I am always forced to navigate through their options hoping to find a way to get to a human to get anything done (and that, as most of us know, is not always a sure thing). Does this sound familiar?

Answering system (A/S): "Thank you for calling XYZ Co. For English say or press 1; for Spanish say or press 2; for Chinese say or press 3; for any other language say or press 9 and hope for the best.

Caller: One.

A/S: "Your call is very important to us. How can we exceed your expectations today? In a few words, please explain why you're calling." Or, you can visit us at www.XYZco.com for the same exceptional service.

Caller: "I'm calling because my car's stereo broke down, and I need to order a part, but your website does not provide the means to do so."

A/S: "I see. Your car broke down. We are sorry to hear that. Please say or enter your name and date of birth followed by your twenty-three digit account number followed by the pound sign. For example, you can say 'John Smith,' March 24 1984, (account number) #."

Caller: "My car did not break down. It's the car's stereo I'm having problems with."

---

* For a humorous list of these and more deceptive phrases commonly in use today by companies everywhere, see Appendix B.

A/S: "We are sorry that you are having problems, but we need a little more information so that we can provide you with the award-winning, world-class customer service we are known for. Let's try this. Please say or enter your twenty-three digit account number, including the dashes, followed by the pound sign."

Caller: "348-55667-6-299490-61-456-32 #"

A/S: "I'm sorry, that is not a valid account number. Please re-enter your twenty-three digit account number followed by the pound sign."

Caller: "0"

A/S: "I'm sorry. Zero is not a valid option. Please enter your account number followed by the pound sign."

Caller: "Agent, please."

A/S: "I'm sorry. That is not a valid response..."

Caller: "I want to speak to a customer service representative."

A/S: "Representative" (annoying digital sound). "Due to an unusually high volume of calls, all of our agents are busy helping other customers. You are number seventeen in the queue, with an estimated wait time of thirty-two minutes. Your call is very important to us. If you prefer, you can hang up and call again between the hours of 8:00 AM and 5:00 PM, Eastern Standard Time, Monday through Friday. Or, you can visit us at www.XYZco.com for the same excellent service. Thank you for your patience and for doing business with XYZ Company (-- Some irritating music starts to play).

Caller: "Click"

Thus, perversely, companies are getting increasingly clever at keeping us from reaching their reps, not to mention how they test our patience by programming their automated systems to ask for information—name, account number, last four digits of social security, and such—only to have the agent ask for the same information all over again when, and if, you get through. They call this *customer service*; I call it customer abuse—more annoyances, more bullshit. The result has been a consumer population whose senses have been dulled, exhausted into submission, or made some bitter, frustrated, and cynical, with low expectations for getting problems solved. But customers are not the only victims of corporate bullshit; workers are, too.

Employee Abuse: Bullshit as Company Policy

On the job, especially in large organizations, employees are subjected to corporate bullshit of a different kind. Working for the Federal Reserve Bank (FRB) for over three decades, I witnessed lots of corporate bullshit, and it got worse as we moved into the twenty-first century. Here is a sampling: Shoving a project that nobody wanted on some poor grunt was referred to as "employee development" and sold to the employee as "an opportunity" or as "a good learning experience." Trying to beat out other FRB offices for the title of stingiest branch (they called it being number one in budget performance)

57

by using draconian slash and burn tactics to reduce costs to please the head office was called "exercising fiscal responsibility" and "contributing to the corporate vision."

And it could get downright ugly and exploitative. Making low-paid staff members do work designated for higher-paid positions was achieved by giving them a job title that included the word "acting." Thus, a senior clerk might end up carrying out the duties of a supervisor, but without the matching pay, by giving him or her the title of "acting supervisor." The same held for low-level supervisors who were made to perform the tasks of assistant managers by calling them "acting assistant managers." The employees took on these responsibilities in the hope that taking a bullet for the bank, and if their performance was good, would result in a promotion fitting the actual job they were doing, although, truth be told, they often had no choice. Even more discouraging, the position was often eventually filled by an outsider, which necessitated the "acting" employee to suffer the indignity of training the newcomer who had just walked right into the open, higher-paying position. Their reward was often a thank you and a phony smile from a manager. I've been always amazed that never once did any of these humiliated employees pop an aneurism, or keeled over from an embolism, or walked in with an Uzi and blew away half the Bank's officers. What self-control!

The bullshit took a condescending tone when employees were fired, with the bad news delivered entirely euphemistically. For example: "We encourage you to seek employment elsewhere," or "The organization is not in need of your set of skills at this time," or "Your performance and contributions to the organization have not achieved a level commensurate with the expectations stipulated in your job description." Indeed, a rather daring executive from one of the FRB offices once observed: "We speak and write like elegant fairies." In essence, as the saying goes, "shit runs downhill," and the bullshit raining down on us from the higher levels of the organization was copious.

Sometimes the bullshit would take ridiculous, even infantile, form. Relatively late in my career, some departments instituted a "reward system" to recognize good performance. If you were reasonably good, you would occasionally receive little gold stars in the form of stickers, just as in kindergarten, that would be tallied at the end of some specified period after which you could take your accumulated little stars and exchange them for prizes. The more stars you had, the better reward you could get. Thus, it was to great astonishment (which quickly turned to laughter) when I realized one day that my star accumulation had entitled me to receive...are you ready for this? A *free dessert* from our cafeteria! Not just a cup of coffee—as some lesser-performing employees might get—mind you, but a complete dessert of my choice. Imagine the enormous motivation generated by such a generous program. The competition for stars, as you could imagine, became fierce. I was afraid it was only a matter of time before we would run out of coffee and desserts!

We also went through a period when outstanding work was rewarded with more than the occasional bonus or gold stars. We could—if our performance warranted it—actually be the recipients of little stickers in the shape of a hand that read: "A pad on the back from Jay," our branch manager, or from another high-ranking officer, stickers that a manager or supervisor would slap on the back of your shirt, and you could wear it proudly around the office, making you the envy of the staff. Fortunately, this program came late in my career, and I was able to cynically laugh it off.

Another form of bullshit in corporate land is the omnipresent pompous rhetoric. From internal office memos to business letters and from status reports to boardroom meetings the jargon and inflated language ooze from the pages in many organizations. FRB management was particularly good at it. It often seemed like a competition to see who could write the longest, most jargon-filled, reports and letters in the most inflated language possible. Here is a sample sentence from a typical piece of correspondence:

> In our most recent communications exchange post budget performance assessments of the preceding quarter, we jointly approved a hitherto untried protocol encompassing a prescribed sequence of fiscal plan adherence verification measures to facilitate and encourage conformity with the directives of forthcoming monetary allocations.

This was officially sanctioned bullshit, and it was the kind that circulated throughout the organization—every day! Here is the translation: *"In our last budget review, we agreed to use a new method to measure budget performance and ensure compliance."* We could even simplify it further by stating: *"In our last meeting, we agreed on a new way to keep an eye on our expenses."* But, of course, that would be too simple, too clear, too free of pageantry.

Actually, that kind of exaggerated language is used by pretentious individuals in just about every field. Such lingo contributes nothing to a conversation (or written document) and in fact works against clear communication, which ostensibly is what we are usually aiming for in human interactions. Consider this statement, which I use as an example to make the point to my students: "My preferred silver screen productions are those dedicated to humor." All this means, of course, is "My favorite movies are comedies." However, the first statement employs ten words and may require a couple of seconds reflection on the part of the listener or reader to understand the message while the second one uses half the words and is instantly understood. The first statement is pretentious, reflecting pure arrogance, in other words, bullshit. It is the type of language that flows from the mouths of way too many, especially those in the public eye and in positions of authority.

Just in case the reader thinks that a field requiring precision, such as science, would be exempt from that kind of convoluted talk, consider the complaints of physicist Richard Feynman, who found unnecessary scientific jargon particularly irritating. He hated that many scientists—for purposes of intellectual pretense—made simple things sound complex. He protested: "Don't say *'reflected acoustic wave*," say "echo." In one occasion, Feynman found himself in a meeting where a sociologist brought a paper and asked everyone to read it. He could barely understand anything on the paper and feared that he was not qualified to be there. That is, until he decided to choose a sentence at random and analyze it closely. In so doing, he learned that "The individual member of the social community often receives his information via visual, symbolic channels..." stood for "People read." Another sentence read as follows: "The medical community indicates that a program of downsizing average total daily caloric intake is maximally efficacious in the field of proactive weight-reduction methodologies." The meaning: "Doctors say that the best way to lose weight is to eat less." If only more people were like Feynman, our quality of communication would improve exponentially.

I'll have more to say about science later. For the moment, let's stay closer to the corporate world and put advertising under the spotlight for a little bit.

Advertising/Marketing: Bullshit Creation as a Profession

Please don't tell my mother I work in an advertising agency — she thinks I play piano in a whorehouse.

—Jacques Seguela

Advertising is the cornerstone of capitalism, and it has been with us all our lives. Most ads, especially from large companies, are cleverly packaged bullshit and largely rely on one of five tactical elements: sex, humor, animals, children, and celebrity endorsements. Some ads successfully blend two, three, four, or even all five. Just as 99.9% of the public, over the years I have been seduced by advertisements and lightened my wallet on many (often unnecessary) products. In effect, they work, but not so much on me these days.

I am suspicious of all ads. I see them as lies, fantasies created to levitate credit cards out of our wallets and purses. In fact, I have become practically immune to them. If a bikini-clad young model were to do the breaststroke on the soap-suds-filled hood of a Chevy sedan, I may appreciate her physical assets and "promotional skills," but I would not be swayed to get the Chevy over another brand. If an insurance company were to amuse us with a funny skit including a cute Labrador puppy, I would probably chuckle and smile, but I am just as likely to not even remember the name of the company that produced the commercial (exceptions to this include Geico's gecko and the Aflac duck, which most people would recognize in an instant). Yet, these gimmicks are still considered successful.

As to the use of celebrities to promote products, I find that concept even more irrational. I could not possibly care less if LeBron James likes Nike shoes, or if Taylor Swift drinks Pepsi, or if Tom Brady endorses a particular brand of jockstrap. It would not make any difference in my decision to rescue a kitten from a shelter if Beyoncé adopted one; I would not contribute an additional cent to the United Way or American Red Cross just because George Clooney says we should do it; and I would not be moved to buy a selfie stick if Kim Kardashian were to say that she carries one with her at all times (of course she does!).

Yet, as puzzling as it is for me, millions of Americans are obviously falling for those absurd endorsements. Why else would companies spend so much on their ads, especially those willing to pay celebrities to push their products? They wouldn't if they were not raking in millions, right? So, I don't get it. Why can't the average consumer cut through the bullshit? Don't Joe and Jane Public get it? There are so many gullible people to fleece it makes one want to open a business, say, Ouija board repair. I think it could work; all I would need to succeed is get Shirley MacLaine or Oprah Winfrey to endorse the venture.

And what about ad claims and disclaimers. Have you ever encountered anything so farcical? Think of drug ads: *Look at the happy people who took our drug!* They are all smiling, the picture of health. And the eighty-year-olds look like they're perfectly fit, bicycle-riding, tennis-playing forty-year-old gym rats. Of course, consult your doctor before using our wonder drug, as it can lead to stroke, heart attack, migraines, severe depression, suicidal thoughts, hallucinations, decreased libido, panic attacks, fits of rage, unrelenting diarrhea, nausea, and compulsive nose-picking. And remember, don't smoke because smoking is bad for you.

We also get to see lots of happy people in advertisements for auto dealerships. And why wouldn't they be ecstatic when they can buy a Mercedes for $99 down and $120 a month and zero percent interest? Why would you not call all your friends to tell them about the sale to end all sales on the 4th of July where you can drive away in a brand new Ford for zero down, and the dealership will make your loan payments for the first six months after which you won't have to send in any money until the car is ten years old! And, remember, they don't sell used cars. They sell quality, pre-owned vehicles that have been professionally inspected by a team of certified, award-winning mechanics.

But you better hurry because the cars are flowing out of the lot like hot lava, surrounded by eighteen-year-old cheerleaders and exploding fireworks, driven by euphoric customers who cannot wait to get home and add up their savings. Just have them rush over and follow the directions of the minimum-wage, high-on-cocaine grunt in the chicken outfit under the gigantic American flag who is frantically waving to motorists outside the dealership. It could be your last chance!

Then we have businesses such as hotel chains, theme parks, and stores that entice customers with "value packs" that, not surprisingly, have little or nothing of value. Often claiming to provide up to $500 in savings, these value packs usually take the form of a shitty coupon book chockfull of worthless offers. There are plenty of examples:

- "One free ride coupon at the XYZ Fair for children under 12 when accompanied by two adults and three senior citizens (must be related) paying regular admission and purchasing two jumbo hotdogs and large drinks each at everyday ultra-low prices (weekdays before Noon only, roller coasters excluded, coupon non-transferable)."

- Take $2 off a bowling game on Tuesday nights after 9 pm; one coupon maximum per customer; lanes 1-5 only when available (redeem at customer service desk)."

- "$1 off a small ice cream cone for wheelchair-dependent, incontinent senior citizens over the age of 75 (before 10 a.m., weekdays; veterans take an additional 10% off; one napkin per customer)."

- "10% off a magazine yearly subscription rate, with agreement to sign up for a minimum of eight additional award-winning magazines for ten years at regular, everyday low supersaver rates* (*restrictions apply)." Additional discounts for members of the LGBT (and Q) community. Be sure to ask about our lifetime subscription rates.

- "Free Internet, one-thousand channels, and cellular service for thirty days..."

- "Free 8 oz. coffee (including decaffeinated!) with purchase of two homerun breakfasts for adults of at least $20 dollars (childless couples must be accompanied by children; cannot be combined with other offers; the handicapped welcomed; Tuesdays after midnight only in participating establishments)."

You've seen many of these, I'm sure. And what about Internet ads? Aren't they a pain in the neck? You can hardly open a page, say some news item that caught your eye, and not have an ad pop right in front of your article, blocking your view, forcing you to find the "x" to close it (sometimes cleverly hidden from view). Activating your browser's pop-up blocker doesn't seem to help either. Sometimes the ad is in the form of a video you must watch before you can get through to what you want to see, which is particularly annoying. It should not surprise the reader to learn that I have *never, ever* bought a single product advertised this way. But somebody must be buying, right? I've also experienced pop up ads that lock you into making one of these choices: [Yes] or [Later], but the "*no*" choice does not exist! Shortly before the 2016 elections I even got one that read: "I support Clinton" with the only choice on the screen: [Yes]

One more thing. How do you feel about the use of the words "premium" and "deluxe" in advertisements? Is deluxe better than premium, or is it the other way around? And are they below or above "first-class"? Perhaps "supreme" or "ultimate" are even better? And let's not forget about product sizes. A few decades ago we had small, medium, and large for most things. However, marketers decided that those designations were not sexy enough, so they created "king size," "plus," "jumbo," "extra large," "giant," "family size," "monster," and "colossal." Would you be able to cut through the bullshit and list these in ascending size order? I'm betting dollars to donuts that very few people can.

To conclude, I have learned to ignore the siren song of advertisers— significantly. I reflexively disregard the bullshit—no effort needed. I have no doubt that if everyone else were anything like I am today, many companies would go out of business, and marketing, as a career and business tool, would soon become extinct. Unfortunately, without these sponsors, we would all have to stop watching television, and I would not be able to see my favorite sports teams in action. Hmmm. You go ahead and keep watching those ads.

"From Our Oceans and Farms to Your Table" — Fishy Smelling Bullshit

Do you know what red snapper takes like? What about grouper? Tuna? If you answered yes, consider yourself lucky, especially if you frequent South Florida restaurants. Back in 2010-12, the last time any serious testing was done, it was found that 33 percent of the fish in the twenty-one states surveyed was mislabeled. Florida's Broward and Miami-Dade counties emerged as "the fish-fraud capital of the nation," where restaurants (especially sushi places) managed to fool their patrons 38 percent of the time. In Miami Herald columnist Fred Grimm's words: "Our fish fraud rivaled our Medicare fraud." Red snapper, tuna, and grouper were specially mislabeled, with the "snapper" turning out to be some other fish a staggering *86 percent of the time!* [15] So, in the case of red snapper, you have a 14 percent chance of eating the real thing in any one visit to a S. Florida restaurant. Any game in Las Vegas offers you far better odds.

Meanwhile, the Tampa Bay Times popped the consumer food fantasy bubble years ago when it revealed that the term "made from local ingredients," means, well, nothing. Grimms explains the findings:

"Florida wild caught shrimp" has been farmed-raised in India. DNA testing found "Florida blue crab" that had come from the South Pacific. Lobster rolls were lobster-free concoctions of cheap imported pollock. Veal items were actually made with pork from who know where. Grouper sushi rolls were composed of tilapia. Dishes that claimed to be "free of hormones, antibiotics, chemical additives, genetic modification" were not. "Grass fed" and "free range" pork and beef weren't. Fresh local fish had been frozen and flown from afar. Restaurant patrons were eating a lot of farm-to-table dishes from farms in Mexico.[16]

But don't put it all on the restaurants. The food industry in general works on deception. Terms such as "free range" and "cage free" do not translate to farm animals that grew in open spaces and wonderful pastures. For instance, all the official USDA definition of free range means is that the animal had "*some* access to the outdoors." And cage free does not mean that the hens could even look outside of where they were kept. Further, "pasture raised" has not been legally defined; "it can mean whatever the producer wants it to mean." And no restrictions exist regarding "natural," "light," or "pesticide free." [17] So, think about all this the next time you visit a restaurant or grocery store. It's mostly bullshit.

Bullshit in Internet News

Are you tired of the copious exaggerations we find in the Internet today? I certainly am. One of the most annoying is the overuse of the word "shock" in the titles of Internet articles. Note these headings from just one small segment of a list of online pieces (appearing on the same day):

- You Will Be *Shocked* When You See These 102 Year Old Photos

- *Shocking* New Snoring Research

- 20 Celebs Who Don't Believe in God: #15 Will *Shock* You

- Merloni: 'Nothing has *shocked* me' with Pablo Sandoval

- *Shocking* joint ingredient could fix knees in just 1 week?

It seems that nothing is surprising anymore, or unexpected or remarkable; everything out of the ordinary is now *shocking*, which has, well, more *shock* value. A similar situation exists with the word "miracle." We have miracle cures for all kinds of ailments, miracle polishes, miracle fertilizers, and lots more. This all gets old pretty fast, and the average reader, I would hope, can see that it's all bullshit.

Another crappy feature of the Internet is the vast number of—there is no other way to say it—stupid, inconsequential news articles. Consider the following from just one day's sampling:

Confirmed: America's 29th President Had a Love Child

Watch Selma Hayek Eat Silk Worms and Frogs

Scientists Have Pinpointed When the World Will End

10 Absolutely Astonishing Feats You Can Accomplish with Kitty Litter

If You Own a Home, Forget About Social Security

And what about targeted ads? You do a little research into a product and next thing you know you are bombarded, daily, with advertisements for the same kind of product. Look up information about a particular brand of shoes, and by the next day you could have difficulties using your computer because so many shoe ads will start popping up on the screen. And it's quite common, as I have experienced, for an individual to discover that he or she somehow signed up to receive emails and newsletters from a slew of merchants, stuff never requested. One way companies slip this deceptive bullshit past the consumer is by including poorly displayed boxes of "choices" that are *already checked*. Thus, the user must find them and uncheck each box. Otherwise, the unsuspecting customer would have agreed to something he or she did not want, such as a change to a new Internet browser or search engine, or to another homepage news source, or a subscription to some worthless publication, and other annoyances.

We also have targeted news stories, something I find particularly disturbing because we risk losing a sense of what is really important and newsworthy for a community, or a nation. For example, because I have shown an interest in international events, a large number of the news articles I see on the internet relate to international affairs. That's not altogether a bad thing, but I not only risk missing out on other important news, I am flooded with news pieces from questionable sources, just because the articles fit my profile. Consequently, I will frequently see silly or misleading story lines such as these:

"North Korea Attacks South Korea" (we then learn it was only a verbal attack, which happens every day);

"Putin Prepares for War Against NATO" (has he not always?); and

"China Threatens to Cut Exports to United States" (really? Are they looking for mass starvation?).

The problem is not only the irritating hyperbole, but that what should be important news for everyone (or most everyone) is lost in the soup of personalized news stories, some of which have little journalistic value or real consequence. I have more for you.

Have you ever wondered just how reliable are those top ten, top fifty lists commonly found in the internet? Here is a word of advice: don't pay too much attention. For instance, recently my interest was piqued when I saw a website claiming to rank the twenty smartest presidents in US history. The site listed each president's IQ. Several of the presidents date back to the 1700's and 1800's. For example, the site claims John Quincy Adams', who ranked first on the list, had an IQ of 168. George Washington, placing at number twenty, scored 132. Now here is the rub: the IQ test was not invented until 1905. So how were the old presidents tested? The creators of the article do not bother to explain this obvious problem, apparently not deeming its audience smart enough to object. But it gets worse.

Another website, *Business Insider*, also ranks the presidents according to intelligence, and guess who tops the list? John Adams, our second president (score 178), and NOT his son, John Quincy Adams, our sixth president (as in the other website). This second site at least acknowledges that IQ tests did not exist back in the 1800s. So, where did they get their numbers? Hang on to your hat. Their data come from an American engineer, Lib Thims, "who compiles high IQ scores as a hobby," and who came up with *his own* list based on the work of a psychology professor who *estimated* his own scores of presidents' "intellectual brilliance," "based on certain personality traits noted in their biographies that would *indicate* a higher-than-average level of intelligence, such as "wise," "inventive," "artistic," "curious," sophisticated," complicated," and "insightful,"[18] a suspiciously arbitrary set of factors that is then arbitrarily assigned a numerical value to stand for the subject's IQ. The results of such methodology, I'm sure readers would agree, can produce nothing but bullshit.

Simply stated: its usefulness notwithstanding, the internet is full of *it*. Be careful.

Corporate Billing: Cryptic Bullshit

How many people do you know can truly understand a telephone or cable company bill? Why are those bills so complicated? Could it be, as I suspect, that the various parties dipping into our pockets find it to be a particularly effective way to nickel and dime us with those innumerable fees? Here are a few of the stealthy cable/telephone related charges hiding in my "bundled" monthly communication bill plus an eye-opening list of the many ways government finds means to tax us:

> HD technology fee;
> Internet equipment fee;
> additional receiver fee;
> broadcast TV surcharge;
> regulatory video cost recovery charge;
> administrative fee;
> Federal universal service charge;
> regulatory cost recovery charge;
> 911 service fee;
> county sales tax;
> gross receipts tax;
> county communications tax;
> local communications tax;
> state communications tax;
> state sales tax.

Many of us are unaware of what some of these charges mean, and, just as sinister, telephone and cable services frequently hook customers with a low-ball (insert the word *bullshit* here for better effect) offer of $29 or $49 (or insert any suspiciously low number here) for the first three months, a rate that escalates dramatically at the end of the promotional period, exposing you to a legal soaking of hundreds of dollars more than you expected (and too late to back out; you signed a two-year contract. Ouch!). However, telephone and cable bills are just one example. Have you rented a car lately?

If you haven't rented a car for a long time, prepare to be stunned when your $99 a week rental becomes $180. That's right; the initial price is all bullshit. In a recent vacation, my weekly rental rate of $199 became—after taxes and a slew of fees— $360.85. That's an 81% increase over the advertised price! Aside from sales tax, I was slammed with a government fee, a vehicle license cost, a county tax, and something called a CFC charge (and fortunately I did not allow them to hit me with a refueling service charge). In an earlier trip the final car rental cost exceeded my base rate by 53% and included some of the same charges of the rental above plus a customer facility charge and a concession fee. With that, a $179 rate turned into $275.74. It's all so deceptive—classic corporate bullshit.

I'm sure that most of my readers have at least a couple of billing horror stories of their own, thus it's not necessary to belabor the issue. I just couldn't resist including one small segment to address that irritant. So, with that out of the way, we can now shift to another area where cattle dung can be found without much difficulty: education.

Chapter 3

Bullshit in Education

When I think back to all the crap I learned in high school, it's a wonder I can think at all.

—Paul Simon ("Kodachrome" lyrics)

I have never let my schooling interfere with my education.

—Mark Twain

Bullshit has been creeping into our education system for many years. Nowhere is this more evident than at the university level, which is particularly disappointing, so I'd like to open by listing *just a few* of the bizarre, outright ridiculous courses students can enroll in at universities in the United States:[1]

- "God, Sex, Chocolate: Desire and the Spiritual Path" (UC San Diego)

- "Lady Gaga and the Sociology of Fame" (The University of South Carolina)

- "Cyber porn and Society" (State University of New York at Buffalo)

 "The Science Of Superheroes" (UC Irvine)

- "Interrogating Gender: Centuries of Dramatic Cross-Dressing" (Swarthmore)

- "Zombies In Popular Media" (Columbia College)

- "Oh, Look, a Chicken!" Embracing Distraction as a Way of Knowing (Belmont University)

- "Getting Dressed" (Princeton)

Yes, parents are paying big money, and students are getting into debt, but look at the "quality" content suggested by those course titles! For instance, the course listing for "Cyber porn and Society" explains that "Undergraduates taking Cyber porn and Society at the State University of New York at Buffalo *survey* Internet porn sites." And the description for "Oh, Look, a Chicken!" states that students will listen to the teacher read from illustrated books, and that "students listen to music while doodling in class. Another project requires students to put themselves in situations where they will be distracted and write a reflection tracking how they got back to their original intent." We are talking really thick bullshit here folks, layers.

At the high school and elementary level, things are not any better. For example, in Miami-Dade County in Florida, students are subjected to so many tests that parents and teachers have been loudly protesting the practice for years, to no avail. There is little evidence that this excessive testing improves children's education or preparedness for college, but more and more testing keeps coming, and the time students spend in actual class time continues to decline. This reduced class time—combined with the directive to emphasize mathematics, science, and technology—has forced schools to sacrifice attention to the humanities, subjects such as history, geography, government, philosophy, and literature, even physical education. Consequently, many kids make it to college with little understanding of how our government operates, the influence that history has on current events, and the importance of geography in politics and world affairs.

I have been taken aback in my encounters with college freshmen who obviously never had the most basic instruction in geography, students who are unable to name more than two or three of the world's continents, or identify a state belonging to New England, or even declare with any certainty that Spain is part of Europe. History befuddles many of them, frequently demonstrating a disturbing inability to place major world events in time (e.g. WW II, American Civil War, Moon Landing, Pearl Harbor attack, and so on). I even met a student who expressed amazement when informed that Jesus Christ was a Jew. We are, in effect, producing generations of semi-illiterate individuals (in some cases the prefix semi is too kind). We have a serious case of widespread ignorance, which is particularly risky in a global economy where our young must compete against students from around the world, increasingly more educated, for what is likely to be a declining number of jobs (think rapidly expanding use of technology to replace humans).

Complicating the issue, some student assessment tests are used to evaluate teacher performance and the ranking of schools, ignoring the complexity that factors such as parental involvement and economic status add to the evaluation process. Children from lower socioeconomic communities are at a disadvantage, and that aspect is not part of the assessment formulas, which is unfair to teachers and schools and the children themselves. And we could go on at length about some of the irrational questions students find in these tests, but for brevity's sake, let's make do with an example from Florida's infamous FCAT of a few years ago. The following is provided by a parent sounding off in a Miami Herald op-ed column titled, "One Hump or Two?":

> My daughter recently took the fourth-grade FCAT writing test. The topic that they were given was, riding on a camel. Has anyone seen any camel farms around Florida recently? Wild camels in the Everglades? Pet camels? Does the state have any camels in the K-4 curriculum to at least expose students to the idea of a camel?
>
> Does the state need more F schools to justify firing teachers and cutting funding for education? Any kid writing in a confused style and not receiving a passing grade on the Florida Writes! Exam will have unindicted co-conspirators: the idiot who came up with this topic and all the other idiots who approved it.[2]

Mark Twain captured the sentiment long ago: "In the first place, God made idiots. That was for practice. Then he made school boards."

Warning: What follows may provoke physical distress—dizziness, nausea, even uncontrolled bowel movements—from mere eye contact with the next two paragraphs.

Hence, unless you are absolutely sure you are in good health, please stop and skip to the next chapter. For those who believe they can handle it, here it is.

It turns out that the city of New York doesn't like students exposed to certain words. None of them are four-letter words, mind you, nothing foul, but nevertheless the city's department of education has instructed companies bidding to rewrite their standardized tests to leave out those terms. Now, you must be wondering, what words could they be? What words, other than those commonly accepted as obscene, could possibly receive this much attention from a department of education? Let's look at a few.

The first one is *dinosaur*. No, that is not a misprint. The New York City Department of Education really doesn't like that word. Why? Because not everyone accepts the theory of evolution. Imagine a child coming back home and announcing to his or her ultra-religious parents who believe the earth is only a few thousand years old that dinosaurs roamed the earth millions of years ago. Think of the shock! I hope you're sitting down because the next word is...*birthday*. What? I can already hear my readers complain: "What could possibly be wrong with that word?" Well, the problem is that Jehovah's Witnesses don't celebrate birthdays. We also can find *pepperoni* in the list. Yes, pepperoni for Pete's sake! And that's because it's junk food, and it could be harmful. Ready for more? Let's allow nationally syndicated columnist Leonard Pitts Jr. to supplement the list:

> "Halloween" (too pagan), "divorce" (upsetting to the child whose parents have split), "disease" (upsetting to the child whose Nana has taken ill), "home computers" (not everyone can afford such luxuries), "terrorism" (scary), "slavery" (bad), and "space aliens" (sorry Superman).[3]

You can't say I did not warn you. I'm feeling lightheaded myself just typing this.

Another problem in academia is that school administrators are sometimes way too eager to embrace the latest methodologies and educational strategies concocted by enthusiastic PhDs, usually from major colleges where the student population is often significantly different from that in other parts of the country, and thus the new methods are likely to produce unexpected, often undesired results, at least in areas with high numbers of non-native students. When new methods fail (although it takes years to realize it), new books are written to analyze those failures, followed by additional studies that lead to new ideas and schemes that, presumably, now got it right.

The writing program at the university in which I teach—in particular the two freshmen writing courses required for graduation—is an example of good intentions missing the mark. The school has a large population of students for whom English is a second (or third) language. These students typically are struggling with basic grammar when they first arrive, even if they have somehow passed exams that presumably qualify them for regular first-year English courses. The situation becomes more critical because the school's writing program has gradually deemphasized grammar in favor of "higher" educational concepts, such as critical thinking, reflection, analysis and synthesis (which are absolutely desirable, but when the student is ready). Teachers, therefore, are discouraged from spending too much time on grammar topics, which—not surprisingly—results in a disturbingly high number of students who cannot articulate their thoughts confidently and effectively.

So I ask, If a student cannot express himself or herself adequately, what can be gained from his or her clear thinking, analytical prowess, and capability to synthesize? These students need to walk before they can run! The foundation of a house must be in place before the main structure can be built. It is essential for students to master the basics of written communication before moving on to higher cognitive skills. Just think of the disadvantages some of these young people will have in the *real* world—away from protective, ego-stroking teachers—when competing for jobs if their writing samples are riddled with grammatical issues! This well-intentioned bullshit in education is doing a disservice to students. It is perpetuating a language deficiency, a handicap, that can adversely affect their future.

It is certainly concerning that in 2014 the College Board, responsible for the infamous SAT college entrance exam, decided to "improve" the test to better assess what high school students actually study and learn. In theory, a more "accessible" test will allow more students to make it to college. So what direction did the Board take? According to Washington Post columnist Kathleen Parker, the test will be simplified and take less time, but at a cost. She explains with no lack of sarcasm: "The test no longer will include fancy words, otherwise known as a rich vocabulary, or require a timed essay. The math section will be adapted so that people-who-aren't-so-good-at-math...can pretend they are." She then asks: "If a person can't write a series of sentences to express a cogent thought, does that person really qualify for a college education? For what purpose?"

Parker goes on to suggest that the process of dumbing-down the exam started years ago when, in 2005, they eliminated the analogy segment. She asks: "Again, too hard?" She then stresses that the analogy was intended to evaluate cognitive ability. That is, "Can the kid think?" [4] In effect, the SAT was changed to try to get more high school students to qualify for college, thus reducing the overall college readiness of incoming freshmen. Is that a good thing? I think not.. If anything, the aim should be to address the root causes of low SAT scores in high school, if not before. Lowering standards to get more students to pass is bullshit.

Here is another anecdote from the annals of education. In 1970, the National Science Foundation decided that U.S. fifth-graders needed to expand their cultural horizons and so went about designing a social studies course for that age group. Miami Herald columnist Glenn Garvin offers some of the details: "...the course included a unit of the tribal customs of the Netsiltik Eskimos of Canada, which turned out to include wife-swapping, incest, cannibalism, bestiality and infanticide. That generated a bunch of headlines...." He then jokes: "Pretty quickly the kids were back to doing long division and fractions."[5] That this was even attempted by experienced, highly-credentialed educators is a real head-scratcher, isn't it?

There are other issues in education that are just as aggravating. Take for instance the casual dissemination of "facts." Starting in elementary school and remaining consistent through their university years, students are showered with assertions of truth that, years later, are found to be false—in other words, bullshit. This is popular in the sciences, where the orthodox view is rammed down the throats of unsuspecting students, even when proof is scant. Worse, some concepts are perpetuated even after having been proved wrong. For example, when I was in high school in the sixties I was taught that an atom could be imagined as a little solar system, with the central nucleus acting as the sun and the electrons orbiting around as tiny planets. This is entirely wrong, but the worst part is that while this idea had already been discarded at the time, it was still taught, and—even worse—it is still popularized today. Electrons, unlike planets, don't really orbit; they do not have exact locations or trajectories, but rather "exist" randomly around the atomic nucleus in a sort of probability "cloud."

And is it just me or do many others pick up a scent of bullshit when confronted with "facts," such as this one in the Science section of the *Miami Herald* of January 10, 2016: "...14 billion years ago the entire observable universe was 'roughly a million billion, billion times smaller than a single atom.'" Look at that number again, and again. Chew on that for a minute. Look at it one last time and give it another good chomp. Now, how well does it slide down your throat, especially if you are good in math? The article also reports that one of the *leading theories about creation* holds that "the universe materialized literally out of nothing." [6] This one is still called a theory and not a fact, but give scientists a little time to work out the details of how something can come from nothing, and this may soon be taught as fact. And then there is history.

"History is written by the winners," declared George Orwell. It is no secret that history is particularly malleable, and it's hardly debatable that the material that makes it to school books (or is omitted) varies from nation to nation. But even inside the United States, schools that bother to teach history are highly influenced by the zeitgeist of the times and/or the part of the country where the school is located. Which books make it to students' hands is subject to the whims of the authorities and their personal agendas or their excessive concern for political correctness. For example, events of the Civil War are often presented under a differently colored lens in Southern schools as opposed to Northern schools. In particular, the issue of slavery as one of the catalysts of that devastating war is magnified in Northern states and de-emphasized in Southern states, with the latter preferring to emphasize state rights as a main cause of the war.

Another case in point is how evolution is treated. Secular schools openly accept Darwinian evolution as a foregone conclusion, while religious scholars still teach the creation story, working to debunk the premises of evolutionary theory that science says are solidly established. The preferred theory can even differ from state to state. Hence, what is "true" to Student A who went to a public school may be completely false to Student B who attended a Baptist or Catholic school, and the same conflict may arise between a student from Connecticut and one from Arkansas.

Furthermore, popular myths are perpetuated in schools. These include long-standing ones, such as the one asserting that Edison invented the light bulb (he didn't, but he did create a long-lasting version that was commercially viable); that bats are blind (they're not); and that humans use only ten percent of their brains (it's more like ten percent at a time, and different activities use different parts of the brain, so that if our daily activities are varied, we end up using all—or most—of our brains).

A couple more. During my junior high years I was taught about the seven wonders of the ancient world (e.g. the Great Pyramid at Giza, the Statue of Zeus at Olympia). One of them, the famed Hanging Gardens of Babylon actually *never existed*, but we "learned" about them anyway. As many others, I also grew up with images of Vikings wearing horned helmets. Well, not one such helmet has ever been found, so there is no proof at all. The few Viking helmets unearthed to date do not have horns (what a disappointment!).

I think by now the reader understands that we could make this list very, very long. The message, of course, is that, at least partly, we sort of grew up on bullshit, much of it delivered to us in school. Most of it harmless, yes, but bullshit nevertheless.

We are now ready to move on to the next bullshit-saturated area in our society: the entertainment industry. I expect this section to be *extremely* controversial (we love our entertainers!), and I can foresee bitter opposition from some of my readers; but let's see if I can make a few points convincingly enough to find some acceptance.

Chapter 4

The Entertainment Industry – An Insidious Kind of Bullshit

Think about how stupid the average person is, and then realize that half of 'em are stupider than that.

—George Carlin

Americans no longer talk to each other, they entertain each other. They do not exchange ideas, they exchange images. They do not argue with propositions; they argue with good looks, celebrities and commercials.

—Neil Postman

One of the most prolific bullshit-generating machines in existence is the entertainment industry. It cranks out the garbage with stupefying ease via television, movies, and music, as it feeds our voracious appetite for amusement with the equivalent of entertainment junk food. From TV's sophomoric "reality" programs, dim-witted predictable humor, and banal, lowbrow game shows (excluding a few quality classics like Jeopardy) to the music industry's coarse, unmelodic productions, consumers are served a full plate of low-quality entertainment in a landscape dominated by a mob of troubled personalities. Let's begin with television.

The TV Industry

Arguably, the axis of modern-day entertainment is television, a medium still so young that there are people living today who remember the times before the revolutionary invention became a part of our lives. It has been argued that, intellectually, television is an unfortunate development because due to its passive nature the need to think and process information is reduced. In his book *Amusing Ourselves to Death,* famous educator Neil Postman explains that "a particular medium can only sustain a particular level of ideas," and television, unlike the printed word, limits the level. Consequently, he maintains, "politics and religion are diluted...and 'news of the day' becomes a packaged commodity." Since TV programming is based on ratings and not excellence of content, he further contends that it "de-emphasizes the quality of information in favour of satisfying the far-reaching needs of entertainment...." One of his arguments is that "televisual communication, which rely mostly on visual images to "sell" lifestyles," has changed politics, for now it "has ceased to be about a candidate's ideas and solutions, but whether he comes across favorably on television." [1] In general, television favors superficiality over substance.

Postman goes on to point out parallels between today's insatiable hunger for entertainment and the pleasure-inducing drug "soma" consumed by the people in Aldous Huxley's classic *Brave New World*. He points out that unlike George Orwell's terrifying view of complete control by a brutal totalitarian state, in Huxley's world "people medicate themselves into bliss, thereby voluntarily sacrificing their rights." That is, Postman sees television "as a present-day "soma", by means of which citizens' rights are exchanged for consumers' entertainment." [2] Long-held values, I hasten to say, are also traded in for the sake of entertainment. No matter what trash is thrown at us in the guise of art and diversion we devour with gusto and generally without question.

While for more than seventy years we've feared the specter of Big Brother—Orwell's totalitarian boogie man—Postman argues that we are now closer to Huxley's dictatorship of pleasure. He says:

> What Orwell feared were those who would ban books. What Huxley feared was that there would be no reason to ban a book, for there would be no one who wanted to read one....Orwell feared that the truth would be concealed from us. Huxley feared the truth would be drowned in a sea of irrelevance. Orwell feared we would become a captive culture. Huxley feared we would become a trivial culture, preoccupied with some equivalent of the feelies, the orgy porgy.... As Huxley remarked...the civil libertarians and rationalists who are ever on the alert to oppose tyranny "failed to take into account man's almost infinite appetite for distractions." In 1984...people are controlled by inflicting pain. In Brave New World, they are controlled by inflicting pleasure. In short, Orwell feared that what we fear will ruin us. Huxley feared that what we desire will ruin us.[3]

Television is one of those pleasure mechanisms that would have given Huxley nightmares, for not only has it largely fulfilled his prophecies of creating a trivial culture drowning in irrelevance, it has engendered a culture willing to sacrifice its principles and intellect at the altar of entertainment. We have learned to worship, the coarse, the lurid, and the sensational, as well as the prosaic. Dialogue, especially in the sitcom genre, has become predictable (e.g. the knock on the door interruption that ushers in the character being talked about, and over reliance on sexual innuendo). Humor is not always meritoriously laughter-inducing; it is decreed, ruled by the laughing box, which clues us in when it's time to laugh.

Perhaps even more insidious, we have become humor-dependent, which tends to trivialize even the most serious matters. In Postman's words: "Who is prepared to take arms against a sea of amusements? To whom do we complain, and when, and in what tone of voice, when serious discourse dissolves into giggles? What is the antidote to a culture's being drained by laughter?" [4] If you pay close attention to our interactions, we are often engaged in live sitcoms, and not just when we've had one drink too many.

The TV wasteland has given us programs unthinkable in the early years of television, with the likes of the infamous Jerry Springer Show, which has lasted *twenty-five years* by putting on display the most repugnant, degrading levels of social conduct, and also dating shows, such as *The Bachelor,* that teach young women how to seduce a man and promote the notion that relationships are shallow and short-term, and *The Bachelorette*, which reverses the role playing, but supports the same notions. Then we have the ultimate in mindless television with *Keeping up with the Kardashians*, which requires no commentary about its ability to waste an hour of human life. The "reality" TV genre, in particular, is an effective way of losing vast numbers of brain cells.

Television is also an arena that pits family values and time-honored codes of behavior against the industry's relentless onslaught on such standards. "Adult material" is first introduced in programs that air late in the evening (at least in the major networks), outside the so-called "family hours," but it doesn't stay there long, as it slowly creeps into the time slots when many kids are watching. Humor, a proven vehicle for introducing subject matter people find objectionable (especially parents) is usually the weapon of choice. Once the questionable material has been initiated in comedy settings, the process of mainstreaming is underway, surreptitiously moving into action flicks, dramas and other forms of entertainment. If it's funny, then it can't be all that bad, can it? Thus, as long as a humorous angle can be created to seep the offensive material past the viewers' bullshit filters, that's usually all that is required to avoid making the audience too uncomfortable.

In this way, particularly crude language, sexually explicit content, and graphic violence have wiggled into our living rooms. So, ha, ha, ha, we adults can now enjoy our microwave popcorn while listening to a barrage of profanity as a woman is violently raped and murdered (in as gruesome a fashion as possible, of course), and so can the children if they happen to stay up a little late on Friday night. We can also share some extra quality time with our preteens explaining ads for erectile dysfunction drugs, lubricated condoms, yeast infection treatments, and feminine hygiene, the kind of stuff that has me feeling nostalgic about old ads for constipation aids and hemorrhoidal ointments.

It needs to be mentioned that cable television, which is not bound by the same regulations as major networks, has taken full advantage of their relative freedom to bring the most horrific scenes of sexual violence and torture to the home screen. A leader in this category is the highly-rated HBO show *Game of Thrones*, a medieval fantasy drama that has already accumulated twenty-six Primetime Emmy Awards. Aside from what is generally recognized as the show's overall quality, this program showcases extreme cruelty, which is frequently of a sexual nature. This is intentional, betraying a clear purpose to keep pushing the line and bring as much shock as possible to audiences, as a considerable segment of the viewership can be counted on to always want more. Christopher Orr of *The Atlantic* seems to share this view in an article titled Why Does *Game of Thrones Feature So Much Sexual Violence?* Orr points out that the show, which is based on George R. R. Martin's novel series titled *Songs of Ice and Fire*, goes beyond the original script in its efforts to bring that excess of graphic sexual violence to the viewers. Regarding season five of the program, he states:

> Benioff and Weiss have gone out of their way, time and time again, to ramp up the sexual violence well beyond their source material. New characters have been invented in order to become victims (or victimizers), and existing ones have had their sexual cruelty amplified.[5]

Orr then proceeds to list the characters who were invented or whose roles were augmented by the producers for the purpose of intensifying the sexual violence. An interesting example mentioned is the Bastard of Bolton. He says:

Among the more substantial alterations between page and screen has been the ascendance of the Bastard of Bolton as a central figure on the show. Though he played an important narrative role in the second of Martin's novels...he was left out of the second season of the show. In the third book, by contrast, he was a distant, off-screen character about whom awful things were heard.... It was at this point, however, that Benioff and Weiss decided Ramsay merited ample screen time, dramatizing at interminable length his torture and eventual castration of Theon. Especially notable was a scene in which two naked beauties...arrived to sexually arouse Theon in preparation for his gelding. Since then, the show has taken every conceivable opportunity to remind viewers that Ramsay is a violent sexual sadist. To pick two examples of many, there was the murder of former bedwarmer Tansy, who was hunted through the woods, shot with an arrow, and then eaten alive by Ramsay's dogs in season four; and the rape of Sansa at Winterfell this last season.[6]

Undoubtedly, some television shows (and movies) tamper with source material to pile on the gore, cruelty, sex, and violence, although *Game of Thrones* is perhaps the most salient example of this modern "genre," one that is deliberately designed to dish out the high-shock material for its own sake. A solid storyline and fine acting are simply not enough. The crude, disturbing content is a requirement so that the show is talked about, drawing in the curious and retaining those already addicted to the spectacle. It is also a prerequisite to ramp up the appalling material incrementally, from season to season to keep those TV sets tuned in. Consequently, the viewers' sensitivities are dulled under the unrelenting assault of the shock hammer wielded by the producers, and this, in turn, necessitates a stronger jolt, a higher dose of unsettling audiovisual effects to maintain the high—just as drug addicts.

Other high-quality TV shows—those with engaging, first-rate scripts and actors, and able to deliver quality entertainment without the need to appeal to lewdness or gut-busting violence—somehow still endure (how much longer?), but their numbers are in decline, as the viewership has been gradually trained to expect increasingly "shocking" productions. Once general acceptance of a disturbing theme or previously avoided offensive material is achieved, mainstreaming is complete, and we're ready for the next assault on young minds and families. But that's all okay because, you know, it's the way of the modern and uninhibited, open-minded persona, and besides, some entity with lots of power, but with little regard for what they put out and its societal repercussions, is making money.

I have not a doubt that a sizeable number of people reading these lines have already been effectively desensitized to such programming to the point where they cannot even understand the issue I'm raising. Their sensibilities have been overwhelmed, clouded in distraction, their moral compass disoriented, their sense of propriety stifled. In effect, the bullshit blinders are firmly on. They've unconsciously or consciously come to accept the well-known phrase from *Star Trek*: "Resistance is futile." Consent is given; surrender is complete. The scatological (look it up) rules the airwaves. So, is the movie experience any different? Not really. Why should it?

The Motion Picture Industry

Sometime in 2014-15 I took my then fourteen-year-old grandson to see a movie he had been wanting to see: *300: Rise of an Empire*. As a history buff and admirer of the military accomplishments of the ancient Greeks, especially the Spartans, he was quite interested in the film, and I was only too glad to take him to see it. It wasn't long into the picture when it became evident that, its attempt to tell about a momentous chapter in ancient history notwithstanding, the film was mainly intended to shock the audience with an inordinate amount of gore (and a discomforting sex scene). I was well aware that, being a war movie, there would be plenty of violence, but I was unprepared for what I witnessed that Sunday afternoon. The quantity of blood running through the screen was, in my experience, unprecedented. Blood squirts were visible with nearly every strike of a sword, and there were hundreds of graphic, vicious stabbings. Taking full advantage of 3-D, the crimson bursts aimed straight at the audience. In keeping with modern-day protocol, the obligatory sex scene was also there. Not unexpected, of course, except that this installment was particularly raw, not in the sense of skin exposure, but in the unusual ferocity and blind hatred that accompanied the act. It was also obviously forced into the script, as it had no historical backing nor was it remotely plausible given the circumstances of the plot. All in all, it was a lamentable 102 minutes.

We walked quietly out of the theatre, my grandson and I, as I pondered what we had seen. I believe he was conscious of my reflective mood and did not speak until we took our seats for a pizza at a nearby restaurant. I silently wondered if the story, which would have been highly interesting and intense on its own, needed to have been delivered in such a brutal visual display (even for a war movie). I found that some critics, such as Guy Lodge of *Time Out*, saw what I saw, only in a more positive light. His comment: "It's flesh and carnage that the audience is here to see, and Murro delivers it by the glistening ton, pausing only for stray bits of back story." Doesn't say much for the approving audience, though. Also disappointing is that a Cambridge University professor of Greek culture found parts of the film historically inaccurate.[7] (so much for the history lesson). That said, I should not have been too surprised with the experience because, well...follow me to the next paragraph.

The reader—if old enough—must have noticed significant changes at the theater. A lot could be written about this, but for brevity, let me use an example to illustrate the matter. Looking at reviews of new movie releases in an April 2016 issue of my local newspaper I found that after each of the critic's ratings, there was a list of viewer warnings. The first film was "Everybody Wants Some!" The viewer warnings box contained the following: "Vulgar language, sexual situations, drug use, adult themes." The second film was "Demolition," and its box read: "Vulgar language, sexual content, drug use, adult themes." The third movie was "The Boss," and the trailing box read: "Vulgar language, sexual content, drug use." Finally, the last picture was "Born to be Blue," and its information box included: "Vulgar language, sexual situations, violence, drug use."[8] Okay, maybe it was an unusual week, I thought, so six weeks later, I ran the same survey. Provoking only a mild surprise, the results actually got worse.

Here are the findings: "A Bigger Splash," – Vulgar language, frontal nudity, explicit sex, violence, drug use, adult themes; "The Nice Guys" – Vulgar language, nudity, graphic sex, violence, gore, adult themes; "Neighbors 2: Sorority Rising" – Vulgar language, sexual situations, nudity, drug use; "The Invitation" – Vulgar language, nudity, violence, adult themes. Can you spot a common theme here, a pattern? Is it too naive to ask if that is all the movie industry is able (or willing) to produce? Further, Is that what we, as a society, want to see virtually every time we visit the theatre? It seems that way. Regrettably, the state of television and the movies is just a part of the larger story playing out in our day. To better understand this, let's now delve into the state of today's music and its creators, which is going to require a little more ink than the other sections in this chapter.

The Music Industry

The highly influential music industry is a major peg in the entertainment board. It is hardly arguable that it is a key contributor in shaping popular culture, as it generates many of the prevailing ideas and attitudes, defining what is hip and what is not. Acceptable behavior and manners have been redefined, not by people with our best interests in mind, but by a clan of influential, sleazy, opportunistic bloodsuckers who cash in by appealing to society's basest conceptions.   Thus, good principles and conventional codes of ethics are passé; modesty, moderation, and civility are out; arrogance, vanity, and rudeness are in. It is an era of unabashed ego, and the music industry—with exceptions in country, jazz, and some pop—is a leading participant.

The morally-failed personalities driving a large segment of the music world best illustrate the issue introduced above. Take the recently deceased, much-celebrated music legend, Prince, the virtuoso who swung the raunchiness doors wide open in the 1980's and who some call "the liberator of millions" (I am not counted in those millions). This lewd "genius" was so messed up that he could not recognize his music and drug dependence were not compatible with moral tenets of his religion. He was a Jehovah Witness! How messed up is that? And instead of proselytizing the faith door to door as the religion's adherents are encouraged (if not required) to do, he chose to worship Mammon, raking in millions from his music and the kind of performances for which some of the more militant parishioners in his church would have had him stoned.

But at least Prince was talented, a prolific composer and dazzling guitarist. He is also known to have been generous and, best we know at the moment, mostly law-abiding (there is that question about prescription drug abuse), attributes sorely lacking in many of today's artists, the gods and goddesses the public worships, especially teenagers and pre-teens. These include the likes of Miley Cyrus, Justin Bieber, and a slew of sordid rappers, many of them hoodlums—all millionaires. Oh, and these are not just stars; they are *super*stars! Artists today are so spectacular, so otherworldly, so much like ancient gods, we rarely find mere stars anymore. S*uperstardom* is the norm.

Now, quickly, before some readers get defensive over their music idols and close their minds, I want to go over a few highlights in the careers of some modern-day deities. These characters—consciously or unconsciously—serve as agents for the widespread shunning of traditional values, not to mention the dumbing down of our youth, which threatens to boost the ranks of insensitive, egotistical, intellectually-challenged, selfie stick-wielding, morally-stunted future adults. First pick: the "adorable" and "endearing" Miley Cyrus.

Miley Cyrus

After gaining popularity in Disney's TV show, *Hannah Montana*, Miley Cyrus launched a successful career as singer, songwriter, and actress, amassing many awards. Regrettably, in the process, Miley went rogue—in a hurry. It was a parent's nightmare that the wholesome girl children idolized turned slut literally overnight. One of her "great" moments came in 2013 at the MTV Video Music Awards, where, in a lurid performance, stroked Robin Thicke's crotch with a huge foam finger and then began twerking against his crotch. That some reviewers compared the performance to a bad acid trip and labeled it a train wreck, did not discourage Cyrus one bit, and she soon followed with another of her now "iconic" moments. In February 2014, at a concert in California, Miley again plunged into the sewer when she took her vile antics to the next level—with the full support of her adoring parents, no less. As reported by E Online:

> Miley Cyrus' risqué Bangerz tour has some parents up in arms, but her own mom and dad are totally cool with it! In fact, [the Cyruses] watched proudly Thursday night as their 21-year-old daughter flew through the air riding an enormous hot dog in the Honda Theater in Anaheim, CA. They didn't seem to have a problem, either, with Miley sitting spread eagle on the hood of a car giving the middle finger, while wearing a cannabis leaf covered onesie...[9]

That's hard to beat. Ask most young girls today who they admire, and Miley will often top the list. How could she not, when the media and music connoisseurs bestow some of the highest accolades on her. As early as 2008 Cyrus was included in *Time Magazine*'s 100 most influential people in the world (that's *in the world!*). In 2010, she ranked 13th on Forbes' Celebrity 100 and was declared "Artist of the Year" by MTV. In 2013 she was a finalist for *Time*'s Person of the Year (placed third). By 2014, she listed at number 17 of the most powerful celebrities of the moment (*Forbes*), placing her ahead of Mariah Carey and Taylor Swift, with estimated earnings of $36 million. Not bad for a miscreant who in 2014 spat on her fans during a performance in Monterrey, Mexico and sparked a huge uproar with her infamous "ass whipping" incident, where she had one of her dancers slap her huge prosthetic butt with a Mexican flag. Disrespectful use of the flag is a criminal offense in Mexico, so there was a push to have her criminally charged, but the clueless brat got away with just a fine.

Miley is supposedly so talented and knowledgeable about music that she has been tapped to be a judge in the popular TV show *The Voice*. Yet, when I listen to her intonations, I must agree with critic Lesley Abravanel's report of Miley's performance in Art Basel Miami in December 2014: "At the end of the night, Cyrus wailed out a few tunes...sounding like a feral cat imitating Yoko Ono. It was bad. Really bad. The ex *Hannah Montana* star babbled some profanities and then sang a ballad she claims was only previously sung in her living room but wasn't even fit for her shower."[10]

Still, the celebration of this marvel continued in our country in March 2014, when Skidmore College in New York began offering a sociology course entitled, "The Sociology of Miley Cyrus: Race, Class, Gender and Media", which uses "Miley as a lens through which to explore sociological thinking about identity, entertainment, media and fame."[11] What a load of shit! Let's move on before I shatter my keyboard. While I'm still holding the shovel, let's talk about another little horror polluting our airwaves: The Biebs, JB.

Justin Bieber

Justin Bieber is a modern-day phenomenon. This spoiled brat, a prime example of mediocrity (I'm feeling generous), inexplicably had his first album go platinum in the U.S. and managed to become the first artist *ever* to chart seven tunes from a first album on the Billboard Hot 100. His second collection, released in November 2011, broke in at number one on the Billboard 200. Along the way, he has accumulated several fan-voted awards, such as the American Music Award for Artist of the Year in 2010 and 2012. From 2011 through 2013, he was listed by Forbes magazine among the *top ten most powerful celebrities in the world*.[12] (Take a short break if that statement made your head spin). In May 2016 he won Billboard's Best Male Artist and Best Social Media Artist. A self-proclaimed Christian, Bieber has a mile-long rap sheet. Here is a *partial* list of his troubles:

- Accused of reckless driving around his neighborhood in 2012.
- Charged with vandalism in Brazil in 2013.
- Arrested in Miami Beach in January 2014 for DUI, driving with an expired license, and resisting arrest, while admitting he had consumed alcohol, smoked pot and taken prescription drugs. Toxicology report showed Bieber had THC and Xanax in his system when arrested. All was settled with a plea bargain that reduced the charges, slapped him with a tiny $500 fine and an anger management course.
- Charged with vandalism in California for throwing eggs at neighbor's home in July 2014, causing thousands in damages; paid $80,900 in restitution, served two years' probation, and attended an anger management course (again).
- Arrested and charged with assault and dangerous driving in Stratford, Ontario after colliding with a minivan while on his all-terrain vehicle on August 29. He then "engaged in a physical altercation" with an occupant of the minivan. He was released and his lawyer blamed it all on "the unwelcome presence of paparazzi".
- Charged with smuggling a monkey into Munich, Germany in March 2013.
- Charged with striking a limousine driver in December 2013 (charges dropped).
- Ordered to appear in court in Argentina in November 2014 to give testimony on an alleged assault by his bodyguards on a photographer in November 2013. He failed to appear, and so an arrest warrant was issued.
- As of May 2016, Bieber faces a $100,000 lawsuit for allegedly smashing someone's cellphone at a Houston nightclub.

The obvious question, of course, is Why is this second-rate artist, this self-absorbed delinquent so popular? This is a punk, a stuck-up turd, who held the record for the most retweeted message (250,000) until Obama's famous 2012 reelection tweet pushed it to second place. A legion of psychologists and sociologists could not explain this. No doubt, his parents will one day be honored with a "Parents of the Century" award or similar tribute, or they might make a million or two writing a best-seller about raising children, or both, with Cyrus' parents close behind. None of that should surprise.

So, rock on Justin! Keep swinging on your hotdog Miley! Please help us guide the children well into the 21st century. Who better than you? Well . . . maybe the rappers!

Rap and Gangsta Rap—The Rise of the Thugs

There is nothing more to be said about music. I'm the f---ing end-all, be-all of music.

—Kanye West

The Internet...It's a way to get shit to Southeast Asia and all types of shit.

—Bizzy Bone

The day Obama got elected, the gangsta became less relevant.

—Jay-Z

Light years from the positive, soul-moving music immortalized by black artists during the Motown phenomenon of the 1960s and 70s, we find the negative, narcissistic, thuggish, misogynistic, boastful, and tasteless "music" style called rap. One of the four subsets of hip hop (the others being DJing, B-Boying (i.e. breakdancing), and graffiti writing), this form of "artistic expression" began to gain popularity during the 1980s and, disturbingly, is still with us today. Mostly populated by black performers, the rap arena also includes a few white ("wanna-be-black") entertainers. From the self-aggrandizing Kanye West (interestingly, the son of a Black Panther turned "Christian Counselor," whatever that is) to the pathologically criminal Bobby Schmurda, the history of hip hop is chockfull of unsavory characters. Of particular concern is the criminal element that pervades the genre. The more research I did on some of the most famed names in the world of hip hop, the more criminal rappers I kept finding—a real eye-opening and disturbing realization. Here is but a modest sampling of the criminal pasts of rap artists per Hubpages.com,[13] a website focused on popular topics:

- *Tupac Shakur* – convicted of sexual assault in 1995; gunned down in Vegas in '96.
- *Lil Wayne* – drug charges and conviction for criminal possession of weapon (2007).
- *Gucci Mane* – murder (2005, charges dropped); assault; possession of weapon by a convicted felon (among several other offenses); currently serving time.
- Cassidy – charged with murder, later reduced to manslaughter after a series of legal technicalities worked in his favor (2005).
- *Fat Joe* – arrested for assault and robbery in 1998 and assault in 2002 (neither charge stuck); pleaded guilty to tax evasion in 2012 and served time.
- *T.I.* – Served time in 2009 for gun charges. This rapper's IQ is so low that he "planned on rolling up to the B.E.T. awards with three machine guns and two silencers, and several more machine guns with a large amount of ammunition were later found at his home." He also served time for possession of ecstasy (2011).
- *Bobby Schmurda* – from a 2014 arrest, Shmurda and friends "face...69 charges, from murder, attempted murder, assault, attempted assault, weapons possession, criminal use of a firearm...[to] reckless endangerment, and narcotics sales."

Again, and sadly, that's just a sampling from my early research. As my investigation continued, I learned that a gangsta rapper named *No Limits C-Murder* (that's right; that's his artist name) is serving life in prison for gunning down a young fan at a nightclub in 2002, and also that rapper *Steady B*, having failed to achieve much success in the music business, decided to rob a bank, which resulted in a Philadelphia cop being shot and killed. He is now serving a life sentence with no chance of parole. And let's not forget the ultra-successful **Jay-Z** whose first career choice in life was dealing crack cocaine and whose lawyers got him off with a wrist slap three years' probation for the stabbing of producer Lance "Un" Rivera in 1999.[14] That did not dissuade Beyoncé from marrying him, but *maybe* she'll reconsider when infidelity becomes the issue, as some celebrity watchers are suspecting. She certainly doesn't need his millions at this point.

I also came across *DMX*, whose long rap sheet includes imprisonment "assault, drug possession, animal cruelty, reckless driving, and many more," including impersonating an FBI agent while high on cocaine. And yes, I learned the incredible story of *X-Raided*, who, aside from being a member of the Crips gang in California, in 1992 broke into a woman's home and killed her. The sick part is that even though sentenced to thirty-one years to life, he still managed to release an album, "Psycho Active," that "featured him posing with the murder weapon on the cover."[15] Is that sick, or what? Who says crime doesn't pay?

But I'm just warming up. No discussion of hip hop would be complete without a mention of the legendary *Snoop Dogg*. This character's unsavory history could fill a 16 gigabyte memory stick, so the challenge is to keep this brief. As a previous member of the radical Nation of Islam, Snoop has demonstrated his "wisdom" via his political views and commentary. First endorsing Rep. Ron Paul in the 2012 primaries, he then supported Obama in the general election, a choice he defended on Instagram, saying, "He a black nigga", "He's BFFs with Jay-Z", and "Michelle got a fat ass." He also explained why people should not vote for Mitt Romney: "He a white nigga", "That muthafucka's name is Mitt", and "He a ho."[16] With that kind of insightfulness, sensitivity, and extensive vocabulary, it's surprising Dogg is not in the Supreme Court or at least a United States ambassador.

Snoop Dogg also has a history of being "highly spiritual." Reportedly a member of the radical, racist, anti-Semitic Nation of Islam in 2009, he has claimed to be the reincarnation of Bob Marley and declared himself "born again" as he converted to the Rastafari movement in Jamaica in 2012, a quasi-religion whose way of life "encompasses the spiritual use of cannabis and [are you ready for this?] *the rejection of the degenerate society of materialism, oppression, and sensual pleasures...*"[17] Say what?

Keep that in mind as we look at how Snoop managed in this "degenerate society" throughout his life. The following is straight out of Wikipedia, with relatively minor editing mostly intended to condense and save space:

- After finishing high school, Snoop Dogg was arrested for possession of cocaine and spent the next three years in and out of prison for various offenses. He was also a member of the *Rollin' 20's Crips* gang.

- In 1993, Snoop was arrested in connection with the death of Phillip Woldermariam, a member of a rival gang who was shot and killed by Snoop's bodyguard; Snoop was also charged with murder, as he was driving the vehicle from which the shooting had commenced. But the guys were no dummies; they enlisted the famous high-caliber attorney, Johnnie Cochran (remember O.J.?) to defend them . Not surprisingly, both men were acquitted.

- In 1997, Snoop was guilty of illegal possession of a handgun and was ordered to record public service announcements, pay $1,000, and serve three years' probation.

- In 2005, he was sued for assaulting a fan on stage at a concert in Auburn, Washington. The accuser claimed he was beaten by the artists' entourage while mounting the stage, allegedly after an "open invite."

- In April 26, 2006, Snoop Dogg and members of his entourage were arrested after being turned away from British Airways' first class lounge at Heathrow Airport because some members were not really flying first class. After being escorted out, the group vandalized a store. Seven police officers were injured in the melee. In May, it was decided that Snoop would be denied entry to the UK for the foreseeable future, and his visa was denied the following year. As of 2010, Snoop has been allowed back into the UK., but the group involved in the incident has been banned by British Airways for "the foreseeable future."

- Stopped for a traffic violation in October 2006 at Bob Hope Airport in Burbank, Dogg was arrested for possession of a firearm and for suspicion of transporting an unspecified amount of marijuana.

- The following month, after taping an appearance on *The Tonight Show*, he was arrested again for possession of marijuana, cocaine and a firearm. Two members of Snoop's entourage were admitted members of the *Rollin' 20's Crips* gang and were arrested on separate charges.

- In April 2007, Snoop Dogg was sentenced to a three-year suspended sentence, five years' probation, and was required to perform 800 hours of community service after pleading no contest to two felony charges of drug and gun possession by a convicted felon. He was also prohibited from hiring anyone with a criminal record or gang affiliation as a security guard or a driver.

- Also in April 2007, the Australian government banned Snoop Dogg from entering the country on character grounds, citing his prior criminal convictions. (He was eventually allowed in as an "unlikely risk to the Australian community").

- In July 2012, he was banned from Norway for two years after earlier entering the country in possession of marijuana and 227,000 undeclared Krones.

- After performing in Sweden on July 2015, Snoop Dogg was detained by Swedish police for using illegal drugs. After tests came back positive for narcotics, Snoop still had the gull to upload videos to social media accusing the police for racial profiling. He declared in the videos, "Nigga as got me in the back of police car right now in Sweden, cuz", and "Pulled a nigga over for nothing, taking us to the station where I've got to go pee in a cup for nothin'. I ain't done nothin'. All I did was came...and did a concert, and now I've got to go to the police station. For nothin.'!" [18]

The reader needs to understand that the bullet list above is *not* a complete register of Snoop Dogg's long lawbreaking history. This is not just a petty-crime, dime-a-dozen rap artist we are talking about, but a highly notorious felon, a career criminal.

However, that has not had a negative impact on Snoop's career because his artistry is so amazing, so stupendous, that we have made him a millionaire many times over. Snoop Dogg has produced a huge volume of "music" and received countless awards and nominations, starting in 1994 when he won "New Artist of the Year," followed in 1995 with "Favorite Rap/Hip-Hop Artist." All this was followed with an enormous accumulation of honors (really far too many to list) that extends through the late 1990s and early twenty-first century until the present, 2016, when his last album, *Bush*, was nominated for a Grammy for "Best Recording Package." Although he's never won a Grammy, Snoop holds the record for most nominations (eighteen), which is beyond remarkable, given that a Grammy is considered the highest possible honor in music.

Snoop Dogg has also appeared in numerous music videos (winning various MTV awards), movies, and television shows. Among his big screen successes we have the 2000 film (which he directed), "*Snoop Dogg's Doggystyle*, a pornographic film produced by Hustler. The film, combining hip hop with x-rated material, was a huge success and won "Top Selling Release of the Year" at the 2002 AVN Awards. Snoop then directed *Snoop Dogg's Hustlaz: Diary of a Pimp* in 2002..."[19]

It is exhausting to try to do justice to the gigantic list of honors recognizing Snoop Dogg as one of the greatest artists of this generation (maybe even of all time?). And I ask, quite possibly naively, "Is there something wrong with this picture?" Let's move on to another gem of the hip hop scene, the one and only Eminem.

Called the "King of Hip Hop" and ranked on its list of 100 Greatest Artists of All Time by *Rolling Stone Magazine,* we have **Eminem** (Marshal Bruce Mathers III), the best-selling artist of the 2000s (in the U.S.) and one of the best selling artists worldwide with over 172 million albums sold.[20] Although his past seems tame compared to Snoop Dogg's and other rappers, this hip hop legend is no angel. With a long history of drug addiction to boost his résumé, Eminem was arrested twice in June 2000 on gun charges for carrying a concealed weapon and for assault on a man he saw kissing his former wife outside of a club. He was also arrested for gun possession during a spat with rival rappers from the Insane Clown Posse.[21] Eminem is also famous for his penchant for stirring trouble, even with those closest to him. *Rolling Stone* includes this snippet in its biography of the rapper:

> On his 1999 major-label debut, The Slim Shady LP (Number Two pop, Number One R&B), the Detroit-based white rapper was willing to put anybody in his verbal crosshairs, including not only his detractors but himself, Kim, his wife and the mother of his daughter, and his own mother (who later ended up filing a defamation of character lawsuit against him). The following year's doubly venomous The Marshall Mathers LP (Number One pop, Number One R&B) raised/lowered the bar even more, drawing intense protest from gay, lesbian, religious, and women's groups, even as it became the fastest-selling rap album of all time...[22]

A commendable character this Eminem. That must be why providence has rewarded him with so much success and wealth! Actually, it wasn't until I was doing research on this ultra-popular rapper that I realized the enormous extent of vulgarity that pervades rap music in general. His lyrics were among the most offensive imaginable, and I found about ninety percent to be unfit to include in this book. Nevertheless, here are some cuts from the *most printable* of the lyrics I found in his "great" hit, *Criminal* (a perfectly fitting title):

> Please Lord, this boy needs Jesus
> Heal this child, help us destroy these demons
> Oh, and please send me a brand new car
> And a prostitute while my wife's sick in the hospital
>
> I'm the bad guy who makes fun of people that die
> in plane crashes and laughs
> As long as it ain't happened to him
>
> ...Dre couldn't make it today
> He's a little under the weather, so I'm taking his place
> (Mm-mm-mmm!) Oh, that's Dre with an AK to his face
> Don't make me kill him too and spray his brains all over the place
> I told you Dre, you should've kept that thang put away
> I guess that'll teach you not to let me play with it, eh?
> I'm a CRIMINAL
>
> Windows tinted on my ride when I drive in it
> So when I rob a bank, run out and just dive in it
> So I'll be disguised in it
> And if anybody identifies the guy in it
> I'll hide for five minutes
> Come back, shoot the eyewitness
> Fire at the private eye hired to pry in my business
> Die, bitches, bastards, brats, pets
> This puppy's lucky I didn't blast his ass yet [*dog whines*]

So wholesome! It seems Eminem (and others like him) pass the test for that ideal role model so many parents want for their children. I mean, they are buying the rapper's songs for their teens, so they must be okay with the "messages" Eminem and his ilk deliver, right? Perhaps they don't like what they're hearing (if they can even understand it) but they're helpless to stop it, so they justify it with "Well, it's just for fun."

Rappers provide so much material to work with, it's like shooting fish in a barrel. Let's put the admired **Sean John Combs** (Puff Daddy, P. Diddy) under our microscope. A cursory review reveals that in April 1999 this "family man and philanthropist" rapper was charged with second-degree assault on executive Steve Stoute of Interscope Records over the content of a video. Then, in December, accompanied by his former girlfriend, **Jennifer Lopez** (yes, she), he was involved in a gunfire incident at Club New York in Manhattan. Arrested for possession of weapons (among other charges) he tried to bribe his driver to claim that he—not Combs—owned the guns. Armed with an elite team of lawyers, Combs avoided punishment, being found *not guilty of all charges*, while his buddy, rapper **Shyne**, who was also involved in the melee, was nailed on five of eight charges and got slammed with ten years in the pen. Much more recently, in June 2015,

Combs was again arrested, this time in L.A. for assault with a deadly weapon on one of his son's football coaches because the coach yelled at Combs' son (how dare he!). P. Diddy has received many accolades and much praise, and, not surprisingly in our corrupt, trash-adoring, fascinated-with-hoodlums society, even got his own Hollywood walk of fame star in 2008. Imagine that! Further, to honor him for charity work (something ill-famed celebrities do to soften their image), Chicago Mayor R. Daley, in an embarrassing display of sucking up to these hooligans, named October 13, 2006, as "Diddy Day."[23] Revolting. Only in America.

Now let's aim the lens toward yet another hip hop "superstar," *50 Cent* (real name Curtis J. Jackson). This darling of the hip hop scene, has had so many run-ins with the law, it would take several chapters to cover them all. In June 1994, 50 Cent was arrested for selling cocaine and then arrested again only weeks later for possession of heroin, crack cocaine and a gun. Sentenced to three to nine years in jail, he ended up spending only six months in a boot camp for rehabilitation. On New Year's day, 2003, he was arrested once more, charged with two counts of criminal possession of a weapon. In July 2005, he was sentenced to two years' probation stemming from three counts of assault and battery on members of an audience after he was hit with a water bottle on stage. Then, in 2013, he pleaded not guilty on charges of domestic violence and vandalism (four counts), and he was looking at up to five years in prison and $46,000 in fines.[24] However, his legal team advised him to take a no contest plea, which got him off easy, a sweet deal where he did some community service work, attended counseling, and was put under _unsupervised_ probation—say that again—_unsupervised_ probation for three years. Later, in June 2016, 50 ignored profanity laws in St. Kitts, cut loose a "motherF...." on stage and was arrested.

Now, some readers might think the public would be turned off by such a character, but they would be wrong. 50 Cent's "talent" and "music" are so out-of-this-world that in spite of his violent, criminal past we are willing to idolize him, and thus—as is the norm with these hooligans—he has collected numerous awards: nominations for Best New Artist and album at the Grammies, six Billboard Music Awards, ASCAP Songwriter of the Year, and *Curtis*, his third album, earned him Best-Selling Hip-Hop Artist in 2007. In fact, he has received 83 awards resulting from 135 nominations![25] Not bad for a crook who once said; "I have less compassion than the average human," and whose most famous quotation is the following: "Niggas think Jimmy Iovine's my boss. Nigga, f--- Jimmy Iovine, nigga! I'm from 134th street, nigga! I ain't got no motherf--in' boss." I couldn't have said it better myself.

Naturally, it should not be surprising that so many of these thugs, I mean rappers, have a criminal history. Just listen to their songs, if you can understand them, and ask yourself: What are these "singers" promoting? How do they get away with this crap? The website "The Root," (self-described as "...the premier news, opinion and culture site for African-American influencers.") carries the article, "Hip-Hop's Finest: 30 Great Rap Lyrics." The lead-in states: "We asked three hip-hop tastemakers to name their top 10 favorite lyrics of all time" (tastemaker defined as *one who determines or strongly influences current trends or styles, as in fashion or the arts)*. Accordingly, even though opinions about best lyrics abound and favorite compositions are highly personal, the list may still provide a representative sample of what are generally considered *milestones* in rap lyrics. Feeling particularly cynical, let's have fun with a sampling of what the article considers among the top rap lyrics of all time: [26]

"Brooklyn's Finest" – *Jay-Z and the Notorious B.I.G.*

LYRICS: Jay-Z
"Peep the style and the way the cops sweat us (uh-huh)
The number one question is can the feds get us (uh-huh)
I got vendettas in dice games against ass betters (uh-huh)
and n--gas who pump wheels and drive Jettas
Take that with ya"

Notorious B.I.G.
"Hit ya, back split ya
F--k fist fights and lame scuffles
Pillowcase to your face, make the shell muffle
Shoot your daughter in the calf muscle
F--k a tussle, nickel-plated
Sprinkle coke on the floor, make it drug related
Most hated"

These are words to cuddle by the fireplace with your loved one, aren't they?

"Rebel Without A Pause" -- *Chuck D, Public Enemy*

LYRICS: "Smooth—not what I am
Rough—'cause I'm a man"

Deep. Really deep stuff. No wonder it found its place among the *greatest* hip hop lyrics of all time.

"Remember Me?" – *Eminem*

LYRICS: "Sick, sick dreams of picnic scenes
Two kids, 16 with M-16's and 10 clips each
And them s--ts reach through six kids each"

Absolutely Inspiring! Reminiscent of the Youngbloods' 1967 immortal, "*Come Together.*" Possibly even better.

"*Come on people now / Smile on your brother / Everybody get together / Try to love one another right now.*"

"Raising Hell" -- *DMC, Run-D.M.C.*

LYRICS:
"The unbelieving receiving prophecy so true
I cut the head off the devil and I throw it at you."

"Ain't No Half-Steppin'" -- *Big Daddy Kane*

LYRICS: "Rappers stepping to me, they want to get some
But I'm the Kane, so yo, you know the outcome"

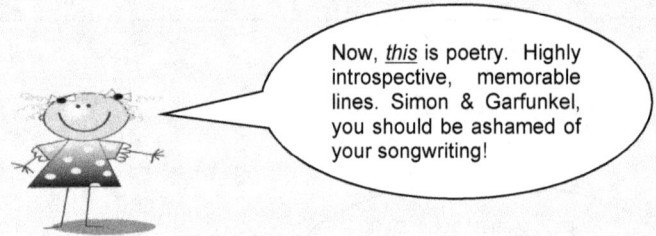

"Judgment Night" -- *Onyx, featuring Biohazard*

LYRICS: "Capture the rapture, come blackness after!
I swear to f--kin' God,
I'll raise hell and make the white man call me master."

Feeling emotional? Touched? In a state of bliss? Just in case you need a little more to push you over the ecstasy edge, consider this: In discussing the *hardest* rap albums of all time, music critic Harold Stallwarth, includes the following commentary about rap icon's **Kool G Rap**'s 1992 album, *Live and Let Die*: "...its cover art depicts upward of a dozen felonies, including kidnapping, conspiracy, murder and even what appears to be animal cruelty....Live and Let Die is rarely canonized, but its influence casts a long shadow over both the horrorcore and mafioso subgenres, the latter being a conduit for *several of the greatest rap albums of all time.*"[27] Uplifting, to say the least. Just imagine the enrapturing feeling their fans must experience after listening to such soul-elevating lyrics, not to mention that vintage rap beat in the background.

Without one iota of exaggeration, there are so many criminals in the hip hop landscape that I've had to leave many out of the discussion because I felt overwhelmed as I did the research. More and more names kept coming up in this fraternity of thugs. For instance, rapper **The Game**, who, among other misconducts, has dealt with assault, battery, and felony weapons charges, and another hip hop darling, **Max B**, now in prison for murder and robbery in 2009. The list is virtually endless.

As to rap music itself, I recognize that tastes in music vary enormously, and so I grudgingly, and greatly discouraged and disappointed, concede that some—okay many—people actually like hip hop's rap style. But it feels like admitting that Hitler had a good side. From this writer's perspective, rap is the lowest, crudest, most tasteless music style ever conceived (that is, to date; who know what's ahead?). It is essentially based on negativity, boastfulness, violence, coarseness, and ill-will. Except for the rhyming, it requires absolutely no musical skills, which is why it has been easily adopted by a slew of talentless imitators who simply cannot sing. In fact, I have tried to argue to some friends and family members that rap is not really music, although I suspect I'll never win that battle.

But *singing it is not*, as it is mostly composed of spoken rhymes accompanied by a background beat that is distinctly repetitive and varies little from tune to tune, to the point that it is often impossible to recognize the "song" until the rapper(s) begin to verbalize, assuming you can understand the lingo. I know I'm ranting, but, hey, this is my book.

A popular shtick of the rap act includes unnatural, exaggerated mannerisms exemplified by the iconic two raised fingers (or two fingers and a thumb) as the performer—knees bending rhythmically—gesticulates spastically, usually bending his torso forward as if to stick his contorted face and flailing hands into the camera, seemingly always in a bad mood. Occasionally, the rapper will bring a hand down to momentarily cover his crotch (or rather, call attention to it), which is supposed to have some significance (Endorsements for jock itch ointments should be one of their specialties.). Also typical is a short, rhythmic patting of the chest that imparts an air of bravado (boasting, really) and self-validation. The inflated facial expressions supposedly convey "attitude," cockiness and anger, a sort of statement declaring, "I'm so hot, so hip, so bad," the type of look that would get you an immediate blow to the face back in my school days. Rap enthusiasts call it "artistic expression." I know full well my dad would have kicked my ass if I ever gave him but a glance of such "artistic expression." We have a name for it in Spanish slang: "soquete." The rap routine is—at a minimum—an egocentric, boastful act. As an aside, I recently saw a few pictures of famous rappers, and none of them—*not one*—was smiling. This unhappy bunch aims to look bad, bad to the bone. Consequently, most look as if they have acid indigestion, judging from their knotted facial expressions.

Also found in the rap business is the practice of attacking other competing rappers (and other entertainers) via song lyrics. It becomes a pissing contest, oozing bravado and threatening each other. That is both childish and reprehensible. Such lack of class.

Adding to the affront on basic decency, the history of hip hop is glorified in the film industry. A recent release, *Straight Outta Compton,* is a good example. In a published review I forced myself to read, I learned that the movie is about an early rap group, **N.W.A.** (Niggaz Wit Attitudes), famous, in part, for their classic *(F-word) Tha Police*, which the article calls "*an anthem for a generation*" (Read that again and digest it—if you can). The review acknowledges that the group's rhymes were obscene, but justifies it saying that "so were the conditions that gave rise to the songs." So, I guess we should excuse them. The article also concedes that in the movie "the women serve solely at the pleasure of the men and are one-dimensional, brainless objects."[28] Another review relates that the film portrays women as "mostly either an annoyance or hedonistic party favors." [29] Based on the justification for the obscene lyrics in the first article, I would then conclude that the women in their lives were, well, worthless and deserving of the treatment depicted in the movie.

According to the second review, the group N.W.A. is credited with bringing gangsta rap to the mainstream, explaining that out of the five main characters portrayed in *Straight Outta Compton*, the three central characters are ***Dr. Dre, Ice Cube, and Easy-E***, guys who grew up in the tough neighborhoods of Compton, CA. It is noted that left out of the movie is "Dre's assault of TV personality Dee Barnes, whom he was convicted of repeatedly slamming against a brick wall."[30] Dr. Dre also got into a contract dispute with Easy-E from which the latter would not release him. So, Dre decided to have his buddy, music executive Suge Knight (not a particularly nice guy) get involved. Knight threatened Easy-E in various ways without success until Knight threatened to get at his mother, and that's when Easy-E put his X on the paperwork. Meanwhile, Easy-E is known to have supported himself by drug dealing after he dropped out of high school. Extremely promiscuous (and obviously unaware of contraception), he fathered seven children with six different women and died of AIDS (what a shame) at age thirty.[31] And yet, the man known as the most ruthless rapper, Ice Cube, does not have much of a criminal record, although in the 1990's he chose to associate with the radical, racist, Nation of Islam,[32] a really fun bunch.

There are many other movies that exalt the kind of life hip hopers claim for their personal backgrounds. For instance, *Hustle and Flow*, features a budget pimp who likes to rhyme about the reality of the streets. The main story line is that, supported by his harem of hookers, plus the appeal of doing time in jail, his street "poetry" becomes highly popular on the radio. The movie features the hit song "It's Hard out Here for a Pimp," by the ***Three 6 Mafia*** hip-hop group, which—I report in total disbelief—landed an Oscar for Best Original Song in 2006! Then we have *CB4*, featuring three aspiring MCs who just can't make it work in the hip hop arena. Aiming to imitate various successful rap groups, they fail to gain any traction "until they take on gangster-rap persona, *invent a criminal past and promise to outrage and offend.*" With the added touch of some Jheri curl wigs and gold teeth, success is theirs. A tremendous plot, isn't it?[33] This is the kind of story that threatens to eclipse *Casablanca* and *Gone with the Wind*. If only my grandparents were still alive to enjoy this.

Social scientists (and fans) justify the antagonistic hip hop genre by pointing to its roots in the tough streets of poor, mostly black, inner cities where gangs, domestic violence, and drug abuse are rampant, and opportunities for economic advancement are limited. The crude compositions, supposedly, are a means of fighting back against the mainstream of a society that simply doesn't care. Perhaps there is some truth in that viewpoint, and how the problem should be addressed has been long debated but with little progress to show. One thing is certain, though; the attitude and actions promoted in rap music are not the answer.

The sad reality is that the message conveyed by rap is a lie. It's bullshit. It offers nothing positive—nothing edifying.   It is intentionally destructive rather than constructive, totally devoid of redeeming value. It exalts everything that is sordid and heinous, and it serves to perpetuate that depressing hopelessness into which so many unfortunate young ones are born every day. Its message of arrogance, lash-out-against-society, in-your-face bravado creates an illusion of defiance and power, but one that creates many more losers than winners. Feeding that attitude of hate, lawlessness, egotism, and misogyny works to keep the vast majority in the very conditions that will hold them back in life—poor, uneducated, and way too often in prison—or dead.

Meanwhile, the rappers (those few who succeed, that is) count their money all the way to the bank. Oftentimes, these "elites" actually live the life of violence and depravity rap promotes—and thus usually end up committing crimes and in jail (although many escape prison thanks to a corrupt legal system that favors the wealthy and famous). A few others, especially the later ones, mostly pay lip service to the tough, bad boy from the hood image, making lots of money, living in mansions, driving ultra-expensive vehicles, mostly at the expense of those who can least afford it, and—according to some critics—acting too "white." Some of these wealthy hoodlums even have the gull to take government assistance for the poor, as in the case of *Ol' Dirty Bastard* who, after having a hit album (tenth in the nation) and making money rapping in various Mariah Carey remixes, cashed a welfare check in front of MTV cameras. Confronted, he had this to say in his defense: "...Why wouldn't you want to get free money?"[34] What a bastard, Bastard is!

To conclude, much of the music industry is dominated by hip hop, and it is disturbing to realize that it's more than music; it's a lifestyle, a culture of its own. Hence, in a sense, we have allowed a criminal element to hijack the attention of our young to sponsor crudeness, anarchy, narcissism, cruelty, violence, shamelessness, devaluation of human life, racism, and degradation of women— just about anything that is vile, abhorrent and depraved. And here is what I *don't* find in rap: kindness, forgiveness, love, modesty, good manners, integrity, compassion, restraint, decency, sympathy, reverence, or spirituality—not ONE of those positive qualities, nothing elevating, inspirational, or humanizing. In effect, there is absolutely nothing of value in this music genre, but there is plenty that is harmful and spiteful. The verdict is in: *rap music and its makers are bullshit*—of the worst kind.*

---

* For a couple more anecdotes revelatory of the slime that populates the world of hip hop, see Appendix D.

Punk Rock

Regardless of their vast differences musically, hip hop and punk rock share similar issues. Punk is, essentially, revolting. It is cheap, toxic, nihilistic, meant to shock, a vehicle for some of the most despicable elements of society to spew their venom. And while punk takes many forms—Anarcho Punk, Classic Punk, Hardcore Punk, Pop Punk, Proto Punk, Post Punk, even Horror Punk—at its core, it's all the same bullshit.

Punk rock, which began in the 1970s, is ostensibly a rejection of mainstream music and stridently anti-establishment, but the genre itself is trash, and the lyrics are just obscenity-shouting disguised as protesting. J. Holmstrom, editor of Punk Magazine explains: "Punk rock was rock and roll by people *who didn't have very much skills as musicians* but still felt the need to express themselves...." [35] So, express themselves they did (and still do), not simply through the acknowledged poor quality of the music and the ridiculous fashion that identifies them, but, as in rap, by seeking attention via the most shocking language possible. The punk vibe also relies on a dress code, which ranges from the satanic to the plain stupid. Here is the excuse: "Punks use clothing as a way of making a statement." Really? What exactly are they stating? Is it, Look what an idiot I am? And, Look at my extreme body piercings, so I'm even more of an idiot?

Scores of fans assert that the most famous punk rock band of all time was the *Sex Pistols*. More diverse in their subject matter than rap artists, they sang—or rather, made loud noises—about violence, anarchy, the music industry, fascism, consumerism, the holocaust, abortion, apathy, and the British Royal Family, all normally delivered via obscene lyrics. Their concerts and other public appearances were often scenes of violence, frequently ending in total mayhem, a true reflection of their drug-fueled excesses and anarchist streak. Other Punk groups that followed imitated their recklessness. All the same, "music connoisseurs" rushed to reward the Sex Pistols' destructiveness and vile, degrading work, inducting them into the Rock and Roll Hall of Fame in 2006. But oh, the Pistols so graciously refused to attend the ceremony, calling the museum "a piss stain."[36] Serves them right, those boot-licking "music experts."

A band often mentioned in the same breath as the Sex Pistols is the *Ramones*, a 1970s bunch of linguistic anarchists from New York. They are credited with truly defining the punk rock sound (whatever that is). By 1996, when they broke up, The Ramones had played in well over two thousand concerts! But, not surprisingly, given their unrestrained lifestyles, all four of the band's original members were dead by 2014. As the Pistols, the Ramones are venerated among *the greatest rock bands of all time*. Honors include a listing in Rolling Stone's "100 Greatest Artists of All Time," and in VH1's "100 Greatest Artists of Hard Rock," and in 2002—and this is heresy—Spin magazine ranked them as the *second-greatest band of all time*, behind only the Beatles! That year saw them inducted into the Rock and Roll Hall of Fame, taking their place alongside the Sex Pistols.[37] For a bigger load of bullshit, you must go to a cattle ranch.

No doubt some of today's punkers, such as *The Royal Headaches, Against Me!, and Teenage Time Killers* will one day be honored. How could they not, with classics such as the opening "song" in Against Me!'s album "23 Live Sex Acts," titled "F...MYLIFE666." Another is "Osama Bin Laden as Crucified Christ." But there's more in the world of entertainment! So let's consider some of today's celebrity-parasites and other characters from this bizarre world of unrestrained amusement we've created.

Kim Kardashian and Other Perplexingly Popular Personalities

Great minds discuss ideas; average minds discuss events; and small minds discuss people.

— Eleanor Roosevelt

There are public figures who are undeservedly famous. They are what I call "celebrity-parasites," because they have no particularly exceptional artistic talent (some are referred to as "personalities" and "socialites") but are good at exploiting our thirst for bullshit. They are "famous for being famous," with two of the most glaring examples being Kim Kardashian and Paris Hilton. Kardashian, of reality TV fame, the voluptuous wife of the harebrained Kanye West, is the quintessential example of these limelight vermin. Unarguably sensual and married to an unfathomably famous celebrity, she has an enormous following and has been nominated or received many awards, including "Choice Female Reality/Variety Star" and "Choice Tweet" by Teen Choice Awards, and in 2012 won the People's Choice Award's Favorite TV Celeb Reality Star. According to Kanye, Kim represents powerful women, and that's why she even inspires Beyoncé!

Continuing, Kardashian listed as #33 (#30 of non-athletes) of highest paid celebrities ($54.5 million) on Forbes 2015, having made more money than *ever* before. She is also the #11 celebrity most followed, with 33 million Twitter and 37 million Instagram followers.[38] A large chunk of her earnings came from her iPhone and tablet game named after her, a game in which players create their own celebrities. This self-absorbed prima donna also wrote a book; it's *comprised entirely of selfies* (of herself, who else), quite appropriately titled, "Selfish."[39] (Kim would fit in beautifully in my home city of Miami, a vanity-soaked town that ranked #3 *in the world* in selfie-taking, based on a study of Instagram pictures by Time Magazine).[40] In March 2016, Kardashian scraped the bottom of the sleaze and vanity barrel by posting nude selfies of herself, prompting singer and actress Bette Midler to comment that Kim "would have to 'swallow a camera' to show off any more of herself." All considered, life's been good for socialite Paris Hilton's ex-assistant and hairdresser.

And speaking of Paris, it's no secret that much of this Beverly Hills phenomenon's fame comes from her lurid, flamboyant lifestyle, her infamous 2003 sex tape (and the Hilton name, of course). This was enough for her adoring fans to flock to the bookstores In 2004 to make her book "Confessions of an Heiress" a New York Times Best Seller.[41] While I have not had the pleasure of reading her magnum opus, I'm sure it must be a stylistic tour de force, a spellbinding display of Paris' writing prowess. Yes, this is the same reality TV Paris, and the one who, having been detained several times for driving with a suspended license and on probation for drunk driving, showed up late to court and told the judge she could not be bothered to look at her emails because she was too busy and had other people do that for her (good thing the judge gave her 45 days jail time). What a role model!

Question: What does this say about a society obsessed with such individuals, the millions who cling to every celebrity tweet, every Facebook and Instagram posting? Are our personal lives so boring, so empty and devoid of meaning? While you ponder that, let's continue with the bizarre by casually flinging a dart at the celebrity dartboard. Pop! Kanye West. Not too impressive a hit, for he occupies over half the board.

Kanye West

But my greatest pain in life is that I will never be able to see myself perform.

—Kanye (yes, him)

Everyone knows Kanye for his unbridled narcissism and staggering declarations, such as, "I ain't concerned about anyone who's living. I ain't going after no one on the radio. I'm going after Walt Disney, Howard Hughes, Shakespeare." Interestingly, in February 2016 Yeezy admitted to a $53 million debt, but that did not deter him from asking billionaires, such as Mark Zuckerberg, to invest a billion in his ideas because he "is the greatest living artist and greatest artist of all time." [42] And, of course, who can forget the infamous: "If I don't win, the award show loses credibility," and when he lost the award for Best New Artist in 2004, he graciously declared: "I felt like I was definitely robbed, and I refuse to give any politically correct bullshit ass comment. I was the best new artist this year." What an eye and ear for talent, Mr. West!

Kanye is also credited with some head-scratchers: "*I don't even listen to rap music. My apartment is too nice to listen to rap in,*" an interesting comment about the music that's fattened his bank account. [43] And more cash is coming his way from a bizarre June 2016 video in which he appears in bed with naked or semi-naked doppelgangers of Taylor Swift, Donald Trump, Bill Cosby, G.W. Bush, and others. Sick, sick stuff.

This paragon of vanity has actually compared himself to Jesus Christ and is even considering a 2020 run for president: "God chose me. He made a path for me. I am God's vessel." (Well, Jesus did say something like that) Given the epidemic adulation of celebrities in our country, I would not bet against West winning the presidency (consider Trump's popularity). After all, he's got the solutions: "...I got the answers. I understand culture. I am the nucleus." Kanye's grossly inflated ego and accompanying fame is symptomatic of our distorted priorities. I can't see it any other way.

This is how shameful it gets. Journalist Micah Singleton, former senior writer at *The Daily Dot*, former founder and editor-in-chief of *CE,* whose articles have made it to highly regarded news sources and who's been called a "rising star" in the "future of journalism" by *The Huffington Post*, had this to say when asked if he thought West was really going to run for president: "...It would be the greatest thing ever to happen in politics." [44] He's added: "Kanye is...one of the most influential people young people have today. He told a paparazzo he had nice shoes, and then they sold out....Kanye's influence is undeniable..." So, don't be surprised if Yeezy takes a shot at the presidency.

I wonder who'll be Kanye's running mate in 2020. I suggest Miley Cyrus or Justin Bieber. What a ticket! Scary that such a pairing would have a real shot at the White House. Don't doubt it dear reader; our star struck, trash-loving nation could easily vote them in—by a landslide! And envision this: Kim Kardashian as first lady! The circus would be complete. Would there be enough time in the media to keep up with them? Would 24/7 be sufficient? Would the nation's economy and security even matter?

Do we need to say any more about Kanye? No. Let's leave him in his alternate reality and blindly toss another dart at our celebrity board. And...Lo! Howard Stern! Now, here is an interesting specimen, one who doesn't sing, dance, or act, and does not fit the mold of socialites. I can't wait to see what the envelope reveals. Come along.

Howard Stern

I don't think there is one thing I've ever said on the radio that would have been found indecent or obscene.

—Howard Stern

Late night television is ready for someone like me...standards have gone to an all-time low.

—Howard Stern

It is easy to be original by violating the laws of decency and the canons of good taste.

—Oliver Wendell Holmes, Supreme Court Justice, 1891

We live in an indecorous time. We are not easily taken aback by crude language and uncultured behavior, but there are still some characters who manage to drag us even lower. Among these is one of the most disgusting personalities to infest the entertainment industry, the ultra-popular radio and television personality, Howard Stern. A true phenomenon of our dim-witted, morally bankrupt society, this nauseating, hard-to-look-at, perfect specimen of unmitigated vulgarity is high on the list of celebrity money makers. Just as Bieber, Cyrus, Kanye, and many in the rap gang, this shock jock has amassed awards almost too numerous to list, including Billboard's Nationally Syndicated Air Personality of the Year *eight times.*

Self-described as "King of All Media," a title he filed a trademark for, the highly intelligent Stern (graduated magna cum laude from college) has found success, not just in radio but in television and as an author, by taking full advantage of the current moral climate and a largely vacuous, frivolous audience. His two books, *Private Parts* (1993) and *Miss America* (1995) went straight to number one in the best seller list of the New York Times as soon as published, with each selling in excess of a million copies (and who knew his audience can read!). Shakespeare would run a distant second to Stern if the famed English playwright were alive today. Due to his enormous following—and not because of any special ability or credentials to evaluate talent—Stern became a judge in the popular television program *America's Got Talent* in 2012.[45] It was, essentially, a stab at ratings by the network.

Howard Stern also boasts of being the most fined radio show host of all time, with station licenses having been slammed with approximately $2.5 million by the FCC for indecent content (please refer to Stern quotations above). Another side of him that probably has helped endear him to bottom-feeding American audiences is his admitted experiences with drugs, which, aside from the relatively harmless cannabis, included Quaaludes and LSD, a habit he claims to have quit after overdosing on the latter.[46] Nevertheless, a drug abuse history remains part of his résumé, which is a plus in our times.

As most readers probably know, much of Stern's fame comes from being an outrageous radio jock who aims to be vulgar and challenge obscenity guidelines in the industry. For example, in his early career, Stern began working at WNBC in 1982.

Having been warned about discussing certain topics, including religion, he was nevertheless disciplined (suspended for a few days) in his first month, for producing a sketch, "Virgin Mary Kong" "about a video game where a group of men pursue the Virgin Mary around a singles bar in Jerusalem. Notwithstanding management's tight leash on Stern, he managed to get away with enough of his antics to achieve great popularity, and in 1984 got a big break when he was invited to David Letterman's late night show. This boosted his status even more, and in 1985 Stern achieved the highest rating in four years for WNBC. However, he soon was fired. Although not told specifically why, it is believed it came as the result of the station's chairman having heard Stern's "Bestiality Dial-a-Date" segment only a few days prior to his firing (the segment's title says it all).[47]

Nevertheless, it wasn't long before good old Howard signed a juicy five-year contract to host shows for station WXRK (in the New York market). His show soon became nationally syndicated and ran for about twenty years, reaching a peak audience of 20 million fans, and, as the saying goes, the rest is history. During those years, he was red hot, producing extremely successful videos (e.g. *Butt Bongo Fiesta*) and hosting the highly popular "The Howard Stern Show," essentially a mindless hour of course, sexually-loaded material aimed to shock (although he appealed mainly to an already desensitized audience) and test the boundaries of obscenity laws. Sticking to his formula of crudeness, Stern produced many other lowbrow pieces of entertainment, including *The Miss Howard Stern New Year's Eve Pageant* on December 31, 1993, a pretend beauty contest that grossed $16 million on pay-per-view television—a record. The show marked a low point in televised content, with the *New York Post* calling it "the most disgusting two hours in the history of television." [48]

However, the American public's worship of this sordid, repugnant individual did not stop there. People actually followed Stern's advice in politics when he strived to influence the race for governor of New Jersey in 1993, helping Christine T. Whitman win the election (in repayment for his endorsement, Whitman shamelessly named a rest stop on I-295 after him!). But that was small stuff for Stern, as in 1994 he announced that he was running for governor of New York as a Libertarian. At the nomination convention, Stern swept 287 of 381 votes on the first ballot. He was well on his way to challenging Mario Cuomo's reelection when he decided to withdraw from the race because he refused to file a required financial disclosure form. But that did not stop him from knocking out Cuomo. Stern threw his support behind George Pataki who went on to defeat Cuomo in the November 1994 election. This is stupefying political clout wielded by one of the most nauseating creatures to ever inhabit the airwaves.[49]

In spite of his intelligence, Stern could do some pretty stupid things. In 1995, only days after the famous Mexican singer, Selena, was shot dead, Howard angered the Hispanic community with comments regarding her death while in his show he played Tejano music that featured gunfire sounds over her songs, In his words: "This music does absolutely nothing for me. Alvin and the Chipmunks have more soul...Spanish people have the worst taste in music. They have no depth." Only three days later, faced with strong media reaction and threats of boycotts, he issued a statement (written in Spanish!) explaining that he was just being satirical in his statements and really did not mean to offend Selena's fans.[50] Total bullshit. It was like trying to clean the mess by throwing more shit on it.

Stern continued to be Stern in 1995, that is, he offended and angered more people, his modus operandi. Given a chance to appear in Jay Leno's *The Tonight Show* in late November, he showed up "accompanied by two bikini-clad women who kissed each other and received spanks from Stern." Clearly displeased with the antics, Leno requested that the acts be cut out of the taping before the final broadcast. Then, at the conclusion of the show, clearly upset, he walked off the stage without acknowledging Stern.[51] I could not be more pleased with Leno. He displayed the gumption so lacking today to stand up to the likes of Stern, the bottom-feeders who get their jollies (and their wealth with the support of a culture breastfed on crudeness and vulgarity) from thrashing traditional values in the filth of their own ethics-deprived sewers.

In 1996, the morally crippled Stern worked hard to produce and promote more trash to sustain his attack on family values and common decency. This time it was a comedy film based on his book, *Private Parts*. When it was released in March 1997, legions of his adoring, lobotomized zombies made it number one at the US box office, grossing $14.6 million in the first weekend alone. Later, In 1998, Stern received a slew of recognition awards, which included a nomination for a Golden Satellite Award for "Best Performance by an Actor in a Motion Picture (Comedy)," although he also received a Golden Raspberry Award for "Worst New Star." Meanwhile, Stern was laughing all the way to the bank, as the film's soundtrack was a tremendous success, selling 178,000 copies in just the first week and jumping in right at No. 1 in the *Billboard* 200 chart. Moreover, the album achieved certified Platinum status, another devastating blow to decorum in the nation.[52]

But Stern was just warming up! He managed to finally avoid FCC regulations by signing a contract to broadcast his show via Sirius Satellite Radio starting in 2006. Exceeding subscriber targets for Sirius brought Stern many, many millions of dollars. And, not coming as a shock to anyone, that year his recognition continued, with Time Magazine including him in its Time 100 list and Forbes' placing him seventh in its Celebrity 100 list. Later, in 2012, Stern was inducted into the National Radio Hall of Fame and, as already noted, became a judge for *America's Got Talent*, staying with the show until September 2015.

From 2013 to 2015, Stern was in first place on Forbes' list of highest-paid television personalities. Tied with Simon Cowell for the honors in 2013-14, he stood alone at the top in 2015 (fifth worldwide), at earnings of $95 million. Imagine—ninety-five million in one year for being a sleazy asshole! In the words of Russian comedian Yakov Smirnoff: "What a country!"

Howard Stern's monumental success is—at least to some of us—utterly perplexing. It is an amazing performance for a man whose career has been essentially about feeding the thirst for obscenity of a disappointedly large segment of the public, promoting depravity, and undermining traditional values and standards of decency. He is an insidious bullshit machine of the worst kind. And if his career says a lot of unpleasant things about him as an individual, perhaps it says even more about us as a society. His enormous success is an indictment of the base culture we have created. Just discussing this repulsive character makes me nauseous, so let's talk about something else.

Bullshit in the Sports Business

Take the overweening ambition of some athletes, mix it with the all-American obsession with sports and money, and it's no wonder we're producing a country of self-entitled "monsters" who think they're above the law.

— Dr. Norman Wyloge, New York psychoanalyst

No treatise about the entertainment industry could be complete without touching on the business of sports in the United States. It's no secret that athletes, in football, baseball, basketball, hockey, soccer, boxing, and other sports, make phenomenal salaries, and the advertising dollars that go into it are staggering. When it comes to advertising costs, football is essentially out of control; it cost companies $10 million per minute to advertise their products during Super Bowl 50 in 2016. That is outrageous— also big business. And how can the networks get away with charging so much? Because football is no longer a sport; *it is a religion.*

On Sundays, real churches cannot compete with the fervor induced by a football game as people gather around their modern-day altars, complete with high definition televisions and comfy recliners, to worship their God-athletes." Who cares about the soul's fate when pizza, beer, hotdogs, and a bowl of potato chips await in front of the big screen? I've prayed at that altar many fall and winter Sundays myself, but the football gods rarely hear my pleas as my beloved Miami Dolphins perennially have trouble finding the end zone while their opponents seem to have GPS guidance to the goal line.

As to the extreme salaries of athletes, the obvious question is, Are they worth it? Well, from the standpoint of the average Joe, no, they are not. But somehow the leagues and especially the team owners must think they are. Why else would they be willing to cough up the millions? Think about this: In 2012, quarterback legend Peyton Manning signed a five year contract worth $96 million (about $19 million per year).[53] And yet, this pales in comparison to Pittsburgh Steelers' quarterback Ben Roethlisberger's $46 million in 2016, which pales in comparison to boxing champion Floyd Mayweather's $285 million the same year.[54] And by the way, these figures do not include revenue from their endorsements.

Those numbers are for athletes at the top of their profession, of course, but the rest of the players are not doing too bad. Let's look at averages. The *average* salary of a football player is over $2 million; it is $5 million for a basketball player; $4 million for a baseball player; and $2.7 million for a hockey player.[55] Compare that to the average salary of the American worker of approximately $50,000 in 2015 (with no chance for endorsements, of course),[56] and to the $400,000 salary of the president of the United States. It bears asking again: at least from the perspective of the sports fans, are those guys worth it? After all, their salaries are a large part of the reason why it is a financial sacrifice for a family of four to attend an NFL game today, where the average admission is $80.00 (over $100 in several cities), and where a hot dog costs $6.00 and beer sets you back $8.00 or more. And don't forget about parking fees!

Just for grins, Do you know how much a seat cost for the first Super Bowl? Six dollars. That was 1967, and the game did not even sell out! How much was the average ticket cost for Super Bowl 50? About $5,000. But what's a little inflation, right?

Much more troubling, it's no secret that scandal plagues many sports. From the illegal use of performance-enhancing drugs to wife beating, even murder, athletes keep making headlines: Minnesota Vikings star running back Adrian Peterson, child abuse; New England tight end Aaron Hernandez, first-degree murder; Baltimore Ravens receiver, Ray Rice, one-punch knockout of wife in an elevator; heavyweight champion Mike Tyson, rape; Los Angeles Clippers guard Lance Stephenson, sexually abused a student when in college and later, as a pro, was charged with felony assault after pushing the mother of his child down a flight of stairs; superstar New York Yankees slugger Alex Rodriguez, illegal steroid use (and lied and lied denying it); Colorado Avalanche's hockey goaltender Semyon Varlamov, savage beating of girlfriend. The list goes on and on and on. In fact, since the February 2016 super bowl, at least twelve football players (that's just NFL players) have been arrested, with charges ranging from drunk driving and illegal drug possession to first-degree battery. [57]

This shameful issue extends to the college ranks, where athletes frequently get away with crimes, oftentimes sexual assault of co-eds, with victims finding it difficult to bring charges against their tormentors due to athletes' exalted status on campus, particularly star players. A relatively recent case, that of 2013 Heisman Trophy winner quarterback Jameis Winston of FSU (now a professional quarterback for the Tampa Bay Buccaneers), is a good example. When rape allegations were raised against him, the accuser had a tough time getting through the school's smoke screen typically employed to protect its prized athletes (and the institution's reputation). Aside from the rape charge, she alleged that FSU "in concert with Tallahassee Police, took steps to ensure that Winston's [alleged] rape...would not be investigated either by the university or law enforcement. She further accused the school of failing to respond when she became a target of hostility." The victim's family also reported that "a detective warned her attorney that Tallahassee is a "big football town" and that life could be miserable if she pursued the case."[58] In fact, the victim became persona non grata on campus (remember, we love our athletes) as Winston's precarious status threatened FSU's football season (we can't have a mere rape get in the way now, can we?), and she ended up transferring to another school. Eventually, the university, citing potentially prohibitive legal fees and the need to "look ahead toward its very bright future," opted to pay a $950,000 settlement rather than let the case go to trial. And so, instead of sitting in a jail, Jameis Winston today counts his millions and basks in the adulation of NFL fans.

FSU and the Tallahassee police are notorious for covering up athlete delinquency, but the problem is common in universities across the country, as it seems that these kinds of incidents are perennially in the news. The likelihood of athlete misconduct—in college and the professional level—is augmented by a culture that prefers to look the other way when the accusations arise, sometimes further victimizing the victims by calling their integrity into question. No doubt, there have been, and will always be, frivolous lawsuits by unscrupulous opportunists trying to cash in at the expense of wealthy sports figures, but it is undeniable that athlete abuse of their deified social standing to behave like bullies and act as if laws don't apply to them, is a major problem today.

Particularly disgusting is that at least some of these criminals and cheaters get away with their foul actions or win reduced penalties thanks to the high-power lawyers they can readily afford. Unfortunately, along with the conceited, criminal element of the music industry and other equally nauseating celebrities, these sports icons represent another segment of today's "role models," the very people children want to—and are often encouraged to—emulate. What's wrong with this picture? This is a tall mound of bullshit, and the smell is unbearable.

Final Thoughts About the World of Entertainment

Having lived through the entire history of television and modern music (modern music I am defining as beginning with rock and roll in the 1950s), I've witnessed the social events to which the products of those channels of popular culture served as a backdrop (or is it the other way around?). Over the years I've seen a lot of bullshit reach our eyes and ears through the airwaves, and with the benefit of hindsight has come the realization that what some would call social liberalization and progress has been, in no small part, an erosion of traditional values. I am not talking about the changes that advanced human rights and ideals—the civil rights movement, women's liberation, the struggle for peace emphasizing love over war, the rejection of all forms of discrimination—all worthwhile and edifying, real contributions to improvement of the human condition. I'm talking about the insidious onslaught on former standards of decency and propriety—the loss of class, decorum, and elegance. I have seen the gradual transformation over the years: innocence supplanted by lasciviousness, discretion displaced by lewdness, modesty replaced by boastfulness, virtuousness crushed by debauchery, the wholesome pushed out by the depraved, the aesthetic lost in a sea of the grotesque, and intellectuality exchanged for triviality. And the entertainment industry—with some exceptions, I concede—has led the way.

A culture requires a defined set of values and principles, but unfortunately, it is the menagerie of characters, many of them hooligans, who now create socially-shared patterns of thought as they define pop culture and bring us the latest in music, television, fashion, and behavior, in the process defining what is socially acceptable for the undiscerning masses. Consequently, the trivial, the dumbed-down, the shallow, the profane, the vulgar now rule. My take—and this is arguable—is that we are not experiencing cultural evolution but *de*volution. Of course, it depends on how we define this concept of evolution and progress, and it hinges considerably on our individual standards and aspirations.

From a purely personal standpoint, cultural ascendency requires a striving for improvement, for refinement, for the elevation of that which distances us from animals and savages, from a lower to a higher degree of sophistication. Thus, for real cultural evolution to take place, the direction must be from the coarse to the aesthetic, from selfishness to unselfishness, from mob mentality to discretion and thoughtfulness, from cruelty to compassion, from anarchy to order, from the insensitive to the insightful, from the crass to the refined and graceful, and from the arrogant to the humble and discreet. With exceptions of course, I don't see those trends reflected in our entertainment diet or entertainers' lifestyles. What I see is the opposite, a reversal of the qualities that enrich a civilization.

Consider today's nearly obligatory abuse of language. The use of profanity is at an all-time high. I'm not talking about the occasional expletive uttered in the company of friends, in the locker room, on the football field, or when we accidentally miss the nail and smash our fingers with a hammer. Even Mark Twain recognized that profanity can sometimes offer a degree of relief denied even to prayer. Instead, I'm referring to the pollution escaping people's mouths in everyday communication and in settings where they should know better, even directed at people they have just met for the first time. And yes, I'm including public figures and celebrities. The issue is a common debate item, and in defense of such undignified language, much ballyhooing is made about the first amendment, which extends its blanket of protection to such vernacular (although I'm sure our forefathers had more lofty considerations in mind). Consequently, many individuals take the stance that because I can, I will use vulgar language, and I will do so often and in your face. The underlying reasons vary.

It could be simply that, in an obscenity-friendly society, in certain circles, a person does not want to be perceived as a prude; it's just that all-too-common need to fit in and not be viewed as an outsider. Or, as with some television personalities, the objective is to appear liberal and uninhibited, or possibly simply to make other, "less enlightened individuals" uncomfortable. Why? Because they can; the constitution and current pop culture norms have their back. Finally, it could be symptomatic of the environment in which these individuals grew up. That is, they don't know better, sorely lacking the vocabulary to express themselves and/or lacking parental guidance in their formative and teenage years. However, there is a growing problem with this unabashed use of foul language. Kathleen Parker of the Washington Post made this observation after being subjected to a "verbal fusillade" by a woman berating her son in an elevator:

> "...her actions were neither singular nor disconnected from a broader range of cultural pathologies. Lack of civility in words bleeds into a lack of decency in behavior....Good behavior is nothing but good manners, simply consideration for others. Recently out of vogue, manners get hauled out the way most people attend church—at Easter and Christmastime. But manners aren't just gray-haired pretension practiced by smug elites on special occasions. They are the daily tithes we willingly surrender to civilization. An "MF" here or an "FU" there might not constitute the unraveling of society, but each one uttered in another's involuntary presence is a tiny act of violence against kindness, of which we surely could use more." [59]

Thus, fully supporting the first amendment and people's right to ooze slimy words from their mouths, I assert that courteous, considerate people who are self-assured and unimpeded by fashionable social trends avoid crude language and possess awareness of when occasional swearing is okay and even effective. Paradoxically, in spite of the current fad to decorate our everyday conversations with vulgarity, the true champions of courtesy generally will be perceived to have more class (not to be confused with money), than their more semantically emancipated counterparts, but now, lamentably, they are a rare breed. In few words, *language reflects changes in culture*, and the lexicon now in popular use speaks for itself. Let's go a little deeper into our present social condition.

Heavily influenced by mass media, ours is a hypocritical society. For instance, we over sexualize nearly everything in the airwaves, pushing the boundaries of propriety, but, ironically, we have decided to censure pornography, which, depending on how you define it, is arguably just a small step or two away from what we increasingly see broadcasted today. We laugh with, and even crave, the use of profanity in all forms of entertainment but tell our young children they can't use such language at home because it is disrespectful. We exhort pre-pubescent children, especially young girls, to become adults before their time, dressing them provocatively well beyond their years, teaching them sensual looks, postures and language, and then we sanctimoniously throw in jail anyone eighteen or over who has *consensual* sexual relations with someone under that age, and we look down in disgust at the sick minds who relish child pornography (a perverted mindset we have indirectly encouraged), which we have decided to criminalize because—at least at this moment, and only at this moment of our moral descent—it exceeds our collective tolerance (but our views on this too will be eventually relaxed).*

Societal hypocrisy is also manifested when we undervalue marriage and family, treating them as quaint rites of past generations, while exalting infidelity and the casual one-night stand, making unfaithfulness fun, erotic, and adventurous, throwing caution to the wind. But we don't like irresponsibility—nooo sir—and we condemn cheaters! Yes, cheating is *baaaad.* Thus, we expect loyalty from spouses, significant others, friends, customers, and employees. And here is a word for those who condemned Donald Trump's vulgar language during his campaign: Stop the hypocrisy and stop listening to that crude rap music and enriching those hooligans. These double standards are bullshit—double bullshit!

Furthermore, fueled by new social guidelines endorsed by pop psychologists and ethically-challenged entertainers, we fan the flames of permissiveness and moral relativism, blurring the line between right and wrong. So, we can't stop our fourth graders from engaging in sex after school? No problem, give them sex education and teach them how to use a condom. Oops, girl got pregnant anyway? Don't sweat it; have an abortion! We don't want little Susie to compromise her promising future just because of a fetus, do we? Can't deal with the social pressure to be an adult before your time? Relax, we've got your back. Make an appointment with a child psychologist or psychiatrist, our modern-day priests. There are therapy sessions and legal drugs to help. But whatever you do, never swim against the pop culture tide; keep your focus on sexy, and keep looking to your entertainers for how to conduct yourself. They have your best interests in mind (and your money). There is more.

We glorify violence and wonder why our society is so aggressive and cruel. We expose our children's developing minds to extreme violence in television, movies and savage video games, completely desensitizing some and reducing the meaning of empathy, and then we ask why middle class Johnny in the fifth grade stabbed his friend after school or why Billy heartlessly tortured puppies and drowned kittens in the neighbor's swimming pool. But, hey, Johnny's and Billy's hand-eye coordination are off the charts! So it's not all bad. And, of course, someone is making money—big money.

---

* It would not surprise me to see child pornography becoming increasingly tolerated within a decade or two, maybe sooner, once the entertainment industry decides the public is ready for the next step down into its moral muck. I expect that it will be introduced via humor, likely in a prosaic sitcom similar to those aired today, possibly one starring Howard Stern or some other degenerate celebrity, or maybe in a cartoonish show such as Family Guy or the Simpsons.

In effect, through the irresistible allure and power of the entertainment industry our values and the innocence of our young have been seized by a depraved coalition of shameless criminals, frauds, and morally-stunted performers (the latter sometimes victims of the system themselves). These agents are surreptitiously enabled by an ethically-bankrupt but powerful industry elite that cashes in on the voracious appetite for amusement (that Huxley feared) of directionless, powerless, entertainment-addicted individuals—the industry-programmed automatons who dutifully sit in front of their televisions or turn on their stereos and plug in their headphones to consume their daily ration of bullshit. The elites are the active, culture-shaping producers and the masses are the passive, undiscerning consumers.

As the assault on "old-fashioned" principles is stepped up year after year, each subsequent wave of productions (movies, TV shows, videos, music lyrics) pushes the boundaries. Such material we have agreed to call "edgy," a cute euphemism that lends it acceptance, or even view it as "avant-garde" to embellish it with a sense of sophistication. Euphemistic language, by the way, is a nifty tool that timid music and film critics use to tell viewers/listeners what a crappy product they're being sold without incurring the wrath of the ultra-liberals and crap aficionados. For example, when writing a movie critique these garbage connoisseurs use highly-restrained phrases such as "It explores the boundaries of good taste," and "It challenges our conceptions of what constitutes 'proper' entertainment" to communicate what they consider crude and offensive, below sensible standards. They thus avoid been labeled as prudish or passé; they don't have the courage to really call it as they see it for fear of antagonizing the hordes of indiscriminating entertainment guzzlers that make up a large segment of their readership. It's weak, cowardly, bullshit commentary.

As the next "line" is crossed, and then the next, few stop to ask, Where does it end? To this disenchanted fogy, the answer is until every social taboo has been broken; until the innocence has been completely eradicated from our young; until adults have lost all sense of propriety; until the words ethical and moral have lost their meaning and could be effectively removed from all dictionaries; in effect, until "la chusma" ** prevails.

In essence, the fabric that makes a society strong, principled, vibrant, cerebral, is tearing, and this is reflected all across society, from corrupt. incompetent politicians and unprecedented corporate greed to the degenerate entertainment icons and morally-compromised families of today. The ethically feeble, amusement-at-all-costs generation, now aided by rapidly expanding technologies that outpace people's ability to properly integrate them into their lives, has chosen to endorse the kind of entertainment and behavior toward which "la chusma" has characteristically gravitated. It has chosen to empower and worship—even immortalize—the sordid celebrities that bring us down to their level. One of the great thinkers of our generation, Nobel Prize laureate Mario Vargas Llosa stated that our "culture of entertainment" has trivialized literature, journalism, politics, and sex. In a 2012 interview, Vargas Llosa told *Miami Herald* columnist, Andres Oppenheimer, that

---

** La chusma" is a Spanish language term referring to the mass of individuals who have no conception of—or don't care about—good manners or decorum, easily stirred into mob mentality, low in sophistication, and attracted to uncultured entertainment and activities.

"...nowadays, 'light literature' designed to amuse audiences is killing literature as an art form. In today's 140-character Twitter world, there could not be a new Leo Tolstoy, James Joyce, or Luis Borges, among other things because the Internet is shortening people's attention span, and making it increasingly difficult for many to read books." In Vargas Llosa's own words, "It is creating an audience that no longer tolerates a big intellectual effort, an audience that finds itself fatigued, bored, distracted by books." [60]

As to sex, he finds that it has become a banal activity, a sport. It's "losing its mystery." He states that we are trivializing it, and warns that "unless it maintains a certain dose of mystery and of privacy, it can take us back to animal sex and to the disappearance of eroticism, which is the civilized and humanizing form of sex." [61] So, as Vargas Llosa sees it, sex is now just for recreation, with little emotional involvement or moral consequences, and today that notion is being encouraged—check that—forced-fed down young throats (and old, too) via the entertainment conduit.

I am not so naive as to believe there is a realistic possibility to turn things around as a society and regain any level of civility and moral footing, although, as quixotic as it may sound, I believe that we should aim to do just that. As suggested earlier, it is imperative that we ask the obvious question: Where does it all end? Can a propriety line be permanently drawn? It doesn't seem likely. There will always be that urge to push it further out, with the main driving force, the entertainment industry, spearheading the thrust, relentlessly redefining and relaxing generally-accepted standards of decency and behavior. And so, eventually, there will be few, if any, boundaries, and the logical end is moral anarchy—a complete breakdown of principles where anything and everything goes. This notion is captured by the deceptively simple Chinese proverb: *"Unless we change direction, we are likely to end up where we are headed."* I hope to be buried by then.

This section has been long and opinionated enough, and yet it has not even included an examination of the underlying reasons why western culture is experiencing such a nihilistic trend. Consequently, for interested readers, I have relegated such analysis to Appendix E (although admittedly way too brief for such a heavy topic). Also, be warned: the contents are highly subjective, and it gets philosophical. Furthermore, save for having lived almost seven decades and given it a fair amount of thought, I claim no expertise on the subject.

But please don't put the book down yet (or throw it away) because the next topic is about bullshit in science, something I would hate for you to miss.

CHAPTER 5

Bullshit in Science

There is something fascinating about science. One gets such wholesale returns of conjecture out of such a trifling investment of fact.

—Mark Twain

A new scientific theory does not triumph by convincing its opponents and making them see the light, but rather because its opponents eventually die...

—Max Planck

A lie told often enough becomes the truth.

—Lenin

The year was 1973, and a previously unknown comet had made its appearance in our solar system. It was named Kohoutek. Astronomers predicted that, once in Earth's neighborhood, Kohoutek would produce a spectacular display in the skies. It was called "the comet of the century," and it was preparing to outshine the famous Haley's comet and other previous visitors to our part of the solar system. In fact, it was predicted to shine so bright that it would be an obvious object in the sky in full daylight! Entrepreneurs jumped at the opportunity, printing T-shirts by the thousands (millions?) that read "I saw Kohoutek," or "I survived Kohoutek," and such. The news media kept the public at high levels of expectation, with regular updates on the coming phenomenon. Sales of telescopes and binoculars soared. Millions around the world, including me, just couldn't wait. Finally, in December '73, Kohoutek arrived, and—well—it was a dud.

The eagerly anticipated and much ballyhooed spectacular "sky show of the century" never materialized. It was a huge disappointment. People were incensed, and the criticism and ridicule of the "experts" were loud. My family and I tried our very best to catch a glimpse of the sky wanderer, but, alas, we never saw it. After Kohoutek's failure to dazzle as foretold, the vastly toned-down claim in the media was that it could be seen at night with a little effort, but I never spoke to anyone who actually saw it. Official excuses for the prediction's failure were eventually issued, but no one was buying. It was pie in the face for scientists, the experts—a severe blow to the credibility of astronomers. In effect, it was simply one more piece of bullshit tossed at the general public by so-called knowledgeable authorities.

A strongly held paradigm of our times is that science is infallible, or nearly so. Once hypotheses become theories, and particularly when the latter are moved to the category of facts and laws, it is generally understood that truth has been established. However, the history of science does not support that, and there are many examples in the records that serve to bring a modicum of humility to more than a few smug scientists. Still, it is hard, especially for those of us educated in western societies, to accept the notion that bullshit is also found in science, so let's see if I can change some minds.

In my 2014 book, *Reclaiming the Afterlife*, I dedicate four chapters to debunking the belief in science's infallibility and its uninterrupted ascendance since its beginnings. There I include surprising historical events and anecdotes that demonstrate the stumbling course of scientific progress over the centuries. Contrary to the popular view that scientific advancement could be charted with a fairly straight, upward-slanting line, it would instead look more like a zigzag, rising over time, but with more than a few backward (or downward) slides. A case detailed in the book is that of the famous astronomer, Johannes Kepler whose mathematical formulations that led to his laws of planetary motion paved the way for Isaac Newton and his cherished laws of motion and theories of universal gravitation. What the general public is not aware of is that Kepler actually stumbled upon correct calculations via a series of elementary math errors that eventually cancelled out into the correct figures—by sheer luck! The famous author and journalist, Arthur Koestler, called it "...the most amazing sleepwalking performance in the history of science...."

Also detailed in the book (from which I am heavily borrowing for this segment) is the case of one of the greatest advances in the history of astronomy, that of Bell Telephone Laboratories' physicists, Arno Penzias and Robert Wilson, who received the Nobel Prize for their 1965 discovery of universal background radiation that provided the proof astrophysicists needed to validate the Big Bang theory. But few people know that the gigantic breakthrough was not the result of a well-designed scientific experiment, but a completely accidental lucky strike. You see, Penzias and Wilson had been testing a highly sensitive microwave detector when they discovered that their device was picking up more noise than they expected, which concerned them. First attributing the noise to equipment malfunction and ruling that out, they eventually blamed bird droppings on the detector as the source of the disturbance. However, that wasn't it.

The researchers soon learned that the noise remained stubbornly the same throughout the year (day and night) in spite of the position changes due to the earth's rotation and orbital movement. Because our planet's motion pointed their equipment to different directions in space, the physicists reasoned—to their growing amazement—that the noise was not only extraterrestrial, but also coming from far beyond our solar system, even beyond our home galaxy. No, it couldn't be bird shit! The origin of the microwaves was, indeed, the radiation from the early universe, light energy that, due to the rapid expansion of the universe, would appear to us as microwave radiation instead of light, something Penzias and Wilson did not fully understand until they talked to Robert Dicke, a Princeton nuclear physicist, but *an outsider* in the field of astrophysics, who had long held a similar idea about the universe's beginnings. The point here is that this fortuitous, paradigm-changing, award-winning discovery was not the result of a meticulously designed scientific experiment, but totally accidental.

Notable examples of closed-mindedness in science—the product of personal pride, peer pressure, and deeply rooted scientific paradigms—are also covered in my earlier book, including Benjamin Franklin being laughed at when he declared that lighting and electricity were related, and the condemning of Joseph Lister, the British surgeon whose support of Pasteur's theory that germs cause infections and whose insistence that surgeons sterilize their instruments and wash their hands before operations was bitterly contested by medical scientists. Also mentioned is the famous British mathematical physicist, Lord Kelvin, who completely rejected the existence of X-rays, calling them a hoax. Moreover, he "mathematically proved" in 1859 that the sun could not possibly produce disturbances in the Earth's geomagnetic field, and, of course, he was dead wrong. Kelvin is also on record stating that heavier than air flight was impossible (Tell that to American Airlines!). And yet, he was so confident of the advanced state of science during his life that in 1900 he stated flatly: "There is nothing new to be discovered in physics now." Now, that's arrogance!

Other famous examples include the 1700s scientific community's opposition to the existence of meteorites because, well, "rocks just don't fall from the sky," and also the concept of continental drift, which was so bitterly rejected until the early 1900s: "How could entire continents move?" The list could be easily expanded.

It is easy to dismiss critiques of the state of science of long ago, believing—as no doubt every generation has—that "modern" science really has it all figured out *now*. Well, we still don't. Such notion is bullshit. There is much to contradict that belief. Here is a case in point (also from my first book). As recent as the late twentieth century, medical scientists refused to believe that a bacteria is responsible for most gastric ulcers. Much suffering would have been prevented if they had listened sooner to Australian doctors Barr J. Marshall and J. Robin Warren who, at a medical conference where they first presented their findings were scoffed at by "experts." It was preposterous to think that a bacterium (H. pylori) is responsible for a condition so obviously due to the burning effects of excess stomach acid!

Well, it took Dr. Marshall to become his own guinea pig, ingesting the bacteria himself and developing the symptoms leading to ulcers that finally got the attention of the scientific world. Nevertheless, even after his findings were published in *The Medical Journal of Australia* in 1985, the idea was considered just another hypothesis for another ten years. As the doctor says, "[t]o gastroenterologists, the concept of germ causing ulcers was like saying that the Earth is flat." Eventually, Dr. Marshall's and Dr. Warren's "crazy" theory became accepted, and they received a Nobel Prize in 2005. Another sad side of the story is that, aside from denying a simple cure (antibiotics) to ulcer sufferers, many deaths could have been prevented, for H. pylori has been shown to be linked to stomach cancer, a killer that has now been substantially reduced in western nations thanks to the Australian doctors.

Now chew on this, and don't bother to floss. Without any comments or apologies, the departments of Agriculture and Health and Human Services removed the recommendation for flossing from their latest (2016) dietary guidelines for Americans. What? Did not our dentists (and the government and our parents) tell us for decades that flossing was necessary to avoid cavities and serious periodontal disease? According to the New York Times, in August 2016 the AP revealed that "officials had never researched the effectiveness of regular flossing, as required, before cajoling Americans to do it..." adding that "...it has been something of an open secret among experts that flossing hasn't been shown to prevent cavities or periodontal disease."[1]

The article points out that the American Dental Association's website states: "Flossing is an essential part of taking care of your teeth and gums." However, the statement does not seem to have scientific backing, as researchers could not find any studies showing that flossing, even combined with brushing, is effective in the prevention of cavities. Dr. Phillippe Hujoel, professor of oral-health at the University of Washington in Seattle offers this comment: "It is very surprising that you have two habits, flossing and tooth brushing without fluoride, which are widely believed to prevent cavities and tooth loss, and yet we don't have the randomized clinical trials to show they are effective." [2]   Does this mean we have been bullshitted into buying dental floss and toothpaste all these years? The answer is yes. Now, these practices may one day be proven to be effective, who knows. But at this moment, the hard scientific evidence to support such claim does not exist, and thus, decades-old expert advice turns out to be...all together now: "Bullshit!"

Unquestionably, there is much reason for celebration among scientists for the significant achievements in many of their fields, but there is also need for humbleness, as there is still so much we do not know, so many mysteries still held by Mother Nature. Nevertheless, the urge to stand out, to make great discoveries, is a part of the scientist's inherent makeup, and this sometimes leads to embarrassing claims. A relatively recent incident is a good example. In March 2014, a group of scientists (known as BICEP2) made the stunning announcement that they had strong evidence for the discovery of gravitational waves that originated within a trillionth of a trillionth of a trillionth of a second of the Big Bang (I have no idea how they can measure that), a finding that could potentially revolutionize physics. International headlines followed, and there was great excitement in the scientific community. But only a few months later, oops, it all crumbled, as it was found that "the signal they'd seen was primarily due to dust in our galaxy rather than to gravitational waves from the cosmic dawn." [3] Oh well, sorry about that.

The understandable human desire to be seen as highly knowledgeable is irresistible, and it can lead to ridiculous pronouncements from those whom we view as particularly objective professionals. Let's consider a few more examples, some straight out of my *Reclaiming the Afterlife*.

In his book *The Third Level of Reality*, scientist Percy Seymour states that the sense of smell in some fish is so highly developed that "the trout can detect smell chemicals of shrimp diluted *a thousand million times*..." And if that does not sound exaggerated enough, he follows with the preposterous assertion that "the sensitivity of the eel is a thousand million times greater than that of the trout."[4]   Scientists occasionally pull dubious numbers like that from who knows where, throw them at the layman, and sit back in their chairs of arrogance to hear our oohs and aahs. What crap! And to think our children are fed this academic hogwash as part of their "education." It gets better.

From the science-oriented magazine, *Discover* (July/August 2014) we learn that "University of Pittsburgh ecologist Jonathan Pruitt has observed juvenile spiders playing make-believe, simulating copulation before reaching sexual maturity to improve their courtship skills. I wonder, how does Pruitt know that the spiders are really "playing make-believe" and practicing sex specifically to improve their courtship skills? Give me a break. All kinds of things could be going on. For instance, they could have been simply playing around, bored!   He also notes that roughhousing seems to make wild Alaskan brown bear cubs more resilient, which is supposedly substantiated by a 2009 study in *Evolutionary Ecology Research* claiming that just 1 percent more time spent playing by those bears correlated with an 18 percent greater chance of survival into adulthood. [5]   One percent more play? Is he serious? Just how precisely can you measure one percent more play time in bears anyway? And then to have the gumption to leap to an association with eighteen percent better survival chances...come on. I have more of this stuff for you.

In a 2014 on-line news article we "learn" that the riddle of why zebras have stripes—*a question that has been debated by biologists for more than 140 years*—has probably been solved. Calling the new theory "by far the best," researcher Tim Caro of the University of California at Davis claims that these animals developed stripes to avoid been bitten by the tsetse fly and other blood-sucking flies. The article cites studies showing that "comparatively little blood from zebras" is found in those flies in spite of their having thinner coats and finer hair than giraffes and antelopes.[6] This could simply mean, of course, that the pests prefer to bite other animals, but that would be too simple.

The piece also mentions that horses and cows are among the most heavily victimized by the insects.[7] So, we should ask: "Why then, if stripes are such an effective deterrent against the flies, didn't horses and cows develop stripes just like the zebras?" And why could there not be other factors that make the zebras more resistant (or less appealing) to the bugs? Or factors that make cows and horses tastier and more attractive to the flies? But the biologists now like the insect-avoidance theory much more than previous guesses; consequently, those older theories claiming that stripes served as camouflage against predators, or to radiate heat more effectively, or for easier group identity, or for mating advantages—each at one time touted as *the answer*—are being tossed aside, so we can expect school textbooks to soon begin "teaching" that zebras evolved stripes to avoid pestering bugs—at least until the next poorly funded, equally incompetent research comes up with a new explanation. Can the bullshit pile up any higher? Oh yes, it can.

As made patently clear by our experience with comet Kohoutek, expert prediction is a pastime where bullshit is abundant. For example, since my high school days in the 1960s, I've been hearing how the world is going to run out of oil. After the 1970s gas crisis (which had nothing to do with the planet running out of oil) we panicked, and many changes were made to our energy policies as we contemplated the impending drying of the oil wells and gas sources. As we all know, not only has the drying out not occurred, we now find ourselves with too much oil, with prices dropping almost daily (at least as of this writing). In essence, it was all an illusion—educated guess, yes, but still bullshit.

Some teachers also terrified us with another generally accepted prediction by "experts": mass starvation around the world due to overpopulation. Well, the world population in 1968 (when I graduated from high school) was about 3.5 billion. Today it is 7.5 billion, which is *more than double*, and yet no global-scale famine has materialized. That we have way too many poor, hungry people all over the word today is a shame, but the situation is no worse today than it was back then. The "experts" did not have the foresight to account for the possibility that improvements in farming technology, fertilizers, and insect control would greatly increase crop yields. In effect, no Malthusian food crisis ever developed; it was all apocalyptic bullshit.

Most of the time, teachers, unfortunately, have no choice but to work with the "authoritative" textbooks they are given, and so when the experts are wrong, which is not infrequently, incorrect information is disseminated and perpetuated. And it seems this is the way it has always been. In fact, I got a good chuckle recently when I learned about a natural historical treatise from 1750 England, titled: "Sirens and Other Monsters." Imagine the bullshit readers were taking in. We are a little more sophisticated today, but certainly not exempt from error, as we have already seen, and as further reinforced by what follows.

From the fields of archeology and anthropology we have just recently realized that, having taught for five centuries that the Irish people are descendents of the Celts, we were, well, just plain wrong. It turns out that, based on DNA evidence from remains recently found in Northern Ireland, the Irish people actually preceded the Celts by more than one thousand years! Yet, the erroneous assertions of "authorities" that the Celts invaded Ireland somewhere between 1000 BC and 500 BC spurred all kinds of stories and customs still perpetuated today. As explained by Peter Whoriskey of the Washington Post, this has created an awkward situation:

> That story has inspired innumerable references linking the Irish with Celtic culture. The Nobel-winning Irish poet William Butler Yeats titled a book Celtic Twilight. Irish songs are deemed "Celtic" music. Some nationalists embraced the Celtic distinction. And in Boston, arguably the most Irish city in the United States, the owner of the NBA franchise dress their players in green and call them the Celtics.[8]

Think about that. *Five centuries* of archeologists and anthropologists spinning that yarn for high school and college students, and it was all bullshit.

Think of the moon. Many people are under the impression that we know just about everything there is to know about it, a notion that more than a few teachers and scientists like to perpetuate. The truth is that, as close as it is to us, the moon remains a mystery. We don't even know how it got to where it is. The theory that it was trapped into Earth's gravitational field after it, and our planet, coalesced from an initial gaseous state in the early stages of the solar system was taught when I was in high school many decades ago. Citing a number of weaknesses with that theory, astronomers eventually pushed it aside with a new conjecture proposing that billions of years ago a big object or lump of space debris happened to come by the neighborhood and the earth pulled it into its gravitational field. Yet another theory states that a Mars-sized chunk of rock actually struck Earth, and the blow produced lots of debris that later condensed into our planetary companion. The problem with the latter two theories is that the moon's composition is nearly identical to Earth's, and that challenges the foreign object notion.

So, no one really knows how the moon formed or came to be where it is located. In fact, there are a number of highly unusual facts about the moon that make scientists scratch their heads. They call these anomalies "coincidences." Among these, we find that the moon is unusually close to Earth (compared to other planet-moon relationships). It is also disproportionally big, in relation to its planet, by solar system standards, and it just happens to be *exactly* the size and distance required to entirely block the sun during a total eclipse, which allows scientists to study solar phenomena particularly well, a striking coincidence. In fact, the moon does not really orbit the earth, both bodies actually orbit each other, which may eventually lead to the moon being called a sister planet (in a twin-planet relationship). The moon's role in the earth's tidal flow and on our planet's tilt (which helps define the seasons) is essential to life on Earth, meaning we would not be discussing this had the moon not been just as it is, and where it is, today. It is no exaggeration that we know less about our closest neighbor than that which we know with certainty. In many ways, the moon remains an inscrutable mystery. Any claims to the contrary is arrogant bullshit.

And what about weather forecasts? "Highly qualified" meteorologists, seemingly unconcerned with their hit or miss daily prognostications, still have the chutzpah to predict the weather a week in advance! Not surprisingly, they are often wrong. However, there is a positive side in this. We can—with a fairly high degree of confidence—assume the opposite of what they predict, especially regarding precipitation. Thus, if the weather report calls for rain in three days, you should aim to plan your outdoor activities for that day. Conversely, if the forecast is for a clear, sunny day, you would be well advised to take an umbrella wherever you go. This has consistently worked for me much better than taking the forecasts at face value. As I'm sure the reader has seen, there is never a shortage of excuses as to why the weather did not behave as forecasted: an unexpected change in air currents; an unforeseen mass of cold/hot air that moved in from the ocean; an anticipated cold front stalled a hundred miles away; an unusual increase in moisture in the upper atmosphere, and such.

The same holds true for predictions dealing with hurricanes, which is of special interest to those of us living in states bordering the Gulf of Mexico and the Atlantic coast. Over the years, meteorologists have changed—and slightly improved—the way they assemble their hurricane forecasts, but they have a long way to go before they become truly reliable. For instance, in recent years it has become popular to draw a "cone of concern" on a map once a tropical system has reached the status of tropical storm (sometimes earlier depending on how alarmist is the news station you're watching). The cone's narrow end marks the nearest location to the storm, and its width increases with distance. The farther out from the storm, the wider the cone of concern because reliability decreases (actually plummets) as the projected path of the weather system is extended out into the future.

In the early stages, these cones are essentially useless in estimating likely location of landfall several days ahead, as they are rarely—I dare say never—right, if taken as initially drawn up. At least we can benefit from the knowledge that the early cones will always be wrong. Thus, if the first or second version of the cone places your city dead center in the projected path of the storm, you can be quite certain, possibly with as high as 95% certainty, that your town will be spared. It has *always* worked for me. Eventually, as the hurricane or tropical storm moves across the ocean over several days and begins to threaten land areas, the cone becomes more reliable, at least for short distances, but it will almost never strike regions most threatened by the early projections. So, if you were to follow the reports about a hurricane closely, you would see the cone shift, up and down, thirty degrees, forty-five, then back to thirty and so on. Do that next time a storm threatens the U.S. It's quite amusing, really.

Hanging on to the topic of hurricanes just a little longer, I know readers will love this next anecdote. In a paper published in *Proceedings of the National Academy of Sciences*, researchers at the University of Illinois, Urbana-Champaign and Arizona State University report that of ninety-four hurricanes that struck the U.S. between 1950 and

2012, "hurricanes with feminine names kill[ed] more people than those with masculine names." Why? The theory is that "storms with feminine names may be perceived as less threatening, so people may take fewer precautions," adding that "on average, a storm that would kill an estimated fifteen people if it had a masculine name would kill forty-two if it had a feminine name." [9] Really? Really? If you believe this bullshit, please skip the rest of the chapter.

It should be noted that much of today's bad science is not the result of poorly trained scientists, but the consequence of the power of paradigms (and our reluctance to challenge them) and a culture that chastises, both professionally and economically, those who dare question the prevalent scientific models. Even Einstein—often recognized as the personification of genius—was not exempt from the "paradigm effect." He was so influenced by the then standard model of a static universe, that when he originated his famous general theory of relativity, he changed his equations to be consistent with that belief. He introduced a "fudge factor," (the cosmological constant) to find agreement. He felt obligated to do so because his revolutionary theory predicted an expanding universe, an idea now fully accepted, but highly objectionable to the scientific authorities of the time. To his credit, Einstein later rejected the changes he made, calling it "his greatest mistake." In fact, clinging to existing paradigms is so strong among scientists that sometimes a new idea cannot be fairly evaluated until most of its opponents have died. As famous physicist Neils Bohr once observed: "Science advances—funeral by funeral."

One of the most strongly entrenched paradigms in science today is materialism, which, in effect, states that only the physical exists and reduces all complex processes and phenomena to physical components (reductionism). In this worldview the mystery of consciousness—the concept of mind—is diminished to the status of an illusion created by electrochemical processes in the brain. Thus, the mind is powerless and cannot influence "the real," the physical. Yet, this picture of reality held by many scientists is proving to be bullshit, as it does not stand to obvious objections, the tough challenges that materialists prefer to ignore. One of these is the placebo effect, which has proven, over and over, that beliefs and expectations can influence what happens in the brain and the body. For example, a study done at the University of British Columbia focused on patients with a severe form of Parkinson's disease, individuals with a 70% to 80% destruction of the nerve cells responsible for producing dopamine, which means they were significantly impaired, barely able to move and experiencing severe tremors. Neurologists running the study then told some participants that they were going to receive a new drug that could be extremely effective in treating their condition. The "drug" was only *distilled water*. Here is what happened.

Only minutes after the injection, the subjects' underwent brain scans, and the amazed researchers found that dopamine was being released into the patients' brains in amounts comparable to young, healthy individuals. Soon came improvement, with reduced tremors, increased strength, and better mobility. Did the distilled water accomplish this? Of course not. It was their beliefs and expectations that acted on the brain, which then acted on the body, that produced the surprising results.[10] It was a clear case of mind over matter (the brain being matter in the form of an organ). Imagine that. A non-physical factor—a belief—causing changes in a physical system. R. E. Tanzi, Harvard professor of Neurology, encapsulates the notion: *"You are not your brain; you are the user of your brain."* Think about that evocative statement—deeply.

112

And here is another interesting fact. We know that external stimuli—a sound, touch, or picture—will register brain activity that is measurable with instruments in the lab. However, as neuroscientist and science writer David Eagleman has pointed out, "Most things we care about—reminiscences, emotion, drives, plans, and so on—can occur with no external stimulus and no overt output that can be measured." These can happen with the brain at rest (at its "'baseline' activity" level).[11] Interesting. More than interesting, as it is supportive of the idea that the brain is a tool; it is not who or what we are.

Psychic events also challenge the materialist worldview. Parapsychologists have shown that extrasensory perception (ESP) phenomena—also referred to as psi—such as telepathy, precognition, clairvoyance, near-death experiences, and channeling are quite likely real, even if their findings are doggedly rejected by the mainstream and attacked by skeptics.* But even if *just one* of these aspects of psi is genuine, it would be sufficient to establish that our minds transcend physicality, helping to bring down the wobbly edifice of materialism—the bullshit upon which the dominant view of reality is based. Unfortunately for those who are more interested in the truth than in maintaining the status quo, decades of serious research into ESP are persistently ignored or disparaged by mainstream science, which has decided to label such work as "pseudoscience."

It is painful to see that such resistance has even led to perpetrating lies about what is going on in the field of parapsychology, and tragically, the popular media parrots the "official" declarations of the radical skeptics. A case in point deals with the interesting work of Professor Robert Jahn at Princeton, which found positive results for psychokinesis (mind-matter interaction). Toeing the standard scientific line that no such phenomenon exists, a 1995 *Newsweek* cover story about the paranormal flatly stated that "Other labs using Jahn's machine, have not obtained his results." As Dean Radin, senior scientist at the Institute of Noetic Sciences (IONS) and founder of the Consciousness Research Laboratory at UNLV reveals, it was a boldfaced lie. He states: "The statement, however, is pure fiction...Jahn's research has been replicated by more than *seventy* researchers worldwide."[12]

Research into telepathy/clairvoyance has been particularly successful in demonstrating the reality of the phenomenon. Increasingly rigorous methodologies demanded by skeptics who keep raising the bar on psi experiments have been implemented, and the positive results persist. The Ganzfield method, which places a "receiver" in isolation under mild sensory deprivation and then has a "sender" transmit mental images from a remote location, has been particularly successful, with the method being refined over the years to respond to escalating demands by skeptics who are dumbfounded by the continual success of the trials. In fact, some hard-nosed skeptics, when confronted with irrefutable data from tightly-controlled experiments indicating the reality of some aspect of psi, have gone as far as calling for a revision of scientific methods of inquiry because psi manifestations just cannot be true. It is remarkable how unwilling to let go of deeply-held beliefs humans can be. For those interested in what is going on in this fascinating field of investigation, I highly recommend Dean Radin's *The Conscious Universe*, which is loaded with information about past and present work in parapsychology.

---

* For an in-depth examination of psychic phenomena and current research in the field, I urge interested readers to read my first book, *Reclaiming the Afterlife*.

It's too bad that dogmatism abounds in the sciences. Many potential scientific discoveries have either been delayed or entirely shelved because scientists are oftentimes unwilling to accept experimental data that conflicts with expected results (usually based on prevailing paradigms). As noted by historian and science philosopher Thomas Kuhn, the anomalous data become virtually invisible to the researchers. Or, if the atypical data is all too real, with alarming frequency the scientists outright refuse to accept the results, quickly jumping to the conclusion that errors were made in the experiment, or, remarkably, if the reason for the "error" cannot be found, the data is simply tossed aside! Consequently, interesting, possibly significant, discoveries are time and again ignored by those who should know better. Science, in a way, is a religion, and its tenets cannot be easily challenged by its members because most have been heavily indoctrinated. There could also be hell to pay.

Financial considerations are also a factor affecting the way science is practiced today. Researchers working, or wanting to work, in fields considered outside of the mainstream find it quite difficult to gain funding for their projects, not to mention the potential harm to their professional reputations if their area of interest is viewed as "on the fringes" of conventional science. This is too bad because new breakthroughs and ideas are often conceived at the edges of the prevailing scientific paradigms, not inside.

I could go on about the not-so-stellar history of scientific progress and the bullshit that permeates the way science is done today. However, I know that many readers are still not convinced that science is not as precise or infallible as they have been led to believe all their lives. So, for those still reluctant to accept this idea, I include a section from my book *Reclaiming the Afterlife* in Appendix C that will leave you aghast and dismayed. What you'll find there will help you understand part of the reason why humanity's efforts to defeat cancer have not yielded better results. Don't miss it.

I am cognizant that some readers may have felt unwillingly dragged through this brief section about science, especially the strong believers in the certainty of scientific laws and theories, but I stand by its contents. That said, there is another area to be covered that can be even more controversial—religion—and I will keep that discussion brief because I do not expect to change any minds in such an abridged discussion, and, being a typically sensitive, contentious topic, some readers may feel their faith is under attack.** Nevertheless, at the risk of tallying a few unhappy readers (not intentionally, please understand), I must examine, even if in an uncomfortably concise manner, bullshit's role in religion, which historically has been an enormously influential social force and an important part of many lives.

** For an extensive discussion about religion, interested readers may want to review the several chapters dedicated to the subject in *Reclaiming the Afterlife*.

CHAPTER 6

Bullshit in Religion

With or without religion, you would have good people doing good things and evil people doing evil things. But for good people to do evil things, that takes religion.

—Steven Weinberg

I like your Christ. I do not like your Christians. They are so unlike your Christ.

—M. Gandhi

Imagine there's no countries; It isn't hard to do; Nothing to kill or die for; And no religion too; Imagine all the people; Living life in peace...

—John Lennon ("Imagine")

In my book *Reclaiming the Afterlife*, I devote several chapters to a close examination of religion, and I have not the least doubt that I unnerved some readers with my less-than-favorable report card. As promised, I will keep this section quite short, just enough to make some key points, and I refer interested readers to my earlier book for a much more in-depth discourse on the subject.

One of the first things about religion that would surely confuse a visitor from another world is that we have so many faiths in such a small planet. It is nothing short of astonishing that there are approximately 4,200 religions today. [1] Many of these share similar beliefs, but there are also significant differences easily identified. Some of these religions count with only a small number of members, while others have millions of followers. Thus, it is commonly said that the world has "only" twenty-one major religions, and among these, there are five really noteworthy in terms of their numbers of believers:

> 1. Christianity (2.1 billion); 2. Islam (1.3 billion); 3. Hinduism (900 million); 4. Chinese traditional religion (394 million); 5. Buddhism (376 million). (Judaism, in contrast, has only 14 millions adherents.).

However, it should be noted that the Secular/Irreligious/Agnostic/Atheist category counts 1.1 billion people, which would place it third in the list, just behind Islam. [2] Also, while Christianity ranks number one in total number of followers, it is split into many denominations (e.g. Protestant, Catholic, Baptist, Methodist, Lutheran, Mormon, Eastern Orthodox, Evangelical, Jehovah's Witnesses, Seventh-day Adventist, Quakers, and more), all sharing similarities, but also having specific, and not insignificant, variations in their beliefs.

Ask genuine believers of most denominations, and you will often get the affirmation that theirs is the one true religion. Who, then, is right? Therein lies the crux of the problem. While in modern times we may encounter more and more religious individuals willing to say that "all religions lead to God," which is nice and inclusive, many still hold to the notion that if you are not a believer in their particular faith, you will surely never reach Heaven or whatever state of ecstasy is reserved for true believers of the *true* religion. Instead, you will likely be cast into Hell or another similarly unpleasant place, usually for eternity. That's where the bullshit really begins to smell. Need we even open a discussion about why that notion is absurd?

Now, to avoid misunderstanding about this author's views about religion, let me make a point as clearly as I possibly can. At its core, the concept of religion—at least in the forms we are most acquainted with, such as Christianity—is good. Religions, with the best of intentions, provide moral guidance, behavioral guidelines, and usually hope for an afterlife. Who, other than a few depraved souls, would disagree with the idea that killing another human being is wrong? Or taking away his or her possessions? Or lying, particularly in a way that is harmful to another? These and other moral codes are wise, rational, and essential to a healthy society.

However, it is when religions claim exclusive rights to the truth, when they assure us that their faith's prophets, usually from ancient times, received direct guidance from God that I begin to resist. One obvious question is this: if God interacted that much with us in the past (as the Bible would have us believe), why does He not do so anymore? If God loves us so much, Why does He not come visit and set us straight on all these differences that we have in this anxious, confused modern world? It would be so simple, and so much pain and distress could be avoided! Also, we need answers to the troubling age-old questions of why the world experiences so much senseless violence, disease, and natural disasters. The resulting toll in human suffering is overwhelming, and much of it is inflicted by a whimsical, seemingly indifferent Mother Nature. These tragedies strongly challenge our religious-based conception of a merciful, protective, involved deity who looks after us. It is in these fundamental areas of human concern that I more sharply divert from religion.

Ironically, while virtually all religious doctrines promote peace and good will, ecclesiastical leaders have historically contributed to the initiation of wars, many leading to enormous bloodshed and the most fanatical and brutal war crimes, including torture and genocide. The sadistic Islamic terrorist organization, ISIS, is today's extreme example of fanatical religionism, but you could pick any century (at least in the A.D. period) and find religious wars. Christianity itself has a rather dark history, highlighted by the bloody Crusades (from late in the 9th Century to at least the 13th Century) and the shameful period of the vindictive and merciless *Inquisition* (which ran from the 12th to as late as the 19th Century!). These were religiously-sanctioned wars, torture and executions ostensibly in the name of God.

It is unfortunate—tragic really—that religion, despite its contributions, has been the source of so much human suffering. The ever-cynical Mark Twain put it this way:

> Man is the religious animal. He is the only religious animal. He is the only animal that has the True Religion – several of them. He is the only animal that loves his neighbor as himself and cuts his throat if his theology isn't straight. He has made a graveyard of the globe in trying his honest best to smooth his brother's path to happiness and heaven.

I have argued that for a religion to be "the one true religion," a God-endorsed faith, it must be unchanging. You either have the God-given truth from the get go, or you don't. Many denominations of Christianity fail in this account, as they have evolved (even if reluctantly) to incorporate secular values and desires that have proven too strong to combat. The oldest, the Catholic Church, is notable for this. For example, during the Dark Ages widespread literacy, science, even hygiene were considered evil, but they are now encouraged; insistence that the Earth sits at the center of the solar system (part of Church dogma for centuries) eventually yielded to the heliocentric system that Copernicus and Galileo championed; divorce, once a mortal sin, is now increasingly accepted; homosexuality, severely condemned for centuries, is now treated with increasing tolerance. Who knows what other changes the doctrine's future holds. Consequently, this self-assigned title of "the one true religion" that Catholics and others arrogantly claim for themselves reeks; it's nothing but pious, self-righteous bullshit.

And let's not even go into details of the scandalous behavior of popes of the past, especially during the middle ages, which include murder, larceny, concubinage, incest, cruel mutilation, simony, massacres of heretics, and more, and priests of today, with the numerous cases of sexual abuse of children that has plagued the Catholic Church in recent decades. We also have Pope Pius XII who not only failed to condemn Nazism, but has some serious allegations hanging around his neck about his collaboration with Hitler. This from "the good shepherds" of generations upon generations of believers.

Protestants and their many branches should not feel too smug. Claiming to have justifiably split from a corrupt Vatican hierarchy, their progenitors—specializing in the control of minds through superstition, fear, and guilt—are on record as exuberant participants in the brutal Inquisition, the treatment of women as essentially evil, the spread of paralyzing superstition, and for the most vicious witch hunts in history, not to mention spawning the TV Evangelist generation that has swindled so much money from the gullible and the needy.

Protestantism's founder, Martin Luther, has a distinctly dismal record of anti-Semitism, bigotry and sexism. He once proposed the enslaving or banishing of Jews from Christian lands, along with the destruction of their synagogues, and he argued that human beings should be ranked according to gender, class, race, and beliefs, asserting that these "indicated superior and inferior states of being." (So, it seems that by the sheer grace of God, Luther belonged to the superior gender, the superior race, the superior class, and held the superior beliefs—how lucky!). Defending his belief in male superiority, he wrote in 1533: "'Girls begin to talk and to stand on their feet sooner than boys because weeds always grow up more quickly than good crops.'" Even worse, regarding the dangers of childbirth in those days, he stated: "If [women] become tired or even die, that does not matter. Let them die in childbirth—that is why they are there." [3] And those were the thoughts of a follower of Jesus Christ?

John Calvin, another exalted theologian of the Reformation, is not much to celebrate either. Calvin instituted a police-state theocracy in Geneva, a system that presided over the torturing and beheading of Jacques Gruet, an atheist critic of Calvin, and over the burning alive of a well-known Spanish physician and theologian, Michael Servetus, due to strong disagreements with Calvin over religious issues. He also made efforts to counteract scientific progress by declaring Copernicus' heliocentric theory incompatible with the Bible (just as his Catholic enemies had tried to do). Furthermore, and incredibly from such a prominent Christian figure, he argued that not everyone was created equal, and that God predestined some to everlasting life (presumably he was among that elite group) while others were appointed to perpetual damnation—*guilty or innocent.* [4] So much for belief in Christ's teachings and a fair and compassionate god.

It is less than inspiring that religious leaders have such a dismal record of corruption and unchristian behavior, and that should be enough reason to view with suspicion whatever these individuals, present or past, have to tell us. Furthermore, holy books are completely open to interpretation. Take the Koran, with its varied renditions of the many Islamic sects that span the gamut from the most peaceful to that practiced by the most extremist elements we see today, such as the unfathomably savage ISIS. As to the Bible, there is much argument among scholars regarding its origins, and those debates are exacerbated by the fact that as various scriptures were being assembled to compose the holy book, men with agendas and political considerations made decisions as to what texts would be included and excluded. Thus, you would be wasting your time and breath trying to convince me that every step in the Bible's creation, every decision, was God-inspired or directed, and that the result is the definitive word of God.

Briefly stated, if religious tenets evolve alongside social, cultural, and political developments, then religion is but another human invention, subject to human error and correction, and not a depository of facts and God's unalterable wisdom and laws. Thus, oftentimes, as history has shown, religion has nothing to do with God, especially the merciful, benevolent one. Leonard Pitts Jr., the insightful, nationally syndicated columnist, makes this clear:

> ...God and religion are not synonymous. God is...the sovereign creator of all creation. Religion is what men and women put in place, ostensibly to worship and serve Him. Too often, though, religion worships and serves that which has nothing to do with Him, worships money and serves politics, worships charisma and serves ego, worships intolerance and serves self.

Finally, a word about those TV Evangelists. How is it possible that there can be so many of these television parasites with so many followers? So many people willing to send them money? Have the scandals of the past not been enough to make believers ultra-cautious? Borrowing again from my first book, let's briefly touch on this.

Judging from the ongoing popularity of TV Evangelists, it seems we've forgotten about indignities of not so long ago. The immensely popular televangelist Jim Bakker's sex scandal, where Jessica Hahn was allegedly paid off (with donation money, of course) to keep silent about her charge that Bakker had raped her comes to mind. This forced him to resign as Assemblies of God minister in 1987 as well as from the PTL Club TV show he hosted for years with wife Tammy Bakker. Compounding the sins of this "man of God," Bakker was also convicted of fraud (1988) and sentenced to prison.

Perhaps we've also forgotten about Pentecostal preacher and televangelist Jimmy Swaggert, who had the nerve to publicly chastise both Jim Bakker and fellow Assemblies of God minister Marvin Gorman for sexual indiscretions. Why the nerve? Because in 1988 Swaggert himself was forced to step down from the pulpit after he first denied and later admitted soliciting prostitutes. What a hypocrite.

And I guess our memories have already forgiven Oral Roberts, the charismatic televangelist and faith healer who claimed to have raised a child from death and who professed visions from, and conversations with, God. The same preacher who in 1987 told his television audience that he had to raise $8 million in donations or "God would call him home." His followers, in a panic, responded to this outrageous claim with donations of $9.1 million, their immense gullibility saving him—not from God "calling him home" early—but from having to explain to his followers why he was still in this world had he fallen short of the target figure. (Too bad we did not get the opportunity to see him in that awkward situation!)

While apparently those who still send their hard-earned money to these shady individuals have forgotten about those scandals, American Indians certainly learned the lesson about evangelizers, albeit too late. In the words of Chief Dan George, a Native American author: " When the white man came, we had the land and they had the Bibles. Now they have the land and we have the Bibles." What a powerful statement, one that expresses the power of bullshitters so poignantly.

Today, since many of the faithful cannot donate land, money will do. Consider this statement in a video where preacher Leroy Thompson screams, "God said: 'It is time to tell the money you don't belong to the wicked, you belong to us.' Money, come to me now!" Then we have televangelist Mike Murdock asking his viewers to donate $1,000, asserting that—are you ready for this load?—God will erase a donor's credit card debt if he or she will donate with a credit card: "As you use your faith, God is going to wipe out your credit card debts." [5] How can people believe the fecal torrent spewing out of those bastards' mouths? Just how often do people have to be fleeced before they get it? I hope all those preachers have a nice warm place reserved for them in hell.

Here is a little religious humor from Herb Caen, a popular San Francisco journalist: "The trouble with born-again Christians is that they are an even bigger pain the second time around." I couldn't agree more. Let us resolve to put this holier-than-thou parasites out of business. Whenever we hear one of those Bible thumpers make statements about what he or she assures us the Bible says, let's not respond with "Amen," but rather with "Bullshit!"

To conclude, all too often religion has little to do with God. Invoking the Almighty is pure propaganda, part of a ploy to further an agenda. As individuals, we would be much better served by following our conscience and the spiritual instincts inherent in all of us.

Chapter 7

Social Media

"Life today has become a series of spectacles to be viewed, not actions to be lived."

— Pete Sanders

Social media has turned all of us into Dogs. The moment a single dog is unhappy with something, it starts barking, and then hundreds of others join the barking immediately. We no longer use our brains, we just join the chorus."

— EverSkeptic

It was a lazy Sunday afternoon at the mall's food court. My wife and I sat comfortably, enjoying coffee and a pastry, trying our best to ignore the intrusive reggaeton, now ubiquitous in our community, blaring from the overhead speakers. At one end of the long table across from us sat a middle-age couple, their attention fixed on the tiny screens of their cell phones. At the other end sat two young girls, age about fifteen or so, also transfixed by their phone displays, but in addition, they intensely interacted with the devices, thumbs gliding across the screens with lightning-fast dexterity. I casually commented to my wife about the current infatuation with cell phones, discreetly pointing out the people in the neighboring table and how they were ignoring each other's presence. However, we had a surprise in store.

Two teenage boys of about seventeen arrived carrying two huge pizzas, soon to be followed by a couple in their twenties carrying drinks for everyone. It was then we realized that the girls sitting at one end of the long table were part of the group. There was some brief small talk followed by the simultaneous reaching for cell phones by the new arrivals. Now everyone had a phone in his or her hands. One of the boys stood up and, as others held the pizzas at a forty-five degree angle, snapped a couple of pictures of the pies, which presumably were quickly posted on social media. After that brief interaction, the picture-taker sat down, and everyone returned to their cell phones. Eight people at the table—not a word spoken. Each sat there, transfixed by the hypnotic power of the tiny screens. Outrageous? Nor really.

Those situations are becoming increasingly common, and consequently, this book would not be complete without some commentary about the social media phenomenon, the electronic venue and virtual gallery that cell phone technology and wireless infrastructure have made possible. This powerful communication medium where millions exchange messages, videos, and pictures every day has become—for many—an indispensible part of life. Hailed as an ultra-effective means of staying in touch with family and friends, the use of applications such as Facebook, Instagram, Snapchat,

Twitter, and just plain texting have grown into time-devouring obsessions, highly addictive. A newspaper article puts it succinctly: "...a generation that texts instead of talks. They've invented a new language. People today tweet the most banal details of daily life. They spend hours on Facebook. They do online dating....It's a poor substitute for personal contact..." [1]

Meanwhile, in the college campus at which I teach, I've been nearly trampled by inattentive students too busy texting or surfing the Internet as they walk down the school's hallways with their heads down, transfixed by the tiny screens. Outside the building, I have actually seen a student riding a skateboard, ears plugged, wire connected to his cell phone, working the gadget with both hands, run right into a girl walking just ahead of him and knocking her to the ground. It's frightening to realize that they are similarly distracted while driving motor vehicles. The way things are going, I wonder how long before dentists and surgeons begin using their cell phones while they work on their patients.

The fascination with social media apps and just plain texting is on the brink of replacing face-to-face communication (There is even a FaceTime app!). I've repeatedly witnessed situations similar to the one described above where couples, even entire families, in restaurants or other public venues are not interacting at all, preferring to link electronically with various others who are not physically present. In effect, whatever comes in via the phones is invariably more important than what the person in front of them has to say (assuming the other person is not on a cell phone as well). Meanwhile, young brain circuitry is being shaped by 140-character tweets with who knows what future consequences. Wake up people! This bullshit is dehumanizing you.

Washington Post columnist Kathleen Parker supports my contention that social media is contributing to our dehumanizing. She laments:

> The more digitally entrenched we become, the less human our interactions. Social media replace human gatherings; online porn becomes a substitute for relationships; email is less trouble than dialing a number and making small talk. Everything at the click of a button has made it less likely we'll take the trouble to exchange pleasantries with a fellow human. [2]

But what else is social media doing to us, especially the young? Are we losing the meaning of friendship? A "friend" is now anybody willing to be counted in a person's collection of pals, and even those who are more than just an item on a list can be easily discarded by choosing to de-friend them. Meanwhile, many people, teens in particular, measure social success by how many "friends" they have. The result is a multitude of shallow relationships (if you can even call them relationships). Some are friends of friends of friends! Young people in particular are hyper-sensitive to the bullshit circulating on social media, with many becoming angry or depressed if they receive negative comments or are "un-friended" by another, and in some extreme cases, teenagers even resort to suicide as a consequence of experiencing too much rejection, shaming, or bullying. Just as distressing, children are frequently stalked online by sexual predators who hide their identities and trick their innocent victims into treacherous rendezvous. That's an abomination.

When it comes to blogs, the connectivity and anonymity contribute to a shoot-from-the-hip mentality where little thinking takes place before opinions are blurted out. Frank Bruni, columnist for the New York Times describes it as "a world in which so many of us, entranced by the opportunity for instant expression and an immediate audience, post unformed thoughts, half-baked wit or splenetic reactions before we can even count to three." And thanks to the anonymity provided by the medium, rudeness is reaching new heights. Bruni states: "...the person you disagree with isn't just misinformed but moronic, corrupt, evil. Complaints become rants. Rants become diatribes." [3] As the quotation at the beginning of the chapter so aptly puts it, we become barking dogs.

Furthermore, think of all the conceited bullshit transmitted via social media. And I don't mean just the senseless comments put out by conceited celebrities now digitally empowered (as if they needed more empowerment) to unload their frequently incoherent thoughts on a population eager to suck up their dim-witted tweets, their mental droppings. I'm talking about everyday folks. As Miami advertising specialist Lauren Ellman explains: "We are constantly bombarded with images of other people's 'perfect' lives. Of all the cool things we could be doing with all the cool people we could be friends with." People throw glaze on themselves, showing the shiniest moments of their lives, or as Ellman puts it: "We manufacture this perfectly varnished version of our lives via social media and then feel bad about ourselves when looking in on everyone else's perfectly varnished version of their lives." [4]

This technological sport can be self-defeating, as it often results in the opposite effect sought by the contestants. Meaning, when people post pictures of all the great things going on in their lives, only a few "friends" will be genuinely happy to see what fun they're having or how great things are going in their lives. More likely the audience will be busy finding ways to criticize and ridicule the sender, all while hypocritically pressing the "like" button on the screen. It's almost perverse.

The Selfie: The Conceited and Irreverent Child of Social Media

The selfie is the ultimate expression of vanity and self-importance of our generation. "Look at me, look at me; forget about the rare sub-Saharan black cheetah racing after its prey across a sun-baked desert in the back of this picture! Let me post this other selfie for the world to see me; and by the way, I'm in Timbuktu, though you can't see anything but my face." And what about the standard, almost-obligatory selfie face, the one where the subject looks as if she just tasted something sour? They call it duck face, and yes, they really do look like ducks—brainless ones.

Aside from the obvious ways that selfies highlight the self-absorbed streak in us, this modern fad has reached disturbing levels, with people now hot dogging for their soon-to-be-posted self images in the most inappropriate of places, as Alabama teenager Breanna Mitchell did with her grinning selfie at Auschwitz, which prompted an entire article by columnist Leonard Pitts Jr. Pitts makes it clear that Ms. Mitchell's irreverence was not an isolated case, saying that "...it has become the modern 'thing,' people clowning, sticking out their tongues, lifting thumbs up, grinning like loons in somber and sacred places." He lists Auschwitz, the New York 9/11 memorial, the

American cemetery at Normandy, the Vietnam War Memorial in Washington, even "grandmother's funeral." [5]

Pitts' anger is palpable in his sharp words of condemnation: "It suggests a cluelessness, a shallowness, and an incapacity for reverence that have come to feel like the signature of our times. It suggests a lack of home training and a surplus of narcissism that have come to feel ubiquitous." He states that "social media have rewritten the social contract," for things that at one time did not need explaining about appropriate behavior now do, and then asks, "Do we take anything seriously?...Is no place so hallowed or holy that we would never think to use it as a stage upon which to showcase the fizzy wonderfulness of our own selves?" In closing, Pitts captures the issue in just a few words: "When you take a picture of yourself grinning and mugging at some sacred place, it diminishes the place and sends a message that has become too common: This is all about me." [6]

I once heard this comment about social media: "You are what you share." So insightful. It reminds me of Kathleen Parker's words when she referred to "...the cultural coupling of narcissism and attention deficit disorder, otherwise defined as an inability to think for more than two minutes about anything more complicated than oneself." [7]

Going beyond the selfie for a moment, but not far from Pitts' and Parker's frustration, it is indeed disappointing that officials at various hollowed sites such as Arlington Cemetery in Virginia and the Holocaust Museum in Washington D.C. have had to petition visitors to refrain from playing Pokémon GO on their grounds. Think about it. Reverence, veneration of the sacrifices of others are notions of the past. Today, our immature, selfish needs for entertainment and pursuit of triviality trump all else. How sad.

Social Media and the Redefinition of Truth

Perhaps the most serious consequence of the social media phenomenon is the routine bludgeoning of the truth at both the personal and the societal levels. At the personal level, the system facilitates the spread of disparaging comments by bitter and malicious individuals who have a personal grudge or nothing better to do than bring others down and create a coarse, vulgar, destructive atmosphere with their vile slander and verbal abuse. Unfortunately, those victimized are oftentimes helpless, with little recourse other than trying to respond in their own defense, a move that could backfire, as such acknowledgments of feeling injured can act as bleeding chum for the cyber sharks, leading to a feeding frenzy of venomous slurs, and damaging lies that could seriously tarnish a person's reputation and ruin careers and relationships, even a business enterprise.

On the public stage, social media's empowerment of opportunistic liars is frightening. Relying on a growing audience of the gullible and those too lazy to verify the many outlandish claims floating in cyberspace, falsehood commandos spread their damaging bullshit faster than a viral epidemic. It's the digital version of the wild, wild west. In a November 2016 newspaper article by author Ana Menendez we learn that "in the final three months of the U.S. presidential campaign, the top-performing fake election news stories on Facebook generated more engagement than the top stories from major news outlets."[8] That is a concerning sign. Social media, full of rumors, innuendo, and plain lies, is increasingly today's source of "information."

In her revealing article, Menendez includes a comment by Paul Horner—an inexhaustible fake news writer who believes he helped Donald Trump get elected—that does not offer much hope: "Honestly, people are definitely dumber....They just keep passing stuff around. Nobody fact-checks anything anymore—I mean, that's how Trump got elected. He just said whatever he wanted, and people believed everything." Regardless of the degree to which Horner's imagination or Trump's boastful lies affected the election, it is undeniable that the degree of unsophistication of a large segment of our population is outright frightening, and many of them vote!

And by the way, Horner makes as much as $10,000 a month from his exaggerated satirical postings, which, due to their viral nature have attracted advertisements, some of which have appeared on Facebook and Google (These entities are now trying to crack down on the malicious websites, but are not finding it easy). In other words, the creation of bullshit is now a real profession. How long do you think before it is offered as a college course (Bullshitting 101) or even a major area of study (the B.S. degree will take on a new meaning)?

Although Horner—the creator of innumerable Internet hoaxes, such as "the Amish lobby," "a gay wedding van," and "a ban on the national anthem"—is a big time power player in the fake-news industry, there is so much money to be made in news creation that he now faces competition from around the world. Abby Ohlheiser of The Washington Post explains that Macedonian teenagers are making as much as $5,000 a month from their fake-news sites, "easy money from American gullibility." Underscoring the growing problem, she provides examples of recent fictitious news stories that went viral:

> The fabricated story posted to a fictional Denver news outlet just before the election "FBI AGENT SUSPECTED IN HILLARY EMAIL LEAKS FOUND DEAD IN APPARENT MURDER-SUICIDE" got more than 500,000 shares on Facebook. "Pope Francis Shocks World, Endorses Donald Trump for President, Releases Statement" is not remotely true, but one fake-news website reeled in more than 100,000 shares with it. A copycat version of the hoax on "Ending the Fed" was even more popular, shared more than 900,000 times on Facebook...[9]

Some of these stories would be simply laughable if it wasn't that counterfeit news can be extremely damaging. Think of Edgar Welch, the North Carolina man who took an assault rifle into a neighborhood pizzeria in Washington D.C. because he read a faux news story "revealing" that a faction of Hillary Clinton supporters were running a child sex ring hidden beneath the establishment. Yes, he actually swallowed that lump of crap. Fortunately, Welch realized his mistake after he failed to find children working as sex slaves and no one got shot.

However, there is another dark, highly concerning side to this episode. As reported by *Miami Herald* columnist Fred Grimm, those child sex ring allegations had been also circulated by no other than Lt. Gen. Michael T. Flynn, Donald Trump's choice for national security adviser! Mr. Trump, by the way, has been a guest at a show whose host, Alex Jones, is "America's leading propagator of insane conspiracy theories." [10] Here is what Jones stated in a YouTube video released just two days before the elections:

> When I think about all the children Hillary Clinton has personally murdered and chopped up and raped, I have zero fear standing up against her. Yeah, you heard me right. Hillary Clinton has personally murdered children. I just can't hold back the truth anymore.

According to Grimm, "Jones has also described blood-drinking Satanic rituals practiced by the Clinton team." He later adds that on an earlier podcast, Trump told Jones: "Your reputation is amazing. I will not let you down." [11] Say what? What was that again, Mr. Trump?

One last example is the popular myth that 3 million illegal votes from undocumented immigrants were cast in the November 2016 elections. A story promoting this whopper appeared in InfoWars, a conspiracy website, and it was shared over 48,000 times at last count (probably much higher by now) as reported by PolitiFact Florida, a partnership between *The Tampa Bay Times* and *The Miami Herald* aimed to verify truth in politics. However, the watchdog agency found that there is no supporting evidence for the outrageous claim, discovering that the InfoWars article was based on tweets from Gregg Phillips (founder of VoteStand, a voter fraud reporting app.), and Phillips would not provide any facts to PolitiFact to support his claim, stating that he was still analyzing the data. The reporters add that "Phillips would also not say what the data is or where it came from or what methodology he used." [12] My translation: InfoWars propagated Mr. Phillips' load of bullshit.

This notion of vast numbers of illegal immigrants voting in elections has been around a while but has never been shown to be true. PolitiFact reveals that back in 2012 Florida Governor Rick Scott's team attacked "the problem." The governor's investigators started by creating a list of 182,000 non-citizens who had possibly voted. However, as they dug into the data, the numbers were revised to 2,700, then 200, and finally only 85 people were dropped from the state's voters list. [13] Something tells me that a few dollars went into this witch hunt, but, what the hell, as we have already seen, Mr. Scott has been very loose in spending taxpayer's money for personal purposes (that is, to pay legions of lawyers to protect him from all his legal entanglements as governor). But I digress.

Though there has never been a shortage of frauds and impostors, the enormous reach of social media (and its instantaneousness) is making it possible for today's charlatans to create widespread confusion and mislead the public about any issue, big or small. It is also creating an atmosphere of distrust that is certainly justified, given how easily blatant lies and half-truths can be disseminated across the social media landscape. Compounding the problem is a not-insignificant number of individuals who choose to believe what they want to be true, asserting that "truth is in the eyes of the beholder." But, as Menendez points out, while a concept like freedom can be interpreted differently and may be determined by culture, "facts are not subject to interpretation." She rightly fears "a post-truth world where everyone is a journalist and mass manipulation is as easy as setting up a website and calling it news."

That the truth is under attack is beautifully exemplified by Trump's former campaign manager, Corey Lewandowski who had the nerve to say at a Harvard University post-election forum that "the literal truth no longer matters." Grimm's article quotes Lewandowski as it appeared in the *Washington Post*: "This is the problem with the media. You guys took everything that Donald Trump said so literally. The American people didn't." [14] Terrifying.

This is the appropriate moment for this author to lament the imminent demise of newspapers in the United States. Even with a biased streak, major, long-established newspapers have traditionally been a reliable source of information. Equally important, they have been our watchdogs, the publics' defenders against corruption and abuse from the rich and powerful as well as government at all levels. Unfortunately, newspapers are under duress from two powerful sources: the increasing dependence on questionable websites, blogs, and social media in general—made possible by rapid advances in communication technology, especially cell phones—and the attacks from politicians (e.g. Trump) when they don't like what they read. In the words of Susan Russell in a *Miami Herald* op-ed article:

> The job of the press has never been to please the reader or win the admiration of the powerful. The job of the press is to be unflinching and unrelenting in searching out the truth of the matter. Without the free press, the water we drink would be dirty, the Everglades would be drained and developed, no one would be held accountable for just about anything....All the more reason to redouble the reporting staff at every major newspaper in the country, knowing the critical importance of their role... [15]

As these venerable institutions continue their decline, we are increasingly exposed not only to the shenanigans of corrupt government officials, powerful financial interests, and other unscrupulous operators, but also to "fake news" (a euphemism for lies), the steady diet of bullshit we are fed today from myriad digital sources, straight to our cell phones and tablets. Most people simply do not read newspapers anymore, and eventually they will disappear, with perhaps a few remaining as anachronisms of earlier days. These are distressing, bewildering times we are living, and I don't think we have even approached the storm's center, the vortex of disinformation that threatens to swallow us into that nightmarish pos-truth world that Menendez dreads.

Some final comments to this chapter. Undoubtedly, our dependence on social media, now almost synonymous with cellular phones, will continue to increase, along with a proliferation of applications that we cannot even imagine at the moment. The gadgets are truly useful, so they have carved a permanent place in our lives for good, practical reasons. Unfortunately, there is a price tag that goes beyond phone replacement costs and monthly service fees, a cost not measured in dollars but in the erosion of truth and the amplification of deception; the waning of personal interactions; the countless hours of "following" public figures and celebrities and their frivolous tweets and postings; the diminishing value of content, context, and serious reflection; and the constant feeding of the insatiable wolf of vanity at the expense of modesty, discretion, and good old common sense.

That's the bullshit part of the deal.

Chapter 8

Vanishing Common Sense and Assorted Bullshit

Lord, please allow me to be the person my dog thinks I am.

This chapter is a collection of factual stories, mixed thoughts, lighthearted gripes, and not so light musings that underscore the bullshit we encounter every day. As my daughter would say, idiocy is running rampant. These days common sense is at a premium, and I know my readers feel the same way.

1. It was the winter of 1988 in New York, and Mother Teresa's nuns, working to help the homeless, located two abandoned buildings that could, after renovations, serve as shelters. They paid $1 each. With funds set aside for improvements, the nuns were ready, but a year and a half later, nothing had been accomplished. Why? New York's building code got in the way. It required an elevator "in all new or renovated multiple-story buildings...." These cost over $100,000, a sum Mother Teresa did not want to spend, as it added no tangible help for the poor. The city refused to waive the law, and a project that would have helped so many homeless people was abandoned, even though there were more than 100,000 walk-up apartments in New York at the time! [1] Chuck another one for the common sense killers.

2. The Occupational Safety and Health Administration (OSHA) is known to be a bastion of irrationality. Over the decades, they have consistently abandoned common sense and produced volumes of bullshit regulations that serve only to harass businesses. For example, OSHA required the Glen-Gery brick factory in Pennsylvania to post large "Hazardous Material" signs on the side of storage sheds holding *sand*. That's right, sand, which OSAH considers dangerous because, even though identical to the one we find at the beach, and which we have enjoyed for centuries, it contains silica, which science suggests could, under certain conditions, cause cancer. But wait! There's more. The factory, among others, was also forced to include forms with each brick shipment that identify what a brick is: "a granular solid, essentially odorless, in a wide range of colors, with a specific gravity of approximately 2.6. Adding insult to injury in that line of business," OSHA issued 19,233 citations in 1994 for not keeping those forms correctly." [2] Nice job!

3. Here is a question I know you've asked: Why are people always smiling in those ads promoting drugs for chronic conditions? I mean, these folks are suffering from incurable diseases, pains and itches, rashes, incontinence, and worse. Why would they be smiling? The medicine cannot possibly be that good.

4. The same may be asked of ads for health insurance and retirement communities depicting old people—pardon me, I meant to say senior citizens. In these promotions we see men and women over eighty exercising as if they were thirty, all cheery, as if—in the case of males, for example—their prostates were not enlarged. Give me a

break. Most of those folk could not make it through a game of checkers without breaking for a nap.

5. Have you ever found yourself at one of those crosswalks pressing a button on an electrical pole, trying to speed up the red light to get across? What do those contraptions "really" do? Do they expedite the light change to allow your crossing? Of course not! The green/red light cycle will continue as programmed. The buttons are useless, just a sedative to keep us from chancing it across the intersection, something to make us think we are in control. They are "un engaña bobo" (Spanish for something to fool the fools).

6. Why do the passwords to my utility companies' websites have to be so secure? Are they concerned someone will break in and pay my bills?

7. From the "say what?" drawer, we have that at a community college in Washington State, invitations were sent out for a "happy hour" to celebrate diversity and combating racism, but—are you ready for this? The invites stated that "white people were not invited!" [3]

8. Ah, those politicians. Popular columnist George Will shares this deuce with his readers: "Alarmed by reports that global warming will cause a 4-foot rise in sea levels, California Gov. Jerry Brown warned that 'Los Angeles' airport is going to be underwater.'" Well, the airport just happens to be over 120 feet above sea level. [4] Think about it. That means his reelection is assured.

9. George Will shares one more head scratcher: "In Seattle, the Freedom Socialist Party, which favors a $20-an-hour minimum wage, advertised a job opening for a Web developer to be paid $13 an hour." [5] Could you run that one past me again?

10. A South Carolina woman was awarded $4.6 million in a lawsuit after having been stung by a needle at a Target parking lot in May 2014. The woman had just stepped out of her car when her 8-year-old daughter picked up a syringe laying on the asphalt. When she tried to knock the needle out her the girl's hands, she accidentally stung herself. [6] Her lawyer initially wanted $12,000, but Target thought that to be unfair and tried to fight it in court. Big mistake. In our litigious, common sense-starved society, Target was found to be at fault and a jury decided the lady deserved millions in compensation. I don't know about you, but I'm seriously considering going to store parking lots around my area to find one of those prized needles.

11. What happened to the predicted paperless society we heard so much about twenty-thirty years ago? Computers were going to do away with all paper, in the process saving the world's forests. Well, I just had to sign my name twice for a gallon of paint recently—once on the electronic pad, and the other on a paper slip. And let's not forget the endless strips of paper coming out of department store registers, some about two feet long!

12. Does it not simply piss you off when you see those clowns on Wall Street televised with their big smiles applauding at the closing bell every business day even when the market took a beating, and you lost ten percent of your life savings? What are they so happy about?

13. Why is there a monthly maintenance fee on savings accounts? What, exactly, are they maintaining to warrant a $5.00 monthly fee? Is it not enough to be using our money for their own gain while giving us as close to zero interest as possible? At today's rates, on a modest sum, the maintenance fee will overwhelm the meager interest earnings, resulting in a negative investment yield. Explain that to your children and apologize for moving their piggy bank funds into a bank account.

14. What is an "exclusive" offer anyway? Why am I so privileged to get such offers? What makes me so special? Who—I wonder—is being excluded?

15. Why does "deluxe" so frequently refers to the lowest/cheapest choice? For instance, a deluxe room at a hotel is often the crappiest room they have, the lowest priced. Does this make any sense?

16. And aren't you tired of the stream of Bullshit headlines in the Internet? I'm talking about stuff like this: *"NASA just found something big hiding out behind Pluto."* Sounds intriguing, even scary, doesn't it? But when you click on the story's link, you learn that it is referring to a tail-like gas cloud that extends for over 50,000 miles. Well, that might be interesting for those who graduated with a PhD in Astronomy, but not that wowing to a general audience. You can find a plethora of this kind of headlines every frickin day!

17. From the files of the ridiculous: a school girl (high school?) in Orlando may face misdemeanor battery charges for pinching a boy's butt in school. The girl has been temporarily suspended from school, and the boy's mother is considering pressing charges. What are we coming to?!? If a girl had pinched my butt in school I would have been wearing a big grin all day.

18. Heard about the boy who got into trouble in school because he pointed his finger at another student, as if he was imitating the act of shooting a gun? No doubt, had these ridiculous overreactions we see today existed back when I was in elementary school, I—and most of my schoolmates—would have been thrown out of school. Let kids be kids!

19. And let's not forget that back in 2009 the city of New York, in its admirable efforts to protect us from predatory capitalism, fined a 10-year-old $50 for selling lemonade without a permit. How dare he! Kids today, I tell you. That's a criminal in the making.

20. Also around 2009, in Danvers, Massachusetts, a local school went through the trouble of calling each student's parents to inform them that a certain four-letter word had been prohibited in the school. The word? "Meep." That's right—a totally meaningless word from the movie "The Muppets," was not to be used by students. When a local lawyer heard about this, he sent the school an e-mail that read: "Meep." I loved that. So, how did the school respond to this offense? Why, they called the police, of course.

21. How about those unwanted emails. Why do I have to opt out of anything when most of the time I did not voluntarily sign up? How do they keep finding me?!?

22. From the files of the absurd and common sense deficiency, we learn that Citigroup has sued AT&T over the latter's use of the word "thanks" in a new customer-loyalty program that Citigroup claims infringes on their trademarks, including "ThankYou." The banking giant has used the "ThankYou" trademark since 2004, with millions of customers carrying credit cards branded with that label. Thus, Citigroup wants AT&T banned from using the terms. Not surprisingly, AT&T is fighting the lawsuit, stating that "the law does not allow one company to own the word 'thanks.'" [7] No shit, Sherlock! And the lawyers cash in on all this idiocy.

23. So, are eggs good or bad for your health? The answer seems to depend on a coin toss about every three to six months. For years now, eggs have switched from being an essential part of our diets to an evil to be avoided at all costs—and then back. "Experts" of all stripes surface every few months to make their contradictory claims. If you like eggs but they happen to be on a popularity down cycle, don't worry; you won't have to wait long until you are again given the okay to eat them without health consequences.

24. And how do you like the rebate system that retail stores use as a customer torture tool? They make the process as deviously difficult as they can, hoping to avoid making good on their promise to send you money back on your rebate-incentivized purchases. Fill out this form, find a number on the box you just threw away, cut part of a box and attach it to the form, and other idiotic requirements. The steps can be so confusing that some customers will simply do it all wrong (thus, no rebate). Why do they do that? Why don't we just get the discount at the time of purchase and be done? Well, as many readers already figured out, it's all part of a game for which the seller writes the rules. Those businesses are counting on a significant percent of buyers to either forget about sending in the rebate forms, or become frustrated with the instructions, or just plain be too lazy to do it. That's all money that stays in the businesses' bank accounts. Even if you do it right, you'll need to wait six to eight weeks for the money. Rebates need to be outlawed. They are bullshit.

25. What about those phone calls from political candidates? Can't they see that what they are doing is bothering the hell out of people, interrupting their dinner time, and probably pissing them off enough so that many will actually vote against their tormentors? How stupid can those candidates be? Well...they are politicians, so....

This list could be much, much longer. Readers, I'm sure, could add a great deal to the register from their life experiences. How could they not? We are all immersed in bullshit!

Chapter 9

In the News Today — 2041

The following are "predictions" for the not-too-distant future based on the trajectory of social change we are seeing today. Looking ahead about twenty-five years, the attempt at humor and obvious sarcasm are not likely to go unnoticed by the reader, who will ultimately decide how effective these future "news" items capture the essence, the flavor of this book. Here we go.

- Superstar actor Rod Jones was awarded the coveted Miley Cyrus Prize for excellence in the performing arts. The former porn star's thirty-year career included six Oscars, twenty-two Oscar nominations, and four Emmy awards. This much admired Hollywood icon, whom *Rolling Stone* has called "larger than life" and "an inspiration to young people everywhere," is best known for his dramatic roles in the blockbusters *Unprotected Sex in Paris, The Broken Condom,* and the hilarious romantic comedy *The Last Tango With My Sister.* The Emmys recognized Jones' unforgettable work in the popular television series *Bedroom Trapeze* and *Loving Fido, and* the sitcoms *Under the Sheets with Harry and Sally* and *Erectile Dysfunction,* the latter sponsored by Viagra for over ten years. After his retirement Jones wants to write illustrated children's books and continue his current family-oriented blog, "Pre-pubescent Sexuality," which has been a hit with pre-teens and a highly acclaimed source of child-rearing advice for millions of parents for years.

- Another superstar, the hip hop artist I. M. Abadass, was released from prison today after serving six days of a forty year sentence for drug trafficking, rape and aggravated assault. His attorney worked out a deal where the remaining thirty-nine plus years of the sentence will be reduced to thirty days of community service and two months of unsupervised house arrest. Abadass was deeply grateful and visibly emotional, declaring: "Praise da'Lord! This nigga here, no never did nothing, so f... da judge, f... da jury, f... da press. Y'all mother f...ers can kiss my badass. And now I'ma gonna make a song 'bout all this' shit and make ten million. God is good..."

- Kim Kardashian was released from the hospital in Beverly Hills earlier today after undergoing her fifth Brazilian butt lift in the last eight years. Kardashian took to Twitter, saying "May be the last time; Hope Kanye happy now." Unlike after her previous buttock augmentation surgeries, there were no "post-surgery" social media postings of her derriere, which has greatly disappointed her fans. The buzz is that the 60-year-old super celebrity is unhappy with the results of her latest procedure, but it is also rumored that she is trying to work out a "pay-per-view" deal with HBO. She is also about to launch her eleventh reality TV show this fall, with an estimated audience of 180 million viewers.

- Running as a Democrat, Oregon ex-convict Rudolph Conman has won his bid for a senate seat with an unprecedented 86% of the vote. Conman, who previously served ten years in jail for his part in a massive 2027 ponzi scheme that cost victims in excess of $8 billion and another four years for child abuse and the attempted murder of his ex-wife, will fill the seat vacated by his previous fellow inmate, Republican Mark Thisdown, who served six years for Medicare fraud and was fined $100,000 for distribution of child pornography without a state permit in 2031.

- Next week, the U.S. Supreme Court begins deliberations on the legalization of infanticide. It is expected to be a highly contentious issue among the justices in what appears will be a very close vote. While opponents view the practice as murder, utterly barbaric, proponents argue from historical precedent—as infanticide was legal in ancient times—and also appeal to the 1973 ruling in Roe Vs. Wade where a mother's wishes trumps the fetus' claim to life. The point is made that an infant is entirely dependent on at least one parent for survival, similar to a fetus. However, unlike abortion, the father's consent would also be required, should the court rule in favor of infanticide. Complicating the issue, these qualifiers could apply to children as old as seventeen, and that is likely to result in bitter debate among the justices.

- In other news, Russia, Iran, North Korea, China, and Cuba condemned Israel for its disproportionate response to Palestinian bombings in Gaza. UN Secretary-General, Mohammed Humanei Kalemini, Nihelameni, called for a cease fire—the fourth this month—until both sides can be brought back to the negotiating table. Meanwhile the United States warned the adversaries for the eighth time since last week that continued hostilities could lead to an embargo on sophisticated rockets the U.S. currently supplies to Hamas as well as defensive missiles it provides Israel to defend against Hamas' projectiles. The Palestinians blame the Israelis for starting the fracas, and the Israelis place the blame on the Palestinians. Nihelameni expressed hope that the three-thousand-year-old conflict will come to a swift end once both parties are brought back to the negotiating table in Geneva for their 647th meeting since 1956.

- The United States will send another 1,850,000 *advisers* to Iraq to speed up the training of 25 Iraqi troops for their sixteenth attempt to retake Mosul from CRAP (Children of Redemptive Allah's Peacekeepers). Adhering to his promise of "no American boots on the ground," President Shady expressed confidence that this latest boost in training personnel will make a significant difference in the course of the war. NATO's air campaign is expected to continue, but White House spokesman Billy Lair expressed concern with recent statements by eighty-nine-year-old Russian President Vladimir Putin that threatened to stop delivery of missiles and spare parts for American fighter jets. Without these, the task of maintaining NATO aircraft combat ready— outsourced to two companies in China last year—could be seriously compromised. Equally concerning is that China may halt delivery of five recognizance satellites the Pentagon purchased last June for over ten billion dollars.

- Meanwhile, due to a recent spike in the number of American tourists visiting South Korea, North Korea again threatened the United States with "a merciless, unprecedented, massive nuclear strike that will bring the North American monster to its knees and shower everlasting glory on the liberated people of the Free and Democratic Republic of North Korea." The Pentagon responded with a one-ship Navy exercise just outside of Hawaiian waters and a surfing competition in Honolulu.

- In a related story, North Korean leader, Kip, Kom, Kum is reportedly angry over a recent U.S. decision to begin providing billions in economic aid to China while disapproving a similar aid package for his nation. He again threatened the "evil, imperialist, capitalist giant" with nuclear punishment of historic proportions, the likes of which "have never, and will never again be seen." The White House, reiterating that it takes all threats to the nation seriously, ordered new uniforms for all service men and women stationed in the Philippines and cautioned sailors to avoid North Korean-owned bars.

- In sports, disgraced Miami Dolphins linebacker Mitch Brown Jr. again apologized for his insensitive statement that he prefers not to date Asian women, a Tweeter comment that went viral in minutes and prompted violent demonstrations in Thailand, South Korea, Vietnam, and China. Nail salons across the United States shut down in protest. North Korea fired three missiles towards the Pacific Ocean (two failed to launch). It is expected that no later than tomorrow the president will be issuing formal apologies to every Asian nation, including California. Meanwhile, the NFL suspended Brown for ten games, and is considering sanctions against the Dolphins. Also, the Beijing Dragons, last year's Super Bowl winners, are considering dropping the Dolphins from next season's schedule. In a statement for NBC News, NFL Commissioner David Pigskin stated: "Such tactless, racist statements cannot, and will not, be tolerated by the league."

- Also in sports, New York Yankees outfielder Ivany Gonzagi has been released on his own recognizance after he brutally beat his ex-wife into a coma and set fire to her apartment. His attorney, the highly regarded H.P. Sleezer, stated that Gonzagi—who only has four other similar incidents of violence in his record, including pushing his misbehaving ten-year-old son over a third floor balcony—should not be suspended from any games pending a trial. Gonzagi is expected to sign a $780 million multiyear deal with the Yankees on Friday.

Let's finish this book.

AFTERWORD

As this book has labored to show, bullshit is imbedded in our culture. It affects nearly every area of our lives—from the corrupt politicians in Washington to those just as sleazy at the state and local levels, from the greedy big banks and heartless insurance companies to the deceitful used-car salesman in our neighborhood corner, from the lowbrow world of entertainment with its offensive music, mindless TV shows, and celebrity-worshipping Hollywood culture to the erroneous "facts" taught in schools and absurd courses offered in universities. Even science and religion contribute their share of bullshit, as does the senseless and egotistical material circulating on social media. The sources are, without exaggeration, too numerous to list.

In particular, the rampant corruption in the political arena and our collective surrender to the damaging influence of the entertainment industry are a concern of mine, as they reflect a growing cultural pathology that, when taken to its logical conclusion, threatens a disturbing future where that which we can still call unethical and depraved today will be completely absorbed into the social code. We are exchanging long-cherished values and standards of conduct for that daily amusement fix that Huxley warned us about in *Brave New World*. The issue is compounded by continuously evolving, dazzling technologies that insistently call on us in an era of diminishing attention spans. Our intellectual muscles are enfeebled by the preponderance of the sound bite, which reduces complex ideas to a handful of words. Thus, the noise makers, the over simplifiers, the outrageous attention-grabbers drown out substance and serious thoughts and opinions. Bullshit today has a much easier path to our over stimulated brains. The ease with which politicians and scammers of all stripes defeat our defenses against bullshit and overwhelm our critical thinking capacity as well as our adulation of debauchers and criminals in the music scene are symptoms of this social malady.

Consequently, while it seems like a quixotic endeavor to attempt to stop—and even more difficult, to reverse—the current trend, it is the responsibility of high-minded individuals to try. At the very least let's stay vigilant, alert to old and new forms of deception, as there are no limits to the imaginative ways with which bullshitters can seize power, take our money, and charm us into moral compromises. We also need to teach our children to see through all the toxic smoke, the deceit, the sensationalism, the contrived and licentious lifestyles promoted by the entertainment media, those warped mirrors of illusion that distort our vision and misdirect our priorities.

Finally, although much of the book may be seen as the ranting of an aging baby boomer, someone who is out of step with today's zeitgeist, I sincerely hope that this text has stimulated some serious reflection, taught you something you did not know; provided validation for a few of your views; raised some earnest, thought-provoking challenges to your beliefs; and that—in spite of its serious framework—it managed to integrate enough humor to elicit a few good laughs. If it managed to accomplish at least a couple of those aims, then, from the standpoint of this author, the book is a success, and the effort that went into writing it was worthwhile.

APPENDICES

Appendix A

The Home Insurance Scandal in Florida

With Florida in the midst of what can legitimately be called an insurance crisis, the state's home insurer of last resort, Citizens Insurance, has been engaged in a program to shed most—and eventually all—its policies since 2012. Ostensibly created because private insurance companies were leaving the state in droves, Citizens is feverishly working to reverse the trend, claiming that should a damaging hurricane strike the state, it may not be able to cover so many policyholders, forcing the state to levy special tax assessments to cover the gap. This has been shown to be essentially bullshit, as the company has a huge funds surplus, the beneficiary of over ten consecutive years without a significant storm striking the state (not to mention that Citizens is additionally protected with backup insurance).

Citizens is "encouraging" its policyholders to move to another company by repeatedly raising premiums, now often reaching ridiculous amounts that make the policies grossly unaffordable. Interestingly, this opportunity to make a kill on premiums has not yet brought too many of the big old players back into the game (e.g. State Farm, Allstate), established companies that left the state to avoid the risks, but the state government is not too worried about that for, you see, young startup companies are willing to pick up the slack. Coincidentally, these new companies are headed by individuals—at least one of which is under suspicion for fraud—with previous ties to government officials and, coincidentally, a number of these companies have contributed to the election funds of some of those officials, including—surprise!—Rick Scott, the illustrious governor.

The final stake in the heart of taxpayers and policyholders is that Citizens is actually paying these companies to do business! One of the companies, Heritage Property Insurance Company, had only been around for nine months, but after contributing $110,000 toward Scott's reelection campaign, it landed a windfall of $52 million, paid by Citizens for Heritage just to take over 60,000 policies. Now, let's pause and ask: Can it get worse and more scandalous? Yes! Yes, it can. Remember, this is Florida. Not only are these new, unstable companies the beneficiaries of handouts, they are actually allowed to "select" (read "cherry pick") the policies that they want—retroactively—so that in effect *they can choose all policies for which there have been no claims.* Translation: Guaranteed profits (incoming premiums without outgoing claims money) plus a direct cash payment for accepting those guaranteed profits.

However, the insults to Floridians continue. As of July 2016, Heritage was working to further squeeze policyholders with a huge premium increase that could reach about

20% in South Florida, even 25% in some cases, even though no hurricanes have struck the state for years. Meanwhile their CEO's compensation *quadrupled* in twelve months to a tune of $27 million! [1] Who says greed has limits? Now, there has been some push back on this scandalous rate hike, and it's possible Heritage will back off (but for how long?).

The stink from this load of home insurance bullshit is intolerable, worse than at a Spanish bullring, and the people of Florida, especially under the rule of the unsympathetic, money-hungry governor Rick Scott, have to breath it all in.

Appendix B

Corporate Euphemism and Lingo

Company Phrase	What it Really Means
Because we value you as a customer ...	Since you're in our mailing list of past or potential buyers, here is a deceptively worded offer that will make us money if we can get you to accept it.
For your protection ...	To safeguard our business, we are going to put you through an annoying process of some kind or take away some benefit, convenience, or advantage.
To serve you better. ..	To lower the cost of our operations and/or make things easier for us, we are going to change the way we do some things that will result in an inconvenience to you.
Your call is important to us ...	Due to vicious staff reductions to cut our costs to the bone, we are going to put you on hold for a long time and then connect you to a low-paid clerk sitting on a desk halfway around the world who can hardly speak your language and who will likely not provide any useful answers to your questions.
To bring you more choices ...	To try to sell you new products and services that you don't really need but will increase our profits ...
If you have any questions, please visit our website at www.xyzzz.com ...	We are steering calls away from our few remaining employees who really know what's going on and leaving you on your own to navigate our indecipherable website for hours, finding "answers" that will rarely satisfy you.
Because we value your opinion ...	Here is a time-consuming survey that will let us figure out what turns you on, so we can sell you more stuff.
The company will be *reengineering* to implement more efficient methods ...	Many employees will lose their jobs or be reassigned to lower-paying positions as we outsource several functions to India and the Phillipines and try to squeeze out of our remaining staff.
Our new and improved product	The same gadget in a different color and design with possibly a few new functions that no one needs.
Our product is guaranteed ...	We assume you will not read the fine print where our team of lawyers has cleverly helped us wiggle out of any responsibility.

Appendix C

The Cell Line Contamination Scandal

(Excerpt from *Reclaiming the Afterlife*)

[Source: Jill Neimark, *Discover Nov. 2014*] [1]

Perhaps the most disturbing of all indignities in modern science is the dogged unwillingness of many researchers to acknowledge that what are known as cell lines—critical for laboratory research—are oftentimes contaminated and thus likely to skew experimental results. This scandalous revelation, however, has been largely ignored for decades. Tragically, many researchers have chosen to look away from the evidence of contamination and turned a deaf ear on those sounding the alarm, and the implications are enormous. In the words of Kenneth Ain, director of the oncology program at the University of Kentucky at Lexington: "Research based on such false cell lines would undermine the understanding of different cancers and possible treatments, and clutter the scientific literature with bogus conclusions.

Considered the "workhorses of biology," cell lines are "immortal" and used in virtually all laboratories to learn about cellular behavior, including in-depth understanding of normal and malignant physiology. According to Jill Neimark, science journalist, author, and contributing editor for *Discover Magazine,* all of today's cancer drugs were initially tested using these cells as models. The problem is that many of these cell lines are not what they purport to be!

Human error is at the root of the problem. Contamination can begin in various ways, including from a researcher working on two cell lines simultaneously, scientists sharing equipment or lab locations, or a dispenser used more than once. Ain himself was an unsuspecting victim, having used contaminated cell lines early in his career, innocently donated to him by the head of radiation oncology at UCLA. Years later, when he learned that much of his work developing highly-valued cell lines for the study of thyroid cancer were not really thyroid cancer cells but melanoma and colon cancer instead, he was devastated. He is now engaged in raising awareness in the scientific community, but his warnings are not always welcomed. In his words:

> I now give regular lectures about cell line contamination...and every last person in the audience is shocked and horrified. But most scientists are not willing to test and verify their lines. The NIH doesn't require it. Very few journals require it. And I can tell you that many scientists are reluctant to disembowel their curriculum vitae, even after they find out a cell line is false. What is an ethical researcher to do?

Neimark explains that in different areas of cancer research, "up to a third of all cell lines have been identified as imposters." The significance of this shocking revelation cannot be exaggerated, but even more appalling is that "this fact is widely ignored, and the lines continue to be used under their false identities." The horror continues.

According to geneticist Christopher Korch, former director of the University of Colorado's DNA Sequencing Analysis & Core Facility, "[t]here are about 10,000 citations every year on false lines—new publications that refer to or rely on papers based on imposter cell lines."

Based on what we've learned about how those who "rock the boat" are treated in the scientific community, Ain is playing dice with his career. Consider what happened to Walter Nelson-Rees, expert in culturing human and animal cells at the University of California, Berkely, and who ran a cell line bank in Oakland. In the period 1975-1981, he publicized the cell line contamination problem and identified the laboratories of origin. This immediately made him persona-non-grata, severely criticized by peers as a "vigilante." Neimark tells us the result: "Nelson-Rees' work made it clear that...contamination was far from the only problem. Eventually, the NIH terminated his contract, and he became so isolated from his peers that he left science and became an art dealer."

Ethical scientists who have honestly reported problems with cell lines they originated have not fared well either. Microbiologist Thomas Klonisch of the University of Manitoba is one example. In 2005 he created a highly-sought cell line to study the effects of estrogen and progesterone in the uterine lining, among other uses, including investigations into endometrial cancer. Unfortunately, his line was tainted, something that came to light years later when some users of the cell discovered the problem. Eventually, faced with the indisputable evidence of contamination, Klonisch "did what a good scientist must: He offered corrections to the relevant journals, which have since published them. 'My reputation was tarnished...and all my research in this field has been shut down. And we never intended any of this."

According to Neimark, cell lines that have been known to be false for almost fifty years are still in wide use today, still carrying the names of what they are supposed to be, "wrong identities regularly invoked in peer-reviewed publications." A consequence of this unpardonable lapse of ethics resulted in the use of false lines in early trials of two cancer drugs (bexarotene and vemurafenib) that were then tested on human subjects suffering from thyroid cancer; not surprisingly, both drugs failed.

It is disheartening that oftentimes, when scientists have been informed that their cell line is an imposter, they try to evade the issue by claiming their line's behavior or appearance does not resemble said imposter. Or they play with the terminology, as explained by experimental pathologist John Master of University College in London who "tells of a normal endothelium line that turned out to be bladder cancer, but researchers still refer to it as 'endothelial-like' so they can use it in studies....They clearly know that these are not endothelial cells, but to get around it and not admit they are bladder cancer cells, they call them 'endothelial-like." I don't know how they reconcile the sleight of hand. It is beyond my comprehension."

A big part of the problem, of course, is that there are reputations at stake, often decades of work that could be rendered useless if the truth emerges. Consequently, these individuals endeavor to erase their scent from a trail of lies and deception by liberally spreading the bullshit in all directions.

More About the Vermin that Populates the World of Hip Hop

It was 6 a.m. at Cheeseburger Baby in Miami Beach, a popular spot for night owls where celebrities can be frequently seen grabbing a bite after a long night of partying. This particular morning early in 2013 saw a famous rapper's posse of five walk in and demand five cheeseburgers, pronto. They also made it clear that they were to be served ahead of other customers because "someone real famous" was waiting outside in the car. The owner, Stephanie Vitori, stood her ground: "First come, first served," she said. So they waited and were eventually given their burgers, which they took back to the waiting vehicle. However, that was not the end of the little story.

Minutes later, the well-known rapper—Busta Rhymes—showed up—angry. He was unhappy because his burger's condiments had been placed on the side (something the restaurant does to prevent the buns from turning soggy), and not on the burger itself as he liked. So Rhymes walked up to the checkout clerk and screamed: "F---you! I'm not leaving until I get ketchup, mayo, salt, and pepper on my burger." Vitori tried to intervene, a mistake, as she was on the receiving end of a classic "F...you, bitch!" The abuse continued until Vitori called 911, and before police could respond, Rhymes and his posse were gone.[1] Let's review one more anecdote.

As amply demonstrated in Chapter 4, in the perverse world of hip hop, nothing is off limits, and crime is glorified. The following example combines a criminal mind with the rap industry's notorious devaluation of women. It deals with Miami rapper's Rick Ross's release of a song titled U.O.E.N.O., a phonetic representation of "You don't even know." The lyrics go like this: *"Put molly all in her champagne; She ain't even know it; I took her home and I enjoyed that; She ain't even know it."* Molly is one of the street names for the drug ecstasy, a powerful hallucinogen that lowers inhibitions. In effect, rapper Ross is singing about date rape

Now, quite surprisingly, in this case there was considerable push back and criticism, with various groups taking action against Ross. The women's advocacy group UltraViolet tried to hurt him in the pocketbook, pressuring Reebok to cancel its endorsement contract with him, and a number of radio stations pulled all his songs off the air. Ouch! said, Ross. That was not what I meant, he tried to explain as he began to bleed dollars. "The people who heard the song made a mistake." "'It was a misunderstanding with a lyric, a misinterpretation. The term rape wasn't used. I would never use the term rape in my records.'" As columnist Leonard Pitts Jr. succinctly complains: "As if not saying 'rape' prohibits him from describing rape."[2] Unfortunately, rapper Ross is just one of many, many examples of the despicable criminal element that pervades the hip hop scene.

Appendix E

All Bullshit Aside: An Increasingly Amoral World—Why?
A Brief Analysis and Commentary

Although my lambasting of the entertainment industry in Chapter 4 might lead the reader to conclude that I'm laying the blame for our amusement-addicted, intellectually-lazy, morally-diminished society squarely on the shoulders of television, movie producers, and narcissistic celebrities (particularly the degenerates who have populated the hip hop scene for decades), that is not an entirely accurate inference. The political landscape lampooned in Chapter 1 and the corporate world condemned in Chapter 2 are also vital pieces of the cultural mosaic of our times. Unethical politicians, corporations, and entertainers, together with a population willing to surrender societal controls to those entities in exchange for reduced civic responsibilities, simple solutions to complex issues, and escapist, brain-dulling amusement, all blend into a perfect storm. Yet, these are only the manifestation, the symptoms, of an underlying existential crisis. What is this crisis about?

Unfortunately, a truly thorough examination of that question is hopelessly beyond the scope of this book, and the simple *why* question in the title of this appendix exposes the inadequacy of any small piece of writing attempting to wrestle with such a consequential theme. Nevertheless, cognizant that succinctness in this matter carries a steep price, I will endeavor to get to the heart of the matter to avoid leaving the reader holding a question mark.

The crisis I'm talking about is about meaning, the absence of a moral compass, and the deeply troubling reality of human mortality. As maintained in my book *Reclaiming the Afterlife*, a significant factor fueling those human concerns is the growing spiritual void created by the waning of religion's influence over the last two centuries (more on that further ahead), a process that has accelerated as science continues to pummel any illusion that there is anything special about planet earth and its inhabitants. Thus, the number of people who practice religion has steadily declined, while many of those who still profess faith are not as steadfast in their beliefs as was more common not so many years ago. Since religion has traditionally been the bedrock of moral guidance for most people, its decline has left millions of individuals living without a firm ethical foundation, without a strong, dependable, higher power to steer them through life and give them hope for a future beyond the flesh. In famed philosopher Nietzsche's words: "God is dead."

Consequently, as a society, we are now essentially hollow. There is an emptiness in our souls that cannot be easily filled. Furthermore, our moral compass is gyrating. We can't find our North, and thus morality is increasingly undefined; it is completely relative, wide open to interpretation. The imperative to be fair, compassionate, faithful, decent, trustworthy, considerate, reliable, kind, and polite—in short, to be as good as we can be—has no solid base. It becomes difficult to justify pursuing and promoting any such high ideals because there is no absolute authority on the matter. Hence, today it is common to hear people say, "Don't preach at me. To you it may be wrong if I [fill in the blank], but not to me, and I choose to [fill in the blank]. It's all relative anyway. Who says I can't? Where is it written?" Thus, conscience is reduced, and having empathy as well as feeling remorse, shame, or embarrassment for having violated traditional norms of behavior are no longer the nearly universal traits of the average person of yore. I'm not talking about prudish behavior; I'm talking about basic decency and integrity.

Unquestionably, many people, religious or not, behave ethically for the most part because that is their nature (or they were very well taught by their parents). Others maintain a degree of civility simply for fear of repercussion. The thinking being something like this: I don't steal because it's against the law, and I could end up in jail. I don't cut in front of you at the supermarket checkout because I don't want it done to me. Furthermore, as a society, we have decided that harming others, such as killing another human being or stealing, is wrong and will be punished, but whereas in the past the justification for such decrees was found in absolute commands supported by scripture, such as the Bible's "Thou shall not kill", these directives are now only defensible under the common sense need to survive and maintain a civilized environment in which to live and thrive.

However, man-made laws do not carry the moral weight of divine laws, and thus, collectively, the enticement to be good—or even the fear and pressure to act ethically—is weaker. Without a mutually accepted set of principles ordained by a respected, authoritative agent (which is the role religion has played stressing fear of God and His judgment and also the potential rewards to be found in Heaven), the communal inducement to observe the laws and uphold those high principles are diminished. How did we get to this point? What happened?

Beginning in the nineteenth century, science, and in particular Darwinian evolution, took God out of the picture and put random, impersonal, natural processes in control. Suddenly, humans were not God's special creatures. Darwin had cut them down to size. Homo Sapiens were highly successful survivors as per natural selection, but so were cockroaches. By sheer luck, our evolving brains outpaced other species, and—along with other randomly-obtained, beneficial physical adaptations—we became the technological ape, able to exert some degree of control over our environment and the other creatures sharing the planet. The rest, as they say, is history.

The first tremors that threatened the notion of human divinity began with the discoveries of Copernicus and Galileo, which took our planet away from the center of the solar system (and later, away from the universal center). This also exposed the Church's limitations in terms of absolute access to the truth, which, together with the disappointing conduct and corruption of so-called religious leaders, saw the rumblings among common folk become louder. It was the beginning of the Enlightenment, the age of reason, which spurred the challenge to religious dogma and the retreat of the Church as a controlling agent in people's lives, increasing reliance on science, promoting the concept of liberty and engendering the notion of the separation of church and state, all revolutionary, positive steps in the development of human thought.

However, it was Darwin's blow to our collective psyche that shattered the pedestal supporting religion and invalidated centuries upon centuries of human exceptionality as a special creation of the Almighty (or the gods). Consequently, fear of death, of personal extinction, soared, as did a pervasive feeling of meaninglessness in a completely indifferent universe where the distinction between right and wrong were no longer so clearly defined. That is when a large part of humanity fell, helpless, into a moral dilemma and a spiritual void.

Later, the twentieth and twenty-first centuries exploded with scientific discoveries that, especially in biology and astronomy, strongly supported evolutionary theory and earth's diminishing importance in the cosmos. This helped further entrench the dominant philosophy of today—materialism, with its view that the universe is purposeless, the concepts of mind and free will are illusions, humans are nothing more than complex biological machines operating randomly, and the idea of an afterlife is just wishful thinking. And we fell deeper into the void.

This period of accelerated scientific advances and technological development also brought us unprecedented carnage in warfare and atrocities against civilian populations. Massive bombing of cities and the systematic mass extermination of human beings, along with the unleashing of the power of the atom—which brought us within a button's push to total annihilation—left humanity powerless, vulnerable, in a state of collective anxiety and paranoia, with nowhere to hide or a deity to protect us. And we plunged further into the abyss.

With no protective heavenly agent, we also found ourselves helpless in the face of the terror and misery that a totally impersonal Mother Nature capriciously unleashed on us—floods that killed thousands in Bangladesh; earthquakes that caved in the roofs of schools full of children in Chile; tornados that leveled towns in the Midwest; famines and epidemics that wiped out thousands in Ethiopia. Deeper, deeper still into the cavernous emptiness of our collective soul.

Consequently, the disturbing thoughts of a limited lifespan imbued with insignificance and purposelessness, ruled by a whimsical and indiscriminate natural world, followed by personal extinction (no hope for an afterlife) have been devastating to the world's psyche—and still are. Since religion has waned (at least in western nations), who or what provides hope and guidance now? There is no universally recognized spiritual guide or moral authority, so what do we do? How do we deal with such overwhelming forces in an uncaring, hostile world? We seek to escape; that's what we do.

Escape mostly takes the form of distraction at all cost; that becomes our refuge. However, distractive activities are limited in duration, and so we are compelled to seek more, and then more, entertainment. Some commit their lives to careers or lofty goals of helping others, finding the cure for a deadly disease, supporting charities, and so on, striving to ease the pain and burden of the human condition; that's their escape route. But as noble and commendable as those pursuits are, they only partially fill the spiritual vacuum, and besides, that is not the path that most people choose, in general. Instead, we get caught in the spinning wheel of pleasure-seeking and endless amusement, and we don't want to get off because, viewed from today's pessimistic, anxiety-riddled perspective, the alternative is grim. We are scared. We are afraid to pose the poignant, philosophical question popularized in the title of a popular sixties' song: "Is that all there is?"

From this writer's perspective, the answer is *no*, that is not all there is. There is more, and that is because, contrary to what materialism tells us, we are much more than just evolved, organic automatons. Our consciousness transcends the physical realm. There is an afterlife. When our physical bodies expire in this phase of existence, our soul's journey through the universe continues. That is a huge claim that takes us well beyond the scope of this book, but I am convinced of its veracity. Years of research led me to that conclusion, and I urge interested readers to look at the results of my investigation in my previous book, *Reclaiming the Afterlife*.

In the meantime, enjoy life, engage in worthwhile activities, be as good a person as you can be, and reject what you know is evil, unethical, and demeaning. And do not be afraid of death; it doesn't exist. Instead, when your time to go is at hand, look forward with joyful anticipation for the next step in your human experience—your life in the afterlife.

About The Author

Roberto J. Herrera was born in Havana, Cuba in 1949 (although he doesn't remember) and migrated to the United States in 1961 along with his parents and younger sister, Liliana. He lives in Miami, Florida with his loving wife, Lourdes and a crazy mutt, Icy. His forty-five year marriage brought a wonderful pair of children—a son, Robert and a daughter, Jennifer—now married adults, and later two bright and energetic grandchildren—Roberto-Andres and Sabrina—from his son. Daughter-in-law, Barbi and son-in-law, Jeff, have brought a great deal of joy to the family. Sports such as tennis, basketball, and occasional cycling keep Roberto active, but reading and writing are his everyday rituals.

Roberto teaches English composition and literature at Florida International University and holds two degrees, a master's in English (2001) and a bachelor's in Economics (1975). His master's thesis, *1984: A Synthesis of George Orwell's Life and Works*, under the guidance of a superb steering committee headed by Major Professor Dr. Asher A. Milbauer and complemented by Dr. Richard Schwartz and Dr. Donald G. Watson, afforded him the opportunity to refine his research and writing skills in a setting far more challenging than the standard classroom. Before joining the FIU faculty in 2004, he was employed by the Federal Reserve Bank of Atlanta—Miami Branch for more than three decades (1971-2004), mostly as a computer systems analyst.

The author's lifelong passion is the pursuit of existential questions, such as Does God exist? Is there life after death? Why is there evil in the world? Do humans have a soul, or are we—as science insists—just biological machines shaped by evolution? Do people truly possess psychic abilities? Are near-death experiences what they appear to be? And who has the better answers to those questions: science or religion? Years of pondering these issues, along with pivotal personal experiences, led Roberto to conduct extensive research in hopes of finding satisfactory answers, and this culminated in his first book, *Common Sense Spirituality in a Secular Age"* (2010), which was revised, updated, and re-titled *Reclaiming the Afterlife* (2014).

Nevertheless, the author's interests span many other areas of human concern, as demonstrated by the book you are holding.

Readers wishing to contact the author, please send emails to the following address: *SpiritLogic@bellsouth.net*

Endnotes

Chapter 1

[1] *"Rick Scott has spent $12.8 million on his own re-election,"* Washington Examiner, *accessed June 22, 2015,* campaignhttp://www.washingtonexaminer .com/rick-scott-has-spent-12.8-million-on-his-own-re-election-campaign/article/ 2555596.

[2] Ibid.

[3] *"Rick Scott,"* https://en.wikipedia.org/wiki/Rick_Scott#America.27s_Health_ Network _. 28AHN.29.

[4] *"Fast-checking the Florida Democrats' Latest Attack on Rick Scott,"* Politifact, accessed June 21, 2015, http://www.politifact.com/florida/article/2010/oct/12/fact-checking-democrats-latest-attack-rick-scott/.

[5] "Crist says Scott pleaded Fifth 75 times 'to avoid jail,'" accessed Sept. 7, 2015, http://www.politifact.com/florida/statements/2014/sep/25/charlie-crist/crist-says-scott-pleaded-fifth-75-times-avoid-jail/.

[6] "Fast-checking the Florida Democrats' Latest Attack on Rick Scott," Politifact, accessed June 21, 2015, http://www.politifact.com/florida/article/2010/oct/12/fact-checking-democrats-latest-attack-rick-scott/.

[7] "Pay Up, Mr. Scott!," *The Miami Herald*, August 11, 2015, 8A.

[8] Steve Bousquet and Michael van Sickler, "Ousted FDLE chief raises new allegations about meddling by Gov. Rick Scott, aides," *The Tampa Bay Times*, January 17, 2015, http://www.tampabay.com/news/politics/stateroundup/ousted-fdle-chief-raises-new-allegations-about-meddling-by-gov-rick-scott/2214084.

[9] Carl Hiaasen, "Scott Picks' the Public's Pockets," *The Miami Herald*, August 16, 2015, 1L.

[10] Michael Vasquez, "Perez, politicians: friends to the end," *The Miami Herald*, November 8, 2015, 1A.

[11] Frank Cerabino, "Dade Medical's fall bad for some pols," *The Miami Herald*, November 5, 2015.

[12] Michael Vasquez, "Dade Medical College's Ernesto Perez pleads guilty," *The Miami Herald*, November 10, 2015, 4A.

[13] Fred Grimm, "Ernesto Perez bought lots of friends," *The Miami Herald*, November 5, 2015.

[14] "In Florida, officials ban term 'climate change', *The Miami Herald*, " March 8, 2015.

[15] "All Statements Involving Rick Scott," *Politifact*, accessed July 28, 2015, http://www.politifact.com/personalities/rick-scott/statements/.

[16] William Douglas and Lesley Clark, "Amid Recent Turmoil, Trump takes a tumble in Wisconsin poll," *McClatchy Washington Bureau*, published in *The Miami Herald*, March 31, 2016.

[17] Andres Oppenheimer, "Analyzing Trump's Hispanic Delusion," The Miami Herald, March 17, 2016, 13A.

[18] Ian Tuttle, "Yes, Trump University was a massive scam," *The National Review*, February 28, 2016, http://www.nationalreview.com/corner/432010/trump-university-scam.

[19] Ibid.

[20] Ibid.

[21] Fabiola Santiago, "Who kissed Trump's Read end? Pam Bondi, AP reports," *The Miami Herald*, June 8, 2016, 3A.

[22] Ibid.

[23] "Donald Trump," https://en.wikipedia.org/wiki/Donald_Trump.

[24] William A. Gaston, "A Myopic Shift Toward Trump," *The Wall Street Journal*, January 27, 2016.

[25] Ibid.

[26] Stuart Anderson, "Trump The Hypocrite: Investing Overseas Fine For Him," *Forbes*, August 17, 2015, http://www.forbes.com/sites/stuartanderson/2015/08/17/trump-the-hypocrite-investing-overseas-fine-for-him/#636c0b87936b.

[27] Fred Grimm, "Hulk Hogan and other great legal issues," *The Miami Herald*, March 22, 2016.

[28] Leonard Pitts Jr. "Not every guy is a piece of scum," *The Miami Herald*, October 12. 2016.

[29] Tony Schwartz, *The Week*, July 29, 2016, pp. 12, first printed in *The New Yorker*.

[30] Carl Hiaasen, "Vote comes down to Liar vs. Liar," *The Miami Herald*, May 29, 2016,

4B.

[31] H. A. Goodman, "If Hillary Clinton Isn't Influenced by Wall Street Cash, Then Why Overturn Citizens United?" *Huffington Post*, accessed May, 2016, http://www.huffingtonpost.com/h-a-goodman/if-hillary-clinton-isnt-influenced-by-wall-street-cash_b_9165672.html.

[32] Open Secrets.Org, Hillary Clinton, accessed May 7, 2016, https://www.opensecrets.org/ politicians/contrib.php?cid=N00000019&cycle=Career.

[33] Anne Gearan, "Can Hillary Clinton Overcome her Trust Problem?" *The Washington Post*, accessed August 6, 2016, https://www.washingtonpost.com/politics/can-hillary-clinton-overcome-her-trust-problem/2016/07/03/b12eeb52-3fd8-11e6-84e8-1580c7db5275_story.

[34] Doyle McManus, "Latest polling has Democrats in a panic," *Los Angeles Times*, (reprinted in *The Miami Herald*, May 26, 2016).

[35] "DC's "Ten Most Wanted Corrupt Politicians," *Judicial Watch*, Dec. 30, 2011, http://www.judicialwatch.org/press-room/weekly-updates/dcs-ten-most-wanted-corrupt-politicians/.

[36]"Nancy Pelosi," accessed Aug. 17, 2015, https://en.wikipedia.org/wiki/Nancy_Pelosi.

[37] "DC's Ten Most Wanted Corrupt Politicians," *Judicial Watch*, December 30, 2011, http://www.judicialwatch.org/press-room/weekly-updates/dcs-ten-most-wanted-corrupt-politicians/.

[38] Lachian, Markay, " Pelosi Subsidies Benefit Husband's Investment in Dem Mega-Donor's Company," *The Washington Free Beacon*, August 15, 2014, http://freebeacon.com/politics/pelosi-subsidies-benefit-husbands-investment-in-dem-mega-donors-company/.

[39] "Ten Most Wanted Corrupt Politicians for 2011," Decembet 26 2011, http://www.judicialwatch.org/corrupt-politicians-lists/washingtons-ten-most-wanted-corrupt-politicians-for-2011/.

[40] "60 Minutes' Reporter Kroft Gets Tough With Pelosi During Press Conference," November 3, 2011, *The Blaze*, http://www.theblaze.com/stories/2011/11/03/60-minutes-reporter-kroft-gets-tough-with-pelosi-during-press-conference/.

[41] *Wynton Hall. "60 Minutes STOCK Act Follow-up Sends Warning Signal to Congress"* Breitbart *28 Apr 2013,* http://www.breitbart.com/big-journalism/ 2013/04/28/60-minutes-stock-act-follow-up-sends-a-warning-signal-to-congress/.

[42] Lee Fang, "Congress Tells Court That Congress Can't Be Investigated for Insider Trading", The Intercept, 7/15/2015, https://firstlook.org/theintercept/2015/05/07/congress-argues-cant-investigated-insider-trading/.

[43] Fang.

[44] Carl Hiassen, "Scott Put the Knife in Some Absurd Projects," *The Miami Herald*, June 28, 2015, 1-2.

[45] Hiassen.

[46] "*25 Scandalous Examples Of Government Pork That Will Drive You Crazy*," Business Insider, *accessed June 28, 2015*, http://www.businessinsider.com/the-worst-pork-of-2010-2010-4?op=1.

[47] Ibid.

[48] A. J. Delgado, "The GOP has not D*efense for its defense spending*," *The Miami Herald*, July 7, 2015, 11A.

[49] Gail Tverberg, "Our Finite World," Feb. 22, 2013, http://ourfiniteworld.com/2013/02/22/twelve-reasons-why-globalization-is-a-huge-problem/.

[50] Ibid.

[51] Lesley Stahl, "The Great Brain Robbery," Jan. 17, 2016, *60 Minutes*, CBS News.

[52] Ibid.

[53] Domenico Montanaro, Rachel Wellford and Simone Pathe, "Money is pretty good predictor of who will win elections," November 11, 2014, PBSNewHour, http://www.pbs.org/newshour/updates/money-pretty-good-predictor-will-win-elections/.

[54] Norah O'Donnell, "Are Members of Congress Becoming Telemarketers?" "Dialing for Dollars," *60 Minutes*, April 24, 2016, http://www.cbsnews.com/news/60-minutes-are-members-of-congress-becoming-telemarketers/.

[55] Amber Phillips, "Congress is as bad as it seems, according to Congressman X," *The Washington Post*, reprinted in *The Miami Herald*, May 31, 2016, 7A.

[56] George Orwell, "Politics and the English Language," 1946, The Political Writings of George Orwell, Ed. Patrick Farley, http://www.resort.com/~prime8/Orwell/>.

[57] "2009 Fort Hood Shooting," accessed Sept. 7, 2015, https://en.wikipedia.org/wiki/2009_Fort_Hood_shooting.

[58] Carol Platt Liebau, "*Obama Uses Euphemism to Obscure His Unpopular Agenda*," September 5, 2011, http://townhall.com/columnists/carolplattliebau/ 2011/09/05/obama_uses_euphemism_to_obscure_his_unpopular_agenda.

[59] Daniel Ruth, "Amendment 1 is proof of real rigged election," *The Miami Herald*,

October 31, 2016, first published in the *Tampa Bay Times*.

[60] "New Hampshire school officials distance selves from 'bias-free language guide'," *The Guardian* 29 Jul 2015, http://www.theguardian.com/us-news/2015/jul/29/ university-of-new-hampshire-bias-free-language-guide.

[61] Robby Soave, "University of New Hampshire No Longer Asking Students to Fix Problematic Speech," Reason.com, 30 Jul 2015, https://reason.com/ blog/2015/07/30/university-of-new-hampshire-no-longer-as.

[62] Ken Tucker, "What the Media Doesn't Get About Donald Trump" 20 July 2015, https://www.yahoo.com/tv/donald-trump-john-mccain-ant-man-hillary-clinton-124576220850.html.

[63] Glenn Garvin, "Sex with robots! What would George Jetson say?," *The Miami Herald*, December 29, 2015, 15A.

[64] Ibid.

[65] Glenn Garvin, "It's a mad, mad, mad, mad world!" *The Miami Herald*, December 30, 2014, 9A.

[66] Ibid.

[67] Michael Gerson, "Clinton's 'short-circuited' apology wasn't sincere," *The Miami Herald*, August 10, 2016, 15A, originally from *The Washington Post*.

Chapter 2

[1] "Life, death and greed; EpiPen cost an outrage," "*The Miami Herald*," Opinion, August 25, 2016, 14A.

[2] "'60 Minutes' Just Attacked High Drug Prices. Here's What You Should Know," Forbes, 5 Oct 2014, http://www.forbes.com/sites/matthewherper/2014/10/05/60-minutes-just-attacked-high-drug-prices-heres-what-you-should-know/.

[3] Fred Grimm, "In Florida, Zombie Pills for Kids an Old Scandal," *The Miami Herald*, September 27, 2015.

[4] "Utah man is charged $40 for 'skin-to-skin contact after son is born'," *The Miami Herald*, October 6, 2016, original article by AP.

[5] Steven I. Weissman, "We must cure what ails our healthcare system," *The Miami Herald*, May 29, 2016.

[6] Ibid.

[7] Ibid.

[8] Scott Pelley, "Denied," 60 Minutes, CBS News, 2 Aug 2015, http://www.cbsnews.com/ news/mental-illness-health-care-insurance-60-minutes-2/.

[9] "Financial Crisis of 2007-08," accessed August 4, 2015, https://en.wikipedia.org/wiki/ Financial_crisis_of_2007 %E2%80%9308.

[10] Ibid.

[11] Gordon White, *The Chaos Protocols*, (MN: Llewellyn Publications, 2016), 20-22.

[12] Ibid.

[13] Matt Egan, "5,300 Well Fargo Employees Fired Over 2 Million Phony Accounts," *CNN Money*, September 09, 2016, http://money.cnn.com/2016/09/08/investing/wells-fargo-created-phony-accounts-bank-fees/index.html?iid=EL.

[14] Matt Egan, "Well Fargo Workers: Fake Accounts Began Years Ago," *CNN Money*, September 26, 2016, http://money.cnn.com/2016/09/26/investing/wells-fargo-fake-accounts-before-2011/.

[15] Fred Grimm, "Farm to table? More like fraud to table," *The Miami Herald*, May 1, 2016.

[16] Ibid.

[17] Ibid.

[18] Natasha Bertrand, "The 15 Smartest US Presidents of All Time," *Business Insider*, Mar. 30,2015, www.businessinsider.com/the-15-smartest-us-presidents-of-all-time-2015-3?op=1

Chapter 3

[1] Tyler Durden, "20 Completely Ridiculous College Courses Being Offered At U.S. Universities," Aug. 31, 2015, http://www.zerohedge.com/news/2013-06-07/20-completely-ridiculous-college-courses-being-offered-us-universities.

[2] Marle Margolis, "One Hump or Two?" *The Miami Herald*, September 26, 2012.

[3] Leonard Pitts Jr., "R-rated column, not suitable for New York's kids," *The Miami Herald*, August 2, 2015.

[4] Kathleen Parker, "New SAT don't care 'bout no fancy words," *The Miami Herald*, March 11, 2004.

[5] Glenn Garvin, "Dropouts from Common Core," *The Miami Herald*, November 30, 2015.

[6] Nancy Szokan, "What came before the big bang?" *The Miami Herald*, January 11, 2016, originally appearing in *The Washington Post*.

Chapter 4

[1] "Amusing Ourselves to Death," Wikipedia, accessed Jan 11, 2016, https://en.wikipedia. org/wiki/Amusing_Ourselves_to_Death.

[2] Ibid.

[3] "Neil Postman," *GoodReads,* accessed June 3, 2016, https://www.goodreads.com/author/quotes/41963.Neil_Postman.

[4] Ibid.

[5] Christopher Orr, "Why does Game of Thrones Feature so much sexual violence?" *The Atlantic*, June 17, 2015, http://www.theatlantic.com/entertainment/archive/2015/06/game-of-thrones-sexual-violence/396191/.

[6] Ibid.

[7] "300: Rise of an Empire," Wikipedia, accessed May 29, 2016, https://en.wikipedia.org/wiki/300:_Rise_of_an_Empire.

[8] Rene Rodriguez, "Letting the Good Times Roll, in 1980," *The Miami Herald*, April 6, 2016, Weekend.

[9] Rebecca, Macatee, "Miley Cyrus' Parents Watch Proudly as Singer Rides Giant Flying Hot Dog, Flips the Bird During Bangerz Concert," February 21, 2014, http://www.eonline.com/news/513433/miley-cyrus-parents-watch-proudly-as-singer-rides-giant-flying-hot-dog-flips-the-bird-during-bangerz-concert.

[10] Lesley Abbravanel, "The Miley show a circus act," Art Basel Commentary, *The Miami Herald*, December 2014.

[11] "Miley Cyrus," Wikipedia, accessed Dec 17, 2015, https://en.wikipedia.org/wiki/Miley_Cyrus.

[12] "Justin Bieber," Wikipedia, accessed Dec 19, 2015, https://en.wikipedia.org/

wiki/Justin_Bieber.

[13] "Ten Rappers with Real Criminal Records," accessed Dec 21, 2015, http://hubpages.com/entertainment/10-Rappers-With-Real-Criminal-Records.

[14] "Jay-Z," *Rolling Stone*, accessed June 18, 2016, http://www.rollingstone.com/music/artists/jay-z/biography.

[15] Rob Fee, "Twelve Gangsta rappers With Criminal Records," October 15, 2013, http://mancave.cbslocal.com/2013/10/15/12-rappers-who-were-actual-criminals/.

[16] "Snoop Dogg," Wikipedia, accessed June 5, 2016, https://en.wikipedia.org/wiki/Snoop_Dogg.

[17] "Rastafari," Wikipedia, accessed June 5, 2016, ttps://en.wikipedia.org/wiki/Rastafari.

[18] "Snoop Dogg."

[19] Ibid.

[20] "Eminem," Wikipedia, accessed Jan 4, 2016, https://en.wikipedia.org/wiki/Eminem #Personal_life.

[21] "Eminem," *The Smoking Gun,* accessed Jan 5, 2016, http://www.thesmokinggun .com/mugshots/ celebrity/music/eminem.

[22] "Eminem," *Rolling Stone,* accessed Jan 5, 2016, http://www.rollingstone.com/music/artists/eminem/biography.

[23] "Sean John Combs," accessed Dec 30, 2015, https://en.wikipedia.org/wiki/Sean_Combs.

[24] "50-Cent," accessed Jan 4, 2016, https://en.wikipedia.org/wiki/50_Cent #Personal_life.

[25] "List of Awards and Nominations Received by 50 Cent," accessed Jan 4, 2016, https://en.wikipedia.org/wiki/List_of_awards_and_nominations_received_by_50_Cent.

[26] Jozen Cummings, " Hip-Hop's Finest: 30 Great Rap Lyrics," June 26, 2014, http://www.theroot.com/articles/culture/2014/06/hip_hop_s_finest_30_best_rap_lyrics.h tml.

[27] "Hardest Rap Album of All Time," *Passion of the Weiss*, accessed Dec 30, 2015, http://www.passionweiss.com/2015/04/30/bracket-hardest-rap-album-of-all-time-the-elite-8-2/.

[28] Dawn M. Turner, "Straight Outta Compton Explains Current Events," *The Miami Herald*, August 23, 2015, originally appearing in *The Chicago Tribune*.

[29] Jake Coyle, "Revisiting the Birthplace of West Coast Rap," *The Miami Herald*, August 14, 2015 (originally an article by *AP*).

[30] Ibid.

[31] "Eazy-E," accessed December 28, 2015, https://en.wikipedia.org/wiki/Eazy-E.

[32] "Ice Cube," accessed December 28, 2015, https://en.wikipedia.org/wiki/Ice_Cube.

[33] Jake Coyle, "Revisiting the Birthplace of West Coast Rap," *The Miami Herald*, August 14, 2015 (originally an AP article).

[34] Earnest Bakes, "The 50 Most Outrageous Rapper Quotes" April 4, 2013, *The Brakes*, http://www.complex.com/music/2013/04/the-50-most-outrageous-rapper-quotes/food-stamps.

[35] "Punk Rock," accessed Feb. 1, 2016, https://en.wikipedia.org/wiki/Punk_rock.

[36] "Sex Pistols," accessed Feb. 2, 2016, https://en.wikipedia.org/wiki/Sex_Pistols.

[37] "The Ramones," accessed Feb. 2, 2016, https://en.wikipedia.org/wiki/Ramones.

[38]"The World's Highest Paid Celebrities," *Forbes*, accessed Dec. 26, 2015, http://www.forbes.com/celebrities/#tab:overall.

[39] "Kim Kardashian," Wikipedia, accessed December 26, 2015, https://en.wikipedia .org/ wiki/Kim_Kardashian#As_actress.

[40] Ana Verciana-Suarez, "What Do Selfies Say About Us? *The Miami Herald*, July 7, 2015 (1E to 2E).

[41] "Paris Hilton," Wikipedia, accessed April 22, 2016, https://en.wikipedia.org/wiki /Paris_Hilton.

[42] Amy Reyes, "Kanye Never Ceases to Entertain," *The Miami Herald*, September 16, 2016.

[43] Earnest Bakes, "The 50 Most Outrageous Rapper Quotes" April 4, 2013, *The Brakes*, http://www.complex.com/music/2013/04/the-50-most-outrageous-rapper-quotes/food-stamps.

[44] Jamieson Cox and Micah Singleton, "Power, pot, and the presidency: breaking down Kanye's VMA speech," *The Verge*, September 1, 2015, http://www.theverge.com/2015/9/1/9239261/mtv-vma-awards-2015-kanye-west-speech-president.

[45] "Howard Stern," accessed Jan 1, 2016, https://en.wikipedia.org/wiki/Howard_Stern.

[46] Ibid.

[47] Ibid.

[48] Ibid.

[49] Ibid.

[50] Ibid.

[51] Ibid.

[52] Ibid.

[53] Doug Farrar, "Peyton Manning, Broncos make it official: Five years, $96 million," March 20, 2012, http://sports.yahoo.com/blogs/nfl-shutdown-corner/peyton-manning-broncos-official-five-years-96-million-155408265.html;_ylt=A0LEVzZhV8JWXxo ASixXNyoA;_ylu.

[54] "The World's Highest-Paid Athletes," *Forbes*, accessed Feb. 15, 2016, http://www.forbes.com/athletes/list/#tab:overall.

[55] Kurt Badenhausen"Average MLB Player Salary Nearly Double NFL's, But Still Trails NBA's," *Forbes*, January 23, 2015, http://www.forbes.com/sites/kurtbadenhausen/2015/01/23/average-mlb-salary-nearly-double-nfls-but-trails-nba-players/#57cb30b4269e.

[56] "Average Income in the United States," Statistic Brain Research Institute, accessed Feb. 15, 2016, http://www.statisticbrain.com/income-in-the-united-states/.

[57] Jimmy Kaylor, "NFL: Here is Every Player Arrested Since the 2016 Super Bowl," *The Cheat Sheet*, accessed July 29, 2016, http://www.cheatsheet.com/sports/nfl-player-arrests-2016.html/?a=viewall.

[58] Elliot C. McLaughlln, "FSU Settles for $950,000 in Jameis Winston Rape Case," CNN, January 26,2016, accessed August 14, 2016, http://www.cnn.com/2016/01/25/us/florida-state-fsu-settles-jameis-winston-rape-lawsuit/.

[59] Kathleen Parker, "What's with these bleeping people?" *The Miami Herald*, August 22, 2011, from *The Washington Post* Writers Group.

[60] Andres Oppenheimer, "Vargas Llosa's case against 'trivial' world," The Oppenheimer Report, *The Miami Herald,* July 8, 2012, 15A.

Chapter 5

[1] Catherine Saint Louis, "Feeling guilty about not flossing? Maybe there's no need," *The Miami Herald*, August 3, 2016, first published in *The New York Times*.

[2] Ibid.

[3] Steve Nadis, "Revisiting Primordial Gravity Waves," Discover Magazine, Sep. 2016.

[4] Percy Seymour, *The Third Level of Reality* (New York: Paraview Press, 2003).

[5] "Twenty Things You Didn't Know About Play," *Discover Magazine* July/August 2014.

[6] Richard, Ingham, "How the Zebra Earned its Stripes," Apr 1, 2014, Yahoo News, https://uk.news.yahoo.com/zebra-earned-stripes-170105914.html.

[7] Ibid.

[8] Peter Whoriskey, "Discovery of Bones Could Alter What We Know About the Irish," *The Miami Herald*, April 10, 2016, first published in *The Washington Post*.

[9] "Did you know that....," Bottom Line Personal, Vol. 35.18, 15 Sep. 2014:13.

[10] Alex Tsakiris, *Why Science is Wrong...About Almost Everything,* (San Antonio: Anomalist Books, 2014), 22.

[11] David Eagleman, "Ten Unsolved Mysteries of the Brain," *Discover Magazine,* Aug. 2007.

[12] Dean Radin, PhD, *The Conscious Universe.* (New York, NY: HarperCollins: 1997).

Chapter 6

[1] "List of Religions and Spiritual Traditions," *Wikipedia,* accessed March 21, 2016, https://en.wikipedia.org/wiki/List_of_religions_and_spiritual_traditions.

[2] "How many religions are there in this world?" *Hub Pages,* accessed March 21, 2016, http://hubpages.com/religion-philosophy/How-many-Religions-are-there.

[3] Hellen Ellerbe, *The Dark Side of Christian History*. Seventh. (Windermere, FL: Morningstar and Lark, 2004).

[4] Ibid.

[5] "10 Crazy Quotes From Televangelists," *BuzzVine,* accessed June 3, 2016, http://www.christianpost.com/buzzvine/10-crazy-quotes-from-televangelists-103645/.

Chapter 7

[1] Linda Robertson, "Tale of Te'o is fascinating—and heart-wrenching," *The Miami Herald*, January 26, 2013.

[2] Kathleen Parker, "Print's longtime passing," *The Washington Post*, 2012.

[3] Frank Bruni, "Twee less—read more," *The New York Times*, December 20, 14.

[4] Lauren Ellman, "Stepping Outside the Social-media Bubble," thestarvingstudent blogspot.com.

[5] Leonard Pitts Jr., "Taking selfies and clowning around in Auschqwitz and other wrong places," *The Miami Herald*, July 27, 2014.

[6] Ibid.

[7] Kathleen Parker, "Look out for the likability trap," *The Miami Herald*, September 13, 2012.

[8] Ana Menendez, "Fake news is dangerous to democracy—learn how to ferret it out," The Miami Herald, November 22, 2016.

[9] Abby Ohlheiser, "This is how Facebook's fake-news writers make money," *The Washington Post*, Nov. 18, 2016, https://www.washingtonpost.com/news/the-intersect/wp/2016/11/18/this-is-how-the-internets-fake-news-writers-make-money/?tid=a_inl.

[10] Fred Grimm, "Reality trumped by lies, conspiracy theories, post-factual president-elect," *The Miami Herald*, December 11, 2016.

[11] Ibid.

[12] Allison Graves and Amy Sherman, "Did 3 million undocumented immigrants vote on Nov. 8?" PolitiFact Florida, *The Miami Herald*, November 26, 2016.

[13] Ibid.

[14] Fred Grimm, "Reality trumped by lies, conspiracy theories, post-factual president-elect," *The Miami Herald*, December 11, 2016.

[15] Susan Russell, "Charge of media bias is unfair," *The Miami Herald*, Op-ed, December 2, 2016.

Chapter 8

[1] Phillip K. Howard, "The Death of Common Sense," Condensed from the book by the same title, *The Reader's Digest*, April 1995.

[2] Ibid.

[3] George Will, "Thanks for the laughs, from group sex to gfruit s'mores," *The Orlando Sentinel*, November 27, 2014.

[4] Ibid.

[5] Ibid.

[6] Nikkie Mayo,"Woman Stuck by Needle in Target Parking Lot Awarded $4.6 million," *Khou*, accessed September 12, 2016, http://www.khou.com/money/ business/woman-stuck-by-needle-in-target-parking-lot-awarded-46-million/317158301.

[7] "Citigroup sues AT&T over saying 'thanks'," *The Miami Herald*, June 11, 2016.

Appendix A

[1] "Rate hike 'greedy'? Insurance firm's CEO is paid $27 million, 50 times Citizens' chief's pay," The Miami Herald, July 2, 2016, 12A.

Appendix C

[1] Jill Neimark, "Trial and Error" *Discover Magazine,* Nov. 2014: 45-51.

Appendix D

[1] Jose Lambiet, "Burger joint: Rapper rude," *The Miami Herald,* April 7, 2013.

[2] Leonard Pitts Jr., "Ignorance seems to be in fashion," *The Miami Herald*, April 7. 2013.

www.ingramcontent.com/pod-product-compliance
Lightning Source LLC
Chambersburg PA
CBHW060625290526
45793CB00001B/144